Raising Kids with Big,
Baffling Behaviors

of related interest

The A–Z of Survival Strategies for Therapeutic Parents
From Chaos to Cake
Sarah Naish
Illustrated by Kath Grimshaw
ISBN 978 1 83997 172 3
eISBN 978 1 83997 173 0

The Seven Core Issues Workbook for Parents of Traumatized Children and Teens
A Guide to Help You Explore Feelings and Overcome Emotional Challenges in Your Family
Allison Davis Maxon and Sharon Kaplan Roszia
Illustrated by Liza Stevens
ISBN 978 1 78775 669 4
eISBN 978 1 78775 670 0

The A–Z of Therapeutic Parenting
Strategies and Solutions
Sarah Naish
ISBN 978 1 78592 376 0
eISBN 978 1 78450 732 9

The Unofficial Guide to Adoptive Parenting
The Small Stuff, The Big Stuff and The Stuff In Between
Sally Donovan
Forewords by Dr Vivien Norris and Jim Clifford OBE and Sue Clifford
ISBN 978 1 84905 536 9
eISBN 978 0 85700 959 3

The Unofficial Guide to Therapeutic Parenting
The Teen Years
Sally Donovan
Foreword by Dr Vivien Norris
ISBN 978 1 78592 174 2
eISBN 978 1 78450 444 1

Superparenting!
Boost Your Therapeutic Parenting Through Ten Transformative Steps
Dr Amber Elliot
Foreword by Sally Donovan
ISBN 978 1 78592 095 0
eISBN 978 1 78450 357 4

Raising Kids with Big, Baffling Behaviors

Brain-Body-Sensory Strategies That Really Work

ROBYN GOBBEL

Foreword by Bonnie Badenoch, PhD

Illustrations by Steve Klein

Jessica Kingsley Publishers
London and Philadelphia

First published in Great Britain in 2024 by Jessica Kingsley Publishers
An imprint of John Murray Press

1

A CIP catalogue record for this title is available from the
British Library and the Library of Congress

ISBN 978 1 83997 428 1
eISBN 978 1 83997 429 8

Disclaimer: The client vignettes that feature in this book are largely composite or
fictional; any real-life vignettes feature with the expressed consent of clients.

Printed and bound in the United States by Integrated Books International

Jessica Kingsley Publishers' policy is to use papers that are natural, renewable
and recyclable products and made from wood grown in sustainable
forests. The logging and manufacturing processes are expected to
conform to the environmental regulations of the country of origin.

Jessica Kingsley Publishers
Carmelite House
50 Victoria Embankment
London EC4Y 0DZ

www.jkp.com

John Murray Press
Part of Hodder & Stoughton Limited
An Hachette UK Company

For all the brave watchdogs and possums.

For letting me see you.

For teaching me to trust you.

Contents

Foreword

Robyn's book is potentially transformative. Period.

I say "potentially" because we have to pause and experience what she is offering for it to work its magic in us. Although it is written to and for parents who are struggling with their children's big, baffling behaviors, her core premise applies to all of us. Grounded in the central discoveries of Relational Neuroscience, she basically says that we are all doing the best we can, given the state of our inner world (as reflected in our autonomic nervous system), what is happening around us, and the support that's available to us. It may be worth pausing to really take this in and see how we feel about it.

Imagine what might happen in this world if we saw ourselves and each other through the eyes of this understanding.

She goes on to say that if people are doing something hurtful, they are feeling unsafe and have been moved by their adaptive nervous system into whatever protective behaviors their system believes will make them as safe as possible. This may feel outrageous at first, but if we begin to look at one another with these eyes, maybe just experimentally at first, we may *feel* the truth of it. The last time we yelled at our child, or said something unbelievably mean, what was happening deeper down inside? If we linger here, we may make some discoveries that help compassion and warm curiosity overtake judgments, blame, and attempts to merely control behavior.

Seeing this way leads us to what comes next. In any difficult situation, any hurtful relationship we need to be concerned with "regulation, connection, and felt safety," the phrase Robyn repeats over and over, on almost every page. When we feel safe, our natural biologically endowed preference for warm, cooperative relationships takes over.

As Robyn says, it sounds simple, but it isn't easy.

She then demonstrates what this journey might look like through the way she writes this book. Anchoring each chapter in the unfolding story of Nat's quest to help her daughter Sammie, Robyn invites us into an intimate conversation that unfolds over many months. (I imagine myself sitting in the hammock in her office to be part of it.) Even though Nat won't know it for quite a while, what she is experiencing with Robyn is exactly what she needs to be bringing to her daughter. There is no better way to learn than to live it.

Robyn offers acceptance and validation for every emotion Nat brings. She holds Nat's anger and her grief as just as true and precious as her joy. She offers tools with the constant assurance that they won't always work (thus reducing shame when things fall apart). She is there to accompany Nat through every step and stage. She brings the living experience of regulation, connection, and felt safety to Nat and to us. There is humor and quiet, along with owls, watchdogs, and possums—the stand-ins for the possible states of our nervous system. (I can't wait for you to meet them! They've become regular companions in our household.) In the midst of all this, Robyn vulnerably shares her own responses in these conversations with Nat and how she, too, experiences moments when regulation slips away. It really helps to hear this in her own voice.

The children Robyn talks about are among the most vulnerable in our society. Kiddos with particularly tender nervous systems that go easily into fear and then into protection—everything from flinging angry words to arms and legs to rocks. Or they may simply slide out of sight into collapse and become lost. These are children who are profoundly sensitive to the world within and around them. To be the parent of a child struggling like this is an exhausting, grief-filled, maddening experience. What Robyn offers in this book is a landing place for parents that is filled with both her accumulated wisdom and felt sense experiences to help parents shift from combatting and correcting behaviors to looking deeper to soothe the frightened roots.

While this book is addressed to parents, Robyn's way of being, embodied in the story of Nat and Sammie, feels like advanced mentoring for therapists, teachers, and anyone who finds themselves in relationships with people who have big, baffling behaviors. Given the way our culture places such value on whatever it considers good behavior and its encouragement to take control and fix those behaviors it does not like, this kind and wise understanding of how change happens from a much deeper relational place is an enormous and absolutely essential shift.

As we live into these challenging times, we need safe companions to accompany us every day—to regulate, connect, and find felt safety together. This book, quite marvelously, provides that. What a gift!

Bonnie Badenoch, PhD, Port Townsend, Washington, author of *Heart of Trauma: Healing the Embodied Brain in the Context of Relationships*

Preface

The first person who taught me to look past someone's behavior to see what's going on inside them was special education teacher and memoirist Torey Hayden. I devoured Hayden's books, checking out one after the next from my high school library.

She seemed like a magician to me. She worked with kids who were selectively mute, kids diagnosed with childhood schizophrenia, kids who had been abused, and kids who hurt other kids. These were kids no other teacher wanted in their classroom. Hayden didn't just want them; she loved them.

My husband was the second person who taught me to look past someone's behaviors. A talented music educator, he's always had a knack for connecting with the kids who need the most connection—and behave in ways that invite the least. I've learned a lot from watching him teach, but I've learned the most from watching him struggle with the devasting impact of a neuroimmune condition. Every single day during his two-year crisis, I leaned into my theory and thanked my lucky stars I'd made a career out of understanding why people behave the way they do. It saved my family.

Most of my professional experience focuses on helping kids with histories of trauma and toxic stress, so this book focuses on how trauma and toxic stress impact the developing brain. These children have vulnerable nervous systems and big, baffling behaviors.

Maybe you're parenting a child with big, baffling behaviors, but as far as you know, they haven't experienced anything you'd consider traumatic. There are different kinds of trauma and toxic stress. Some kinds are obvious, like physical, sexual, or emotional abuse, or chronic neglect. But some kinds are harder to see.

Nervous system vulnerability can result from kids being gifted or otherwise neurodivergent; from sensory processing challenges; from PANS (Pediatric Acute-onset Neuropsychiatric Syndrome), PANDAS (pediatric autoimmune neuropsychiatric disorders associated with streptococcal infections), Lyme disease, or another neuroimmune disorder. Maybe your child was exposed to alcohol or other toxins in utero. Maybe you have absolutely no idea why your child has big, baffling behaviors. Whatever the backstory, you are not alone.

In this book, you'll meet Nat, an overwhelmed mom desperate for help with her child, Sammie. Nat learns about how trauma and toxic stress have impacted Sammie's nervous system and her behaviors. Ultimately, this helps her learn to respond to Sammie's behaviors in a way that doesn't just change Sammie's behavior, but actually changes her brain and her nervous system.

The details of your family's story might be different from Nat and Sammie's, but your struggles are the same: you're parenting children with vulnerable nervous systems who demonstrate big, baffling behaviors. You're overwhelmed and confused, and you sometimes find yourself parenting in ways that shock you. Regardless of what has led to the vulnerability in your child's nervous system, this book is for you.

Everything I know about what behavior really is applies to all big, baffling behavior—regardless of the origin. It applies to our children, our clients, our spouses, and ourselves.

HOW TO BECOME THE EXPERT IN YOUR CHILD'S BEHAVIORS

CHAPTER 1

What Behavior Really Is and How to Change It

I watch your eyes glance around my office as you take in the polka dot carpet, the aerial yoga hammock hanging from the ceiling, and my purple velvet couch. I mentally note that somewhere along the way I crossed the line from "bright, inviting room full of color" to "a circus exploded in here." Oh well.

"Have a seat," I say, pointing to the couch, and we make a trade: one cup of coffee with cream for one worn manila folder.

"I hope it's okay," you say, wrapping your hands around the warm mug and not yet meeting my eyes, "but instead of filling out all your forms I just brought in the history I've typed up before. I think it covers everything your forms asked for, anyway."

I glance at the tab on the folder labeled: "Therapy—Robyn." "Robyn" has been written over with what looks like a lot of scribbles.

I know I'm not your first therapist. I almost never am. It's heart-breaking to know you've been through so many therapists that you have your own intake paperwork locked and loaded. Of course you do. You don't want to keep trudging through your child's past, your past, and the near constant letdown of professionals who say they can help but then don't help.

Despite those continued letdowns, here you are again: in a new therapist's office. Hope brings people to therapy. Parents and care-givers often feel hopeless, but if they truly were without any hope, they wouldn't even call me. They wouldn't come through the door or sit on my couch or make eye contact with me.

Hope brought you here. Hope will bring you back every week.

"Of course it's okay. In this office, you always get to come exactly as you are."

I take a breath, slowly exhale, and imagine what it means for you that you've told your child's story to so many professionals that you have it all written out and ready to go. That sounds really painful and also extremely resourceful. It's so smart not to give away your limited energy whenever possible.

I see you exhale and settle ever-so-slightly-more into the purple couch.

Our eyes connect. We have a moment of meeting. The tiny muscles around your eyes and mouth relax almost imperceptibly. Your shoulders drop just a bit. I feel our energies begin to connect in the space between us. At this moment, you seem to have received my offers of safety.

I remind myself this will continually shift, for you and for me. Felt safety lays the foundation for everything that will unfold in our work together and I can't take it for granted or assume it is always there.

This is a moment I've been in before. A moment of connection with a parent who has done what no parent should have to do: sit on the couch of yet another brand new therapist. A new stranger who receives the most intimate details of her family's life, her child's life, her life. It's completely not fair.

Wait! Before You Go Any Further: A Brief Note on the Format of This Book

You've just met Nat. Nat isn't a real person, yet she's every parent I've ever known. In the pages of this book, you'll have a front-row seat to months of parent sessions between Nat and me.

Nat is going to learn about why her child is acting this way. She will also learn how important she is in changing her child's behavior—not just what she does, but how she does it. By giving you, the reader, this inside view, you'll get to learn exactly what Nat learns, in exactly the way she learns it: in relationship.

Each chapter starts with Nat in my office. I talk to Nat on these pages the way I would talk to her in my office, and that's why I call her "you." My intention is that you will feel like these coaching sessions are actually happening between me and you. Why? *Because this is how the brain changes.*

If you are going to invest hours reading this book, I want you to actually be able to use the tools you will learn. So I'm writing this book in a way that will change you.

In each chapter, after the parent coaching scene ends, I further lay out that chapter's concepts in the way you might expect from a book like this. In those parts, I really am talking to you. The real you—not the Nat you. Have you ever seen *The Neverending Story*? Remember how Sebastian felt like he was in the story? The story became alive in him. It changed him. It's my hope that in this book, you'll feel like you are in the story.

The last thing you need is another parenting book that just tells you what to do without it becoming alive in you and creating real change.

Tell Me More

"The next two hours are set aside just for you and me to be together," I say, as I relax back into my swivel chair. "When you leave here I want to make sure you have a good feel for what it would be like to work with me, so you can decide if you want to. I want to make sure you understand, as much as you want, the approach I take and how important you are in any change that will happen in your family. How does that sound?"

"Oh, I already know we want to work with you," you say. "Our family needs you."

"It sounds like things are hard and you have hope that working with me will be exactly what your family needs."

"Yes...things are just so hard. I mean, I knew they would be hard. We had to take all those classes and even write a book report while we were waiting to adopt. Our caseworker made it clear that this would not be easy. But I didn't know it would be this hard." I see tears well up in your eyes. "And I didn't know that it would be this hard to get Sammie the help she needs. I just don't know how much longer we can take it."

"I hear those exact words from so many families. I'm glad you are here and you haven't given up yet. Working with families like yours is really an honor for me, and I will do everything I can to help you. Can you tell me a little more about what's been happening and what led you to reach out for help?"

We start wherever you need to start. I hear your story, as long or as short as it is.

I'm watching your eyes and your body as you tell me about your child's "bizarre" behaviors. Lying about teeny tiny things, when she isn't even in trouble. Playing with much younger kids. Having no idea how to play at all. Aggression that seems to erupt out of nowhere and leaves you feeling like a hostage in your own home. Your child's complete refusal to do almost anything—sometimes to just respond to your questions. I'm watching your shoulders tense up. You look off into the distance. Your voice gets just a little bit higher and you speak a little bit faster.

You tell me about how your other child is sometimes afraid to leave her bedroom.

You tell me that you and your spouse only talk to each other to criticize how the other one is handling things, but really, neither of you has any idea what to do.

You tell me you've tried reward charts. Time-outs. Even spankings, out of desperation. You tell me how you go to therapists and they give you advice that contradicts what the last one said. They tell you it's your fault. Or that it's not your fault. Or that you are too strict. Or that you aren't strict enough.

Then they tell you they can't help you anymore.

"Thank you," I say. "Thank you for sharing your story again and for trusting me to hold your story." After a moment, I say, "Here's what I'm hearing. Let me know if I'm getting it right. Your child's body and nervous system, and therefore her behaviors, too, feel a lot like this." I reach for my white board and draw some jagged lines.

I glance up and meet your eye to see if we're still connected. Your eyes are wide and you nod in agreement.

"Through my work with Sammie and your family, we'll be aiming to help Sammie's body and her behaviors look more like this." I draw a new wave underneath.

"That would be a miracle," you say.

"Yeah, that would feel like a miracle for sure. But brains and bodies and nervous systems are always available for healing and change. It's just that living with someone whose body feels a lot like this [pointing to the top jaggedy set of lines] leaves your nervous system feeling the exact same way."

Another emphatic nod, and a sigh of relief.

"Well of course it does!" I exclaim. "Fair enough. I mean, you're human too. It's just hard to help your child's nervous system shift when yours looks the same way."

You laugh. I take that as a "yes."

"Luckily," I go on, "I don't live with Sammie." More laughter. "And because I don't live with her, I have a nervous system that looks more like this bottom one. I work really hard on that. So when we come together, me and you, I get to stay pretty regulated. And believe it or not, us just being together will start to help your nervous system shift. One day you'll come here and tell me you can hear my voice in your head, and we'll rejoice because the process is working!

"Eventually, you'll be able to stay more connected to yourself when Sammie's behaviors are the most baffling or frustrating. You'll stay more connected to your thinking brain, which I usually call the owl brain. You'll be able to respond to Sammie's behaviors in a new way. And over time, Sammie's brain and body and nervous system, and yes, her behaviors too, will begin to change."

Before we end this first appointment, I tell you I won't always know the answers, and that sometimes, I'll be as confused as you are about Sammie's behaviors. Sometimes, I'll even be irritated or angry with her behavior. I tell you that my job is to figure out a way to use my own irritation as a clue so that I can stay curious. I tell you that I will stay with you on this journey as long as you want me to, even if I have no idea what to do next. I tell you that I do indeed have some ideas, maybe even some good ideas, about how to help change Sammie's behavior, but that ultimately, you are Sammie's best expert—second only to Sammie herself, of course. I tell you I will teach you what I know about the brain and you will teach me what you know about Sammie, and together we will try to make things better.

You decide you'll come back next week.

I'm so grateful.

What Behavior Really Is

Almost a decade ago, I sat in the back row of a conference room and nearly choked on my lukewarm hotel coffee when I heard author, therapist, and Interpersonal Neurobiology (IPNB) expert Bonnie Badenoch say, "No behavior is maladaptive."

Huh?

Up until that moment, I had used the word "maladaptive" to describe the challenging, overwhelming, and confusing behaviors of the children who came to my office. These were children who had been in other therapists' offices but who still had behavior that was getting them expelled from school. In kindergarten.

I thought "maladaptive" was a generous word.

Implicit in the word "maladaptive" is recognition that these behaviors emerged as protective coping behaviors. They were behaviors that at one point the child needed in order to be okay. They were adaptive then. But they weren't adaptive any longer.

I called a colleague later that night and we mulled this over. I respected Bonnie Badenoch a lot and figured she knew what she was talking about. But...not maladaptive? The fantastical lying? The desk flipping? The poop smearing? Those behaviors seemed pretty darn maladaptive to me.

The next day, I approached Bonnie on that stage and asked if she did consultations. She said yes. That started a relationship of regular training and consultation, 10 years old and still going strong. Bonnie Badenoch has been my guide. My primary mentor. And now, she's a friend.

She was right, of course, and now I understand the science that allows her to make such a bold, liberating statement.

No Behavior Is Maladaptive

In fact, *all behavior makes sense*.

Hard to believe, right?

But it's true.

Even the most nonsensical and eyebrow-raising behavior makes sense. Even the behavior that causes you to drop exhausted into bed at night, wondering how you can possibly do this again for one more day, let alone until your child is 18, makes sense.

It really does. All behavior makes sense. It still needs to be boundaried, or even changed. But if we start with the premise that it makes sense, we tend to approach the behavior with curiosity instead of control.

Curiosity begins the path toward behavior change and must remain our ever-present co-pilot.

Starting with the truth that all behavior makes sense, I then have three core tenets that ground me as I work with families to decode and ultimately change their children's most confusing and even dangerous behavior.

I'll briefly introduce the tenets to you below. By the time this book is done you'll understand how I reached these conclusions. More importantly, these three tenets will completely change the way you interpret your child's behavior and how you respond.

1. Behavior Is Just a Clue

Behavior is simply what we see on the outside that helps us know what is happening on the inside. It's easy to stay focused on just stopping bad behavior any way we can, but unfortunately, that approach keeps us stuck in behavior whack-a-mole. Sometimes we make a behavior go away, but then another one pops right up. It keeps us constantly on our toes, habitually hypervigilant, and frankly, pissed off.

2. We All Need Connection to Survive

Children—people—need other people. We all need connections and relationships. Children especially need big people to survive! They need connection for their brains to grow—and the brain's most important goals are to survive and grow.

Your child is definitely making it very hard to give them connection. Even when I don't understand why a child is pushing away connection, I've learned to stay curious and ask myself "What's up with that?" Always.

If a child is behaving in a way that rejects or pushes away connection, *something's not right*. We want to try to fix whatever that something is.

3. Regulated, Connected Kids Who Feel Safe Behave Well

Really, they do. Not perfect. But...like kids. Over our time together I'll teach you the brain science that convinces me this is true, but for now, I ask you to just take my word for it.

You might be skeptical that all behavior makes sense. You might be skeptical of child development expert Ross Greene's belief that *kids do well if they can.*[1] Of course you are skeptical. Everything we learn in Western parenting culture tells us the opposite is true.

But there is nothing wrong with you or your child.

Without a doubt, there are some major challenges in your family. On the surface, we can easily see that there are behaviors that need to change.

We have to get below the surface to understand that those behaviors exist because a part of your child is hurting. I think the size of their hurt is directly correlated to the intensity of their behavior.

I do want your child's behaviors to change, but more than that, I want their hurt to be seen, known, honored, welcomed, and healed. As that happens, their behaviors will improve. I'm confident this is true because this is simply how humans work.

You Are More Important than You Think

You are an extremely important part of your child's healing journey, not because their pain is your fault, and not because their healing is your responsibility. It is never anyone's responsibility to change anyone else. It's not even possible.

You're an extremely important part of your child's healing journey because healing happens in relationship.

At the most, children and their parents are only in relationship with me about one hour a week. And the rest of the time? Well, it's you. This isn't meant to be pressure; it's just the truth. After all, I'm not moving in with you!

Knowing Isn't Even Half the Battle

We just met, but in a way, I already know you. I know you because I know the parents who would pick up a book like this one.

This is the story of a mom, Nat, who finally finds real help for her child, Sammie. Nat comes every week and tells me her story, longing for me to see her, believe her, and help her. Nat and Sammie's story could be your story. The details are different but the story is the same.

You're probably tired of the parenting book cycle: you read a parenting book, feel briefly empowered with new ideas and techniques, then quickly fall back into real life only to feel like you can't implement what you learned. Like you're failing. Again.

It's not because you are doing anything wrong. *It's because knowing isn't even half the battle.*

Like other parenting books, this book will give you lots of tools. But unlike other parenting books, this book will change you. I just so happen to know how the brain changes, and it's in relationship. Turns out, change can happen even in the relationship that is created between an author and a reader.

I'm not writing this book just to give you more information. You could get that anywhere. I'm writing this book so you and I can create a relationship. Inside our relationship, your brain will change. You'll develop more and stronger connections between neurons (brain cells), and more neuronal connections means more regulation. More regulation means you'll be able to parent the way you want to, like the parent you already are.

Remember how one of my core tenets is that regulated, connected kids who feel safe behave well? That's true about parents, too.

Regulated, connected parents who feel safe parent well. The way they want to. The way that matches their values.

Not Quite That Easy

Without question, offering safety and connection to children with overwhelming, bizarre, baffling, and push-away behaviors isn't easy. Trying to connect with this child is like trying to connect with a cranky possum.

Or maybe a super-scared watchdog.

We now know, though, that it isn't impossible. We know what is happening in the brain that causes people to feel like connection is dangerous. Yet connection is also needed to survive. If something that I needed to survive was also extremely dangerous, I'd act a little bizarre too.

How I Got Here

When I was in graduate school, I didn't plan to have the kind of job that could leave me with a black eye. Yet one day, early in my career, I left the office with what I knew was going to turn into quite the shiner. Yup. A young child gave me a black eye. While I was at work.

"No one taught me how to do this," I thought on my drive home. Back then, like many of the parents who now come to my office, I was woefully unprepared to work with children with vulnerable nervous systems and high levels of intensity and dysregulation. The child who gave me a black eye wasn't a bad kid or even a violent one. It was actually a complete accident. The child was extremely dysregulated, and honestly, the strategies I knew how to do only made the dysregulation worse. The child's intensity escalated and I got hurt.

I had learned a lot of tools in graduate school and my early years of training, things like reward charts and positive reinforcement, but none of them were working. I had absolutely no idea what was causing these intense and sometimes extremely bizarre behaviors. I knew it was "trauma" but I didn't really know what that meant. How was trauma creating these behaviors? I didn't want someone to just tell me what to do to keep from getting another black eye. I wanted to understand *why* that child was behaving that way.

Luckily, I became a therapist at a pretty cool time in history.

Two significant things were happening as I wrapped up my undergraduate degree in 2001. The turn of the century ended what US President George H.W. Bush called "The Decade of the Brain." We were learning so much about the brain! Right about that same time, a child in Colorado died due to an intervention that was supposed to treat her symptoms of reactive attachment disorder.[2] While this child's death was an extreme outcome, it was reflective of the controlling, coercive, and dangerous practices that were being used by desperate therapists and desperate parents who had no idea what else to do with this child's out-of-control behavior.

With new understanding of the brain came new understanding of why these children had extremely challenging, bizarre, and even dangerous behaviors. I got lucky. When I left the office with a black eye, I went on an obsessive search for anything that would help me understand this behavior—and I found something.

Relational Neuroscience

I discovered Interpersonal Neurobiology (IPNB) and the emerging field of Relational Neuroscience—the study of the behavioral, social, and emotional brain. Ultimately, my obsessive search landed me at that Bonnie Badenoch conference with the crappy hotel coffee. I slowly began to develop an understanding for why these kids did what they did. Once I understood what was happening in their brain, body, and nervous system, I realized that changing a child's behavior wasn't actually my goal. How could it be? I'm not in charge of anyone else's behavior. I mean, I hardly feel in charge of my own.

As my understanding of what was underneath the behavior grew deeper, I realized it wasn't the toolbox full of tools that was important—it was knowing what tool to use when and why. Otherwise, a full toolbox just exacerbates the endless game of whack-a-mole.

The parents I was working with needed more tools, but more than that, they needed someone who could help them understand what was going on in their child. They needed to understand some basic brain development, and a little bit about the autonomic nervous system, too. When I teach parents about the brain, they are less dependent on me. They don't have to do so many Google searches and then sift through endless contradictory suggestions from all the different Instagram-famous parent experts.

> If you give a hungry person a fish, you feed them for a day. If you teach that person to fish, you feed them for a lifetime. (Lao Tzu)[3]

I want to empower you to become your child's expert. No one knows them better than you—except, of course, your child. I happen to know a lot about the brain, the autonomic nervous system, and how those things are related to your child's behaviors. I'm going to teach you about the brain and I'm going to teach you some new parenting tools. Then, you can take what you know about your child and combine it with what I teach you about the brain. After that, you'll be fed for a lifetime.

Shall we get started?

(Very) Basic Brain Development
Bottom Up, Inside Out
The brain develops from the bottom up and the inside out. This means that the lowest, most inside parts of the brain develop first, and the highest, most outside parts of the brain develop last. If you're a neuroscientist you'll immediately know that my brief overview of brain development is wildly oversimplified. Luckily, this book isn't preparing you to do brain surgery! This oversimplified understanding of brain development and architecture is enough to help us develop what Dan Siegel calls "mindsight"[4]—the ability to reflect on what's happening in our inner world, make sense of it, and ultimately change it if we want to.

The Brainstem
The brainstem is the first part of the brain to develop. It's located at the bottom of the brain and nestled deep inside, connecting the brain to the top of the spinal cord. Our brainstem is responsible for all of the things our body does without us thinking about it, like heart rate, digestion, breathing, and energy. The brainstem rapidly develops in utero and is mostly wired up and ready for action in healthy, full-term infants. After birth, babies breathe and their hearts beat without any help. Other autonomic functions are still developing. Sleeping, digestion, and temperature modulation are just a few things that come to mind that continue to develop long after birth. This is why we keep babies bundled up for a few months after birth. Eventually we can drop all those extra layers!

The brainstem fuels our body with the energy we need to get things done. It also eases the energy off when it's time for rest. Think of it this way: the brainstem can step on the accelerator to give more energy, or it can step on the brakes to decrease the energy. Babies know how to have energy and how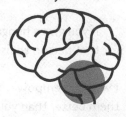

to rest. They cry almost immediately and they definitely don't have any trouble sleeping a lot. What babies need help with is going back and forth between energy and resting. The brainstem continues to develop after birth as caregivers help their baby calm down. Eventually, the energy in the brainstem settles into a nice rhythm.

The Limbic Regions

As brain development awakens further up and further out in the brain, the regions commonly referred to as the limbic regions begin to rapidly increase in neural connections. If the brainstem is at the bottom of the brain and nestled deep inside, and the cortex wraps itself all the way around the outside of the brain, then the limbic regions are nestled in between the two. The limbic regions are involved with relationship, emotion, attachment, and so much more. Both the brainstem and the limbic regions are genetically primed to develop through relational experiences.[5] This means that these regions of the brain are designed to develop in relationship. In fact, leaving babies alone without enough relational experiences can have a devastating impact on their brain development, even if they have enough food, water, and a safe place to live. I think it's pretty awe-inspiring to imagine the impact caregivers have on the development of their baby's brain when they gently and lovingly pick up their baby and soothe the baby's cries.

This crucial time period in an infant's first 18 months of life creates a map for relationships. When babies experience safe, predictable, and loving caregiving, they learn to expect relationships to be safe, predictable, and loving. This impacts the kinds of relationships this child seeks out in the future. They'll look for friends and romantic partners who live up to their expectations about what a relationship should be like.

The limbic regions of the brain are always on the lookout for whether they are safe...or not. When the baby feels safe, the brain gets to focus on growing and developing. If the baby spends a lot of time feeling unsafe, their brain can become so focused on the task of staying alive that other important aspects of development get delayed.

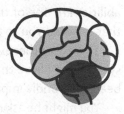

The Cortex

The last part of the brain to come online is the cortex. The cortex is what we would see if we opened up the skull and looked at the outside of the brain. All those ridges and folds you see on the outside of the brain? That's the cortex. The cortex is responsible for complex tasks like reasoning, logic, and understanding cause and effect. It experiences a rapid increase in development between 18 and 36 months old. If you have ever parented a toddler, you know that this is when their language starts to explode. They're asking, "Why? Why? Why? Why?"

This highest part of the brain isn't done developing at 36 months of age! Thank goodness! If we all had the impulse control of three-year-olds, life would be tricky indeed. We'd walk by someone eating dessert in a restaurant and instead of just commenting on how good their cheesecake looks, we'd snatch it up! Luckily, all these parts of the 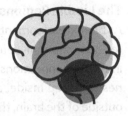 brain continue to grow and develop well into adulthood. More importantly, the connections between all these parts of the brain continue to grow and develop throughout our entire lives.

Trauma and Toxic Stress
A Brief Note on Trauma and Toxic Stress

In this first section on "How to Become the Expert in Your Child's Behaviors," I'll first offer you some insights into how different parts of the brain and nervous system develop. I'll then offer you some insights into how trauma and toxic stress impact those parts of the developing brain and nervous system.

The short version is that trauma and toxic stress lead to vulnerabilities in the developing child's brain and stress response system. These vulnerabilities are one of the factors that contribute to the bizarre behaviors that have led you to pick up this book.

There are other experiences that can lead to a sensitive stress response system, but I have the most experience working with children who have been profoundly impacted by trauma and toxic stress.

You might be asking: "What's trauma?" In his Foreword to Bonnie Badenoch's book *The Heart of Trauma*, Dr Stephen Porges states that trauma is something that disrupts our capacity to feel safe.[6] The treatment of trauma, then, is to enable the person to experience feelings of safety.

Trauma is subjective, but I've worked with children who demonstrate traumatic symptoms after experiences of sexual abuse, physical abuse, neglect, adoption, orphanage care, medical procedures, cross-country moves, divorce, and oh yeah, a pandemic. Trauma also includes the experiences of oppression, marginalization, and "othering" of a group of people due to (but not limited to) race, gender, sexual orientation, and ability.

To be perfectly frank, I'm not terribly interested in defining trauma and toxic stress; it's simply too subjective. What's traumatic to one person might not be traumatic to another. The reality that some people experience traumas that most of us can't even imagine doesn't negate the traumatic impact of the seemingly smaller but chronic trauma of being unseen and not having our relational needs met. I think we can recognize the horrors that the people in Ukraine have experienced during the Russian invasion, or the devastating impact on the families and survivors of the Uvalde school shooting, while also recognizing the trauma of being the only brown child in a family and community of white people. At times it feels like simply being a human is traumatic.

I've spent my entire career working with kids who have experienced complex or developmental trauma. This is trauma that occurs inside the caregiving relationship and happens repeatedly, for a sustained length of time. Complex developmental trauma could include things like physical or sexual abuse, and also neglect. In the context of this book, trauma and toxic stress is any disruption in the attachment and caregiving system that leaves the developing child in a chronic state of uncertainty and without the co-regulation of a safe, secure adult.

The Impact of Trauma and Toxic Stress on Brain Development

The brain develops around what it is experiencing. When a baby experiences safe, loving, nurturing care in an environment that encourages curiosity and exploration, the baby develops a brain that expects safe and loving relationships. Their brain has fun learning and seeks new experiences. They develop a strong brain foundation (the brainstem) that fuels their body with the energy it needs, not too much and not too little.

When a baby's brain develops in an environment of trauma, toxic stress, danger, and chaos, the brain organizes and develops around trauma, toxic stress, danger, and chaos. It expects danger and develops strong behaviors of protection. The rhythm of the brainstem is chaotic instead of predictable, and sometimes it fuels the body with way too much energy or way too little. This becomes a child who punches their friend during a playground game of hide-and-seek (too much energy) or a child who stares doe-eyed off into space because you remind them to do a chore (way too little energy).

A two-story house built on sand would collapse in an earthquake. So it is with the brain. The higher-level cortical and limbic regions seem to simply collapse under strain—strain that a child with a more resilient stress response system could withstand. To make matters worse, connecting with this child doesn't seem to help at all. In fact, it seems like the last thing this child wants is connection.

Remember, we work from the perspective that all behavior makes sense. So first, I will help you understand how that is the case with your child. Then I will teach you specific tools that work with your new understanding of your child's brain. With practice, you'll learn how and when to use them, and you'll be able to come up with your own great ideas. You'll grow in compassion not only for your child, but also for yourself. And you'll do this through a front-row seat to my sessions with Nat.

How does that sound? Good? Well, let's go!

CHAPTER 2

Connection or Protection: The Science of Felt Safety

"Whenever we're considering how to respond to a challenging behavior," I say, "we're always going to start by thinking about Sammie's nervous system."

You look at me quizzically. It's our second session, and there's a lot to cover today. I gesture to the mug of hot coffee with cream I've set out for you. You pick it up, surprised. "Thank you!"

"The nervous system has two modes," I go on, "connection mode and protection mode. We rest in connection mode when we feel safe. But the moment we sense something might not be safe, we shift into protection mode."

You take a sip of coffee, nodding slowly and considering.

"Connection and protection are mutually exclusive. You're in one mode or the other; there is no in-between. It's basically like a light switch that way. But once the switch is flipped and you're in protection mode, it works like the dimmer switch in my kitchen. You can be a little bit in protection mode or a lot in protection mode.

"What kind of behaviors do you think we are most likely to see when Sammie's nervous system is in connection mode?"

"Uh, behaviors I like?" you ask, uncertainly.

"Yes!" I can feel a grin spread across my face. "Exactly! So, what kinds of behaviors do you think we are more likely to see when Sammie's nervous system is in protection mode?"

"Behaviors I don't like!" Now you're smiling too, and we laugh together. This exchange shows me that you, too, are in connection mode.

"Exactly. So, let's say we're trying to figure out a behavior of Sammie's that feels frustrating or overwhelming or just downright baffling. Like when she lies about something that doesn't matter, or is uncooperative about everything, or punches her classmates."

"Or me," you say with a sigh.

"Right. Or you," I agree. "Those are challenging behaviors, and when they happen, we want to pause and ask ourselves why Sammie's nervous system is in protection mode. Then we'll get curious to discover if there is anything you can do to help her come into connection mode."

"Oh, that sounds simple," you say, clearly meaning the opposite.

"Well, it's simple," I say. "But not easy."

"Wait." Your eyes shift as you have an "aha" moment. "Are you telling me that when we're dealing with those behaviors, Sammie isn't feeling safe?"

"Yup."

"So basically, she almost never feels safe?"

I take a breath and speak softly, trying to convey my empathy. "It feels like Sammie is almost always misbehaving? Almost always in protection mode?" You give a little shrug: yes.

"Gosh," I say. "That is just so exhausting. For all of you. People aren't meant to be chronically in protection mode, and when we get stuck there, it's very, very hard on our bodies. And on everyone around us."

"But why doesn't she feel safe?" you ask, sounding frustrated now. "She's been in our family since she was a toddler—she doesn't even remember anything from before our family. And we're safe! She isn't in danger when I tell her it's time to brush her teeth. But then she'll throw her toothbrush on the floor and scream at me like a wild animal. It doesn't even make sense!"

"It doesn't," I agree, "until we understand how the brain works, how it decides if we are safe or not. Then we realize that actually all behavior makes sense. We can always believe what Sammie's behaviors are telling us about what mode her nervous system is in: connection or protection. Being safe and feeling safe aren't the same thing."

Felt Safety

Felt safety is a term that, to the best of my knowledge, first entered the attachment literature via Dr Alan Sroufe. Dr Sroufe holds a PhD in clinical psychology and is an internationally recognized leader in attachment research. Almost 50 years ago, he used the term "felt security" to describe a child's subjective experience based on three factors: internal experience, environment, and caregiver.[1]

Dr John Bowlby was a British psychologist whose work in the 1950s earned him his reputation as the father of attachment theory. Dr Bowlby wrote that children are always instinctively gauging their caregivers' emotional availability—not only at specific points in time, but also over the course of their history with that caregiver.[2]

Decades of related research and literature describe what we now take for granted: a child's sense of felt safety is subjective. It is impacted by their environment, their caregiver, their inner world, and their history. Sure, maybe the child's caregiver is, objectively speaking, safe and available in a given moment. But if that child has a history with a caregiver who was repeatedly unsafe or unavailable, that child might not be able to fully feel their caregiver's current safe presence.

Neuroception

In the early 1990s, Dr Stephen Porges introduced the concept of neuroception.[3] Dr Porges, a psychologist and neuroscientist whose research examines human emotion, stress, and behavior, asserts that the nervous system is continuously making lightning-fast decisions about whether we are safe. It's important to really feel in our bodies how fast the nervous system is making this decision about being safe or not, so let's pause for just a moment.

Dr Porges asserts that the nervous system is continuously asking "Safe or not safe?" but to really quantify this, let's say that the nervous system is asking "Safe or not safe?" four times every second. Actually say those words out loud right now. "Safe or not safe?" Guess how long it took you to say it. One second? Two? In the time it took you to say "Safe or not safe," your nervous system made the decision at least four, if not eight, times! Of course, since it's asking so frequently, that decision can change in an instant based on the implicit data our nervous system is constantly processing.

Implicit data refers to all the things our brains notice and process, and it's estimated to be about 11 million bits of data per second.[4] 11 million! That's such a huge number, I really can't even wrap my mind around it. Obviously, we couldn't possibly pay attention to all of those things. In fact, out of those 11 million bits of data per second, we are only aware of somewhere between 6 and 50.

All that incoming data helps our brains detect safety (or lack thereof) throughout every moment of our lives. That safety detection system—our spidey-sense—is what Dr Porges means by neuroception.

Connection or Protection

When our nervous system decides that most of the incoming information is safe, it keeps us in connection mode. Connection mode is actually our default; it's our preference.

On the other hand, when our nervous system decides that most of the incoming information is not safe, the "danger-danger" system comes online and it flips us into protection mode. I can pretty much guarantee that the behaviors you wish your child would change happen when their nervous system is in protection mode.

Think of the "danger-danger" system like a cute little watchdog that lives in your child's mind. At any possible sign of danger, the watchdog perks up. First, the watchdog wants to know "Is this real danger or a false alarm?" If it's real danger, then the watchdog takes its job very seriously and will do whatever it takes to protect them.

A nervous system in protection mode is trying to stay safe. Opposition and defiance? Those are behaviors that say, "I don't trust this situation and I need to stay in control to be safe." Verbal or physical aggression? Those are protective behaviors, right?

I know that your child has these behaviors—opposition, defiance, control, aggression, and so many more—when there is no reason to think that they are in danger or need to protect themselves!

Still, those behaviors tell us your child is in protection mode, even if it doesn't yet make sense why. If we want our kids to have connection behaviors, we have to get curious about why they are in protection mode and then offer them the opportunity to shift into connection mode. We want to help their "danger-danger" system feel invited into safety.

I know. Way easier said than done! And ultimately, it's their decision whether to accept the invitation of safety or not.

Inside, Outside, and Between

Confirming Dr Sroufe's theory, Dr Porges's research similarly indicates three places the nervous system scans for cues of safety and danger: the inner world, the environment, and the caregiver.

Deb Dana, a licensed clinical social worker who collaborates closely with Dr Porges, has taken his concept of neuroception[5] and translated it for those of us who aren't brain scientists.[6] She calls these three streams of awareness inside, outside, and between.

That's much catchier and easier to remember. Inside, outside, and between.

Inside

Our nervous system is always keeping track of what's happening in our bodies. Are we hungry? Tired? Gotta pee? Any of those cues can flip the nervous system into protection mode and leave us feeling unsafe. Why? Because feeling unsafe motivates us to take action and get our needs met.

We're driven to return to connection mode as soon as possible. Flipping into protection mode because we're hungry means we'll go look for a snack, then come back and return to connection mode. Maybe you've seen someone get "hangry." That's what happened—they couldn't stay in connection mode in the face of the "Find food now!" message coming from the body.

Remember the last time you had to pee really bad? You got pretty focused on solving that problem and probably weren't thinking much about being friendly or kind. And yup, we're all familiar with getting grumpy when we're tired.

There's a lot more going on inside our bodies and our kids' bodies than just being hungry, tired, or needing to pee, though. Our hearts are beating, our lungs are breathing, our body temperature is regulating. Our immune system is working to stay in balance and sometimes it kicks into gear because of a cold or infection. Some bodies develop chronic immune responses like PANS, PANDAS, or Lyme disease.

Any of these internal experiences can flip our bodies into protection mode, too. For instance, when our body temperature regulation is off, our body's regulation system gets to work on fixing it. An immune response sends signals all over the body that basically say, "Something is wrong here! Let's rally the troops and fight it!" This process can flip a nervous system into protection mode. If a body has a chronic or persistent immune response, it spends a lot of time in protection mode.

Ideally, a baby gets to have lots of fun experiences that make their heart rate go up: playing peek-a-boo, knocking over block towers with a crash, or getting tossed in the air and caught by a laughing and safe caregiver. As babies get older, their caregivers wrestle, play tag, or maybe jump on the trampoline with them. These children learn that the sensation of an increased heart rate can mean that they are safe and having fun.

But what about the babies who don't have a lot of fun experiences with their caregiver? Those babies don't learn about safe and fun play. Instead, they learn that a high heart rate only means "danger-danger." Then they grow into kids who quickly shift from having fun at recess to punching their friend.

Outside

We intuitively understand that our environments have a significant impact on how we feel. We decorate our homes, organize school classrooms, or sit by waterfalls to influence our moods and actions.

Our environments have the power to help us feel safe. I have a peacock art print in my office because its vibrant colors and textures bring a sense of joy, and therefore safety, into my body. My husband keeps his music room dim, with a red bulb in one lamp. This lighting brings a sense of calm, and therefore safety, into his body.

The sensory data that we process from our environments—how things sound, smell, look, feel, and even taste—can shift our nervous system in and out of experiencing a sense of safety. This process depends on so many things! Does our unique nervous system like this sensation or that sensation? Does it need more of one? Less of another?

Babies who have an atypical unique sensory processing system or a neurodivergent brain that may later be labeled autistic, developmentally delayed, ADHD (attention-deficit hyperactivity disorder), or even gifted (just to name a few) often experience a mismatch with the environment or even the well-intentioned caregiver. If this mismatch occurs regularly, their developing nervous system begins to spend too much time in protection mode.

Our nervous system also likes to know *exactly* what's in our environment. No surprises, please! One day a new client took the framed art prints off my walls and looked behind them. She was driven by her nervous system to look for danger. When she found nothing but wall, she felt safer. I always show new clients what I keep behind closed doors and curtains for the same reason: to help move their nervous systems out of protection mode.

Another environmental safety cue is a door or window, which our brain perceives as an escape route. Imagine being blindfolded while someone takes you to a new place you've never been. When you take off that blindfold, you find yourself in a room with no windows or doors. You wouldn't like it—and you shouldn't! Your nervous system would flip into protection mode and you'd feel unsettled.

Between

In addition to checking inside (the body) and outside (the environment), neuroception checks out what is happening between you and whomever you're with. For young children, neuroception is laser-focused on the grown-up taking care of them. Kids need grown-ups to literally help them survive.

If your child's neuroception could talk, it would ask the obvious questions about their grown-ups: "Are you going to hurt me or have you hurt me in the past?"

It would also ask questions like:

- Are you (caregiver) present with me?
- Are you paying attention?
- Do you seem to know me, or want to know me?
- Are you behaving in a way that is predictable and makes sense to me?
- Is your nervous system in protection mode or connection mode?

Our children's neuroception spidey-sense knows if their caregiver is in protection mode or connection mode. They don't usually know they know, but they do.

We all have this spidey-sense, actually. When we're with someone whose nervous system is in protection mode, we experience that as a cue of danger, and our own nervous system flips into protection mode. Why? Well, humans in protection mode can be dangerous. They're unpredictable and not focused on relationship; they're focused on protection. If we are with someone whose nervous system is in protection mode, we flip into protection mode ourselves to stay alert to potential danger.

Pause for a moment here. That's heavy.

Maybe you've noticed the irony here: your child's neuroception is determining safety or danger based partially on how safe *your* nervous system feels. And I'll bet your nervous system feels a little ragged right now. Sometimes—maybe a lot of times—it's in protection mode.

It makes perfect sense that your own nervous system spends a lot of time in protection mode. No judgment here—only compassion. As with your child, it's exhausting for your nervous system to be stuck in protection mode. Unfortunately, it's difficult for your child to rest into experiences of felt safety when they are preoccupied with how safe (or not!) you feel to them.

I know. That's heavy. It's a burden. It's unfair.

But it's also science. I've devoted an entire section of this book (Section 3) to helping your nervous system spend more time in connection mode. If it feels like that's what you need, you could even flip ahead and read that section now. What a gift of care and compassion you could give yourself.

"But There's Nothing Unsafe!"

I'm a parent too, and I totally understand that, right now, you might want to yell: "What do you mean his behavior shows he's feeling unsafe? There's nothing unsafe happening here!"

Like the anti-virus software on your computer, your child's neuroception is constantly doing background scans of those three places—inside, outside, and between—looking for malware (danger). There are millions of bits of sensory data for the brain to sort and process every second. Millions of data points every second. Can you imagine how much incoming sensory information our kids are experiencing?

But wait! I have one more layer of complication to add.

Our brain's most important job is to keep us alive, which it does in part by managing energy. Rather than spending energy to react to everything happening in the present, our brain uses prediction to anticipate and prepare for whatever is going to happen next.[7] In fact, more than 80 percent of our perception of reality is actually based on our memories of what has happened in the past.[8]

Picture it like this: one stream of information in our minds contains all our past experiences. Another stream of information in our minds contains the 11 million bits of sensory data that we're experiencing in the present. Those streams merge to create the river that becomes our own unique reality.

Yup, all of us are constantly creating our own reality. Me, you, your kid, and everyone else.

Now, let's imagine that in the stream of the past, there's a lot of scary things. A lot of yelling and mean faces. A lot of discomfort and not a lot of soothing. Remember how I said the brain is mostly focused on keeping us alive? That focus can cause the brain to prioritize cues of danger so strongly that even when the danger is past, the brain still responds to it. The brain's focus on that long-ago danger turns the stream of the past into a crashing tsunami, which overwhelms and floods the stream of the present.

So yes, based on the way *your* mind creates reality, you and your child are safe. But our minds are all different, and your child's experience in this moment of reality could very well be that they are *not* safe. Cue protection mode.

All Behavior Makes Sense

I know your child has some challenging behaviors that don't seem to make any sense. Their behavior doesn't match your experience of reality. But I promise you that it matches theirs.

That's simply how the mind works: we create, and then respond to, our own reality.

When I began to fully understand and embody this truth, my therapeutic practice changed dramatically. In fact, so did my practice as a parent, wife, friend, and even just as a grocery store customer! I realized that behaviors that emerge from protection mode aren't personal and don't reflect a person's character; they reflect that person's felt safety. As I came to fully grasp this idea, I became less judgmental of others and better at setting boundaries for myself. Now, if the grocery store clerk isn't friendly, I assume their nervous system isn't feeling safe. I don't have to take it personally. If I feel up to it, I can respond with authentic kindness—one small gesture toward cultivating more felt safety in the world.

Knowing that all behavior makes sense does not mean all behavior is acceptable or understandable or excusable. It just means that there is a reason for it, that it all makes sense.

When we approach a behavior with the assumption that it doesn't make sense, we feel friction in our bodies: anger, frustration, anxiety, despair. Any of those feelings will push us into protection mode.

But when we approach a behavior believing that it *does* make sense, even if we don't understand it, our own nervous system is more likely to experience safety. We will stay in connection mode longer. Connection mode is healthier, feels better, and helps us make better decisions and set better boundaries.

It is, of course, good for our kids, too. You know what they need to be invited into safety? They need for us to be in connection mode.

Staying in connection mode brings a sense of ease to our bodies. It opens up compassion and curiosity, and allows us to respond to our kids in a way that helps them experience felt safety.

Stress Response System

Dr Bruce Perry's research on the stress response system plays a vital role in making sense of our child's bizarre behaviors, especially in the context of the idea that all behaviors make sense.[9] When your child's neuroception shifts their body into protection mode, their stress response system is called to action. Activation of the stress response system is not bad! The stress response system helps our brain know there is something really important happening that needs attention. All humans, but especially babies and children, are continually exposed to new experiences that makes the brain perk up and ask, "What's up? What's going on here? What do I need to get back into balance?"

Dr Perry states that if the developing child's stress response system is activated in ways that are predictable, moderate, and controllable,[10] then the child will develop a resilient stress response system. Caregivers who respond to their babies' frequent needs in a predictable and consistent manner support resilience in this way. As babies grow, they become toddlers who fall down, have to take yucky medicine they don't like, or get told "No! You cannot go down the stairs by yourself." Those types of experiences, even though they elicit a stress response, are actually good for the developing brain as long as they are experienced as predictable, moderate, and controllable. When those toddlers become teenagers and have a bad day at school, they have a stress response system that can help them manage that stress without freaking out.

Some babies spend a lot of time in protection mode and their stress response system remains activated for too long. Dr Perry states that babies who experience stress that is unpredictable, prolonged, and extreme are more likely to develop a stress response system that is sensitive and vulnerable. These children seem to react to everyday life stressors as if their lives are in danger. The sensitization of their stress response system sends exactly that message to their brain—that their life is in danger because you forgot to cut the crust off their peanut butter sandwich. They react like an attacking watchdog, or maybe they have the opposite response and collapse like a possum playing dead.

Trauma and Toxic Stress

The brain likes to be energy efficient, and continually assessing for safety takes a lot of energy. Eventually, the brain starts to wonder why it should spend energy asking "Safe or not safe?" if the answer has almost always been "Not safe."

Children with a history of trauma and toxic stress have brains that default to "not safe," even when there is information available that could help the brain feel safe. Remember the two streams of information that shape our reality? For these kids, their stream of the past is full of experiences of being "not safe," and it forcefully takes over their stream of the present.

Most of the time, our kids don't know why they don't feel safe. They just don't.

We know they are feeling unsafe because they show us protection mode behaviors like opposition and defiance. They're rude and extremely uncooperative. They lie about things that don't matter, take things without permission, and seem to have little regard for anyone else's feelings.

Or maybe they act maniacally silly—the kind of silly that feels confusing because they are laughing but it doesn't feel fun at all. Maybe they space out and seem like they're in la-la land, sometimes not even remembering conversations you've just had or something they learned in school. Or they're TOO compliant, saying "yes" to things without thinking, even dangerous things.

They might show these or other confusing, disagreeable behaviors that definitely don't come from connection mode. You know it's not connection mode because frankly, when they act like that, you don't want to be connected to them.

The Science of Safety

Understanding the science of safety starts with understanding the autonomic nervous system. The autonomic nervous system, which is controlled largely by the brainstem, is responsible for things that we don't think about and are mostly out of our control, like breathing, digestion, and heart rate. The autonomic nervous system is also in charge of the energy in our bodies. When we don't feel safe, our energy is directed at protecting us in some way. On the outside, that looks like opposition, defiance, lying, stealing, laughing inappropriately, ignoring you, being overly compliant, and other off-putting behaviors.

When we do feel safe, our energy can be directed toward connection. That looks like openness, cooperation, and age-appropriate empathy for others. We are caring toward those around us and open to being cared for.

Changing your child's big, baffling behaviors means shifting their autonomic nervous system from focusing on protection to focusing on connection. The good news is that there are ways to deliberately offer your child cues of safety so that they can easily rest into feeling safe. I'll be teaching Nat all sorts of things she can do to help Sammie experience more felt safety in Chapter 6. Nat and I will work together to help calm Sammie's tsunami of the past, so that her mind has more opportunity to feel safe in the present.

One thing I know for sure: Sammie longs to feel safe. She longs for her protection mode to rest and take a break. It's a lot of work. It's exhausting. A lot of bad things happen because of it.

Maybe the Sammie in your life doesn't seem interested in feeling safe. Maybe it seems like your Sammie enjoys feeling oppositional, controlling, and aggressive.

There probably *is* a part of every Sammie that thrives on the power that comes from those behaviors. It's the part that is desperate to be safe. The point of protection mode is to find a way to be safe. That's what protection is! There is always a part of Sammie that is longing to find safety and connection.

Connection just feels too scary right now.

CHAPTER 3

Trust Me...Your Kid Wants to Be Connected to You

"If she needs connection to survive," you ask, "then why does she do things on purpose that make me not want to have anything to do with her?"

I nod. "Totally fair question. It definitely seems like those two things don't belong together. Can I tell you a little story?" You set down your coffee and settle back into the couch, as I reach over and pick up the baby doll I always keep nearby. I tell this story a lot.

"Teeny tiny babies come into this world so soft and squishy and wonderful that we want to hold them close." I hug the baby doll close to my chest and immediately start swaying back and forth, without even intending to. "If I sat this baby down and walked away, what would happen?"

"They'd cry," you answer, in a tone that says, "Well, duh!"

"Yes of course," I say. "But why?"

"Because they don't like to be alone."

"Okay, yes! And then when a baby cries, what do most parents do?"

"They pick up the baby."

"Right. Why?"

"So the baby will stop crying."

"Sure, but why is being picked up what helps a baby stop crying?"

You think for a second. "Because...they feel better?" you ask.

"Yes! But the connection doesn't just feel better. Babies need safe grown-ups to feed them and to keep them from being gobbled up by a saber-toothed tiger. Babies literally need connection to survive, right?"

You agree.

"Okay," I say, "so we agree that babies need a grown-up to take care of them for survival. But survival isn't just about staying alive. Babies who get their physical needs met but don't have a dependable emotional connection with a caregiver really suffer. Physical connection isn't enough. From the moment we're born—probably even before—we need emotional connection to survive. And that never changes."

You raise an eyebrow at me. "Well Sammie certainly doesn't seem like she needs emotional connection. She pinches me and spits on me. She tells me I'm ugly and a bad mom. Sometimes she says these things when she's mad, but sometimes she says them when I'm trying to connect with her. She pushes away connection—with her words and sometimes literally, like with her feet or hands."

"Yes." I soften my voice. "I know. I can't imagine how painful that is. You also need connection to survive, so having your attempts at connection rejected so aggressively must hurt really badly." Your eyes well up slightly as you heave a big sigh. "It's confusing," I continue. "On the one hand, your heart knows that Sammie needs you. But on the other hand, she sure does try hard to prove she doesn't."

"Exactly." The word catches a little in your throat.

"We talked last week about how the brain has two modes, connection and protection. In a way, these modes work together. When we feel afraid and shift into protection mode, we have two instincts. One is to get away from danger. The other is to get closer to safety and connection."

I hold up the baby doll. "When a baby feels afraid, they cry. They look around, try to find the person who takes care of them, and then cry until that person comes. What do you think happens if the person who takes care of them is also the person who caused them to feel afraid?" You look at the baby doll with some uncertainty. "Oh good idea," I say. "Let's have the baby act this out."

I look at the baby, make a mean face, and yell, "You are a very,

very bad baby!" Looking back at you, I say, "Yikes, that would scare the baby!"

You nod.

"And I'm the one who made her feel afraid." Another nod. "So how does this baby feel if now I go and pick her up?" I shift back to a mean face and start to pick up the baby doll. "Why are you crying?" I yell at her.

I look over at you. "This baby is so confused! She felt afraid, so she cried to get her caregiver to come. The caregiver came," I indicate myself, "but it's the same person who made her feel afraid—and that person is still acting scary. So the baby wants to get away because she's scared." I turn the baby away from me. "But she also wants to get close because she's scared." I turn the baby toward me. "She's kind of stuck. Being close is scary, so she cries for help from her caregiver. But her caregiver is the one making her feel scared." I turn the baby away, then toward me, away, then toward me. "If you had to guess, what do you think this baby is learning?"

You look sad and a little confused. "That her mom," you begin, "...or whoever you are...is mean and scary."

"Yes! This baby learns that connection equals danger. And she learns that when there is danger, there is no way out."

"That makes sense," you say. "But...I'm not mean to Sammie. Well, I try not to be mean." You sigh. "Sometimes it's so hard to take care of her. I get so mad and overwhelmed, and I say mean things I shouldn't." You look ashamed. "Is that why she rejects connection?"

"You know," I say, "for some reason we think that being a parent means we're no longer a regular human with regular human feelings. You're right. It's not great to say mean things to Sammie. I also know that sometimes you get overwhelmed and it feels like you just can't take any more. Sometimes you say things you wish you didn't... because you're human. I wonder if it would be okay for me to feel compassion for both of you right now, for you and Sammie?"

"Well, sure I guess." You pause, thinking. "I mean, yes you can feel compassion for us. Things are pretty hard for both of us I suppose."

"Yup, they sure are," I agree. "My guess is that connection and protection were tangled in Sammie's brain long before you adopted her, right?"

"Yes, that's right. But why does she take it out on me?"

"Well, I know it feels like she's taking it out on you, but that's not exactly what's happening. Because you take care of Sammie now, your relationship with her activates the connection circuits in her brain. But for Sammie, connection is tied to protection. Remember how the baby felt?" I pick up the doll again and turn her toward you, then away. "For Sammie, as soon as her connection circuits get activated, her protection circuits also get activated. Those protection circuits tell her body to go to the person who takes care of her. But then her body remembers that connection is where the danger is, and she goes back into protection mode. She wants to turn toward connection, but the connection is what makes her afraid." I turn the baby doll toward you and away, toward you and away.

"Well, that's exhausting and confusing," you say.

"Yeah, it is," I agree. "Think of it like this. What if my body knew I needed chocolate cake to live? Like, I had to have it or I would die. But the only chocolate cake I have is poisonous. I know it's poisonous, but I have to eat to live. But if I eat it I will die. How do you think I might act around that chocolate cake?"

"Really weird?" you ask.

"Yeah. REALLY weird! My behavior probably wouldn't make any sense at all. Sometimes I'd be mean, sometimes really angry, because why does chocolate cake have to poison me when it tastes so good and I need it? Sometimes I'd feel exhausted by this internal battle. I'd feel like just collapsing next to it, but still not eating it. I might poke at it, yell at it. I might try to make it not be poisonous by being super extra nice to it. I mean really, who even knows what I would do?"

"Sammie thinks I'm poisonous chocolate cake that she needs to live but will die if she eats?"

"Basically."

"Okay so now what?" you ask.

"Oh, we just untangle connection from protection. Piece of cake."

Connection Is a Biological Imperative

We've already established that human beings need connection to survive. Teeny tiny human babies can't physically survive on their own. They need a grown-up to stay connected to them, to feed them, change them, keep them warm, and keep them safe. Compared to other mammals, human children actually need adult connection for a long time. Connection literally ensures our survival.

Physical survival isn't enough, though. Remember how we learned in Chapter 1 that the brain develops through relational connection? When we're born, the limbic regions of our brain, which facilitate interpersonal connection and attachment, among other things, aren't fully hooked up to the rest of the brain. There's plenty of neurons there; they just aren't communicating yet. The brain is sort of like a house with all the outlets, but not all the wiring. Babies need to receive safe, soothing human connection for the limbic regions of the brain to develop properly—for that wiring to go all the way from the basement up to the "second floor," where the higher thinking regions of the brain can come online.

Babies who don't get their emotional connection needs met often demonstrate delayed cognitive development. This delay makes sense when we remember from Chapter 1 that the brain organizes around what is used the most. Not getting connection is dangerous, so the "danger-danger" portions of the brain remain online too long and work overtime. That takes energy away from the development of other brain regions.

Attachment Behaviors

It wouldn't make sense to talk about connections between parents and babies without talking about attachment. Dr John Bowlby, the psychologist who first researched attachment, observed three very distinct behaviors in babies that he considered *attachment behaviors*:

- *Stay close!* One of the primary jobs of the attachment system is to keep babies close to their caregivers. Babies can't stay out of sight from saber-toothed tigers, make their own bottles, or keep the thermostat set at a safe temperature. They need grown-ups for everything! Babies keep their eyes on their caregiver and cry when their caregiver gets too far away for too long, which usually brings their caregiver back. As babies get older, they can crawl, run, and pound on closed bathroom doors with their tiny fists when they feel like they're too far away from their caregiver. Believe it or not, even just being cute supports attachment. Babies are so precious that adults want to hold, snuggle, and gush over them. Being cute keeps caregivers close!

- *Be curious and explore!* Once a baby feels confident in the closeness and dependability of their caregiver, the next attachment behavior is actually to be not so close. When I was in graduate school, we'd take our puppy on hikes in the Wasatch Mountains outside Salt Lake City. I can still picture how she'd run ahead of us a few steps, pause, turn around, make sure we were still there, then turn back around and keep running ahead. She'd go through that routine basically every four seconds until we reached the top. Our pup was using her attachment figures (us) to feel safe enough to explore. Humans (and pups) are naturally curious! When they feel safe and connected, their drive for curious exploration kicks in. As our pup would reach the edge of proximity that felt safe, she'd turn around and check on us. Seeing us would help fill her connection cup back up and off she'd go again.

  Babies and, of course, toddlers, preschoolers, and even high-schoolers and spouses do this exact same thing. As they get older, they need less proximity. They go out a little farther and stay away a little longer, but then there comes a moment when they need their attachment cup refilled. So they toddle back, or the school day ends and they run toward their caregivers at school pick-up, or they send a text message to their caregiver when they're having a tough day at school. But until then, they are out doing exactly what they need to do: explore, learn, wonder, and discover new things, including their own likes, dislikes, talents, and challenges.

- *Feel better!* Going out and exploring the world will inevitably lead to some big feelings! Excitement, surprise, and fear are just some of the feelings that will overwhelm babies and young children. The next attachment behavior is to use the attachment figure to feel better. Imagine giving a toddler their first jack-in-the-box. To the toddler, it looks like a pretty box that plays music. Then, all of a sudden, a clown jumps out. This is so unexpected and scary!

The toddler is startled, cries, and immediately turns toward their caregiver. If they are sitting in their caregiver's lap, they likely turn and bury themselves in their caregiver's chest. If the caregiver is somewhere else, they will first use their eyes to find them and then run toward them—fast!

The "danger-danger" system activates the attachment system and propels the child toward their caregiver. The toddler with the jack-in-the-box wasn't in physical danger but they were scared and needed help feeling better. All humans reach a point where their feelings are too big to handle without help. For babies and toddlers, this happens a lot! As children get older, they need help handling big feelings less frequently, but even you and I sometimes need help with our big feelings. This is a normal attachment behavior. When I'm stressed, upset, or in danger, once I know I'm physically safe, my next instinct is to connect with my husband. First, I go toward him in my mind. His presence actually lives in my mind; I have a neural net (a cluster of neurons) that represents him. A sense of soothing already begins, though it might be very subtle. Next, if I can, I reach out. I call or send a text, or I get up and walk to wherever he is. This process of co-regulation and the internalization of our attachment figures is described in more detail in Chapter 4.

The Attachment Cycle

In the most basic explanation of attachment, a baby has a need. They are hungry or tired or lonely. That feeling prompts the baby to express their need, usually (especially at first) by crying. For a moment or two, the caregiver actually matches that energy. This is important! The caregiver's slight increase in energy sends a message to their own body. "Oh! The baby is crying!" It's enough energy to prompt the caregiver to do something about the crying baby, but not so much energy that they become too distressed to soothe the baby.

After that little burst of energy, the caregiver first self-soothes (this doesn't involve a lot of thinking; it just happens) so they are better able to soothe the baby. The baby's nervous system begins to sync with the caregiver, to regulate, calm, and, eventually, move into a state of contentedness.

This cycle—baby has a need, baby expresses the need, parent meets the need, baby is soothed—is repeated approximately one billion times in the first 12 months of life and ultimately lays the foundation for attachment.

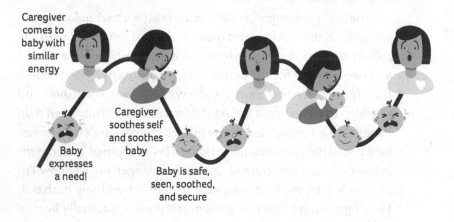

Caregiver comes to baby with similar energy

Baby expresses a need!

Caregiver soothes self and soothes baby

Baby is safe, seen, soothed, and secure

Safe, Seen, Soothed, and Secure

Babies need a lot more than a full tummy and a warm blanket. In addition to having their physical needs met, Drs Dan Siegel and Tina Payne Bryson say babies (and actually humans of all ages) need to feel "safe, seen, soothed, and secure."[1]

Feeling safe, seen, soothed, and secure are the magic ingredients in attachment. When the caregiver feels the baby's distress, holds that distress in their mind and heart, then soothes the baby and meets the need, the baby "feels felt."[2] There isn't a checklist to follow that helps babies feel safe, seen, soothed, and secure. It's a feeling, an experience. It's both doing (like feeding) and being (energetically connected and soothing to the baby).

When the baby has a need, their protection system comes alive. This activates the accelerator side of their autonomic nervous system, giving them the energy necessary to cry or shout or run toward their caregiver. Babies learn that when their protection system gets turned on, going toward the safety of their caregiver helps them feel safe, seen, soothed, and secure. Feeling safe, seen, soothed, and secure turns off the protection system and allows the baby to rest into connection.

When the Need Isn't Met

What happens when the baby's protection system turns on and they have no one to help them feel safe, seen, soothed, and secure? What happens when the baby expresses their need but nobody comes? Or when somebody comes but doesn't meet their need—or maybe even causes more distress?

The connection system and the protection system start to get tangled up. The Circle of Security, an intervention that supports the development of secure attachment between parents and children, describes the kind of caregiver behavior that can cause the connection and protection systems to get tangled as "mean," "weak," or "gone."[3]

Mean

The kind of caregiver behavior that the Circle of Security intervention describes as "mean" includes physical, verbal, and sexual abuse. Mean behavior activates the child's "danger-danger" system. When the "danger-danger" system gets activated, the child wants to go toward their caregiver to feel better. But the child of a mean caregiver doesn't feel better when they go toward that person. This child feels more scared and has no one to help them feel better or be safe.

Weak

The "weak" caregiver isn't overtly abusive and terrifying like the mean caregiver. Weak caregivers are so very afraid themselves that they cannot help their child feel safe. Some weak caregivers are in scary situations, like domestic violence. Some are too scared to set any boundaries with their child and the child ends up more in charge than the parent. Although it might not seem like it at first, this is actually a very scary situation for a child. Children know that in order to be safe, they need their caregiver to be in charge. When the child ends up in charge, the child might act powerful and even scary, but really this is a child who is very, very scared. The end result is similar to the child whose caregiver is mean: the child is left all alone with big, scary feelings and with a caregiver who not only causes those scary feelings, but is also unable to soothe or provide safety for the child.

Gone

This describes a caregiver who is either physically or energetically "gone." The child might be left alone for a very long time, longer than a baby should ever be left alone. Inevitably, babies have needs! They will coo or cry or fuss or do something to alert their caregiver that they need to be safe, seen, soothed, and secure. But what if no one comes? What if the caregiver isn't frightening (mean) or frightened (weak), but actually not even there at all (gone)?

Some caregivers, due to their own significant histories of trauma and terror, are physically present but energetically gone. They may become swept away in their own state of disorganization and ultimately dissociation, which makes them unavailable to meet the baby's needs. As we've learned, having unmet needs activates the child's protection system and propels the child to seek comfort and connection. But an unavailable caregiver cannot meet those needs, so the child is left uncomfortable and disconnected.

A Caregiver in Protection Mode

It's important to take a breath here and remember that caregivers who could be considered mean, weak, or gone are caregivers whose nervous system is in protection mode. It can be hard to understand how caregivers can be mean, weak, or gone until we remember that these systems of connection and protection exist in people of all ages. There are many reasons why a caregiver could struggle to be in connection mode with their child, but the bottom line is that mean, weak, or gone caregivers have vulnerable nervous systems themselves and respond to their children in protection mode instead of connection mode. We can acknowledge the tragedy of children being hurt by their caregivers while remaining compassionate toward caregivers who are swept away by their own nervous system being in protection mode.

Trauma and Toxic Stress

In attachment language, we call this tangle of connection and protection *disorganized attachment*. Disorganizing experiences get stored in the nervous system as experiences of intense chaos and confusion.

Children with these histories often become chaotic and confusing themselves. They are extremely difficult to care for because they send very mixed signals about what they need and want.

It feels bad to be overwhelmed by chaos and confusion, so one way these kids try to feel better is by being controlling and manipulative.

Children who have had a lot of disorganizing experiences don't want to depend on their caregivers for safety. It feels safer to these kids to just rely on themselves, and they control and manipulate others in their attempts to do so. If you're caring for a child like this, it's important to remember that even though part of them wants to stay safe by controlling and manipulating you, another part of them desperately wants to stay safe by feeling connected to you.

The disorganization remains because connection is a biological imperative and there is a part of their nervous system that continues to desperately search and long for connection, while also feeling like connection is dangerous.

Their nervous system is tied in metaphorical knots. They are exhausted. They remain in an almost constant state of activation without any trust or willingness to seek out safety and connection—from anyone.

They spin endlessly in a tornado of disorganization.

Protection Behaviors

When your child has a behavior that isn't inviting or seeking connection, it's a protection behavior. It's pretty easy to tell the difference. Do you want more of that behavior from your child or less? If the behavior is annoying, frustrating, scary, or unsafe, it's a behavior of protection.

Underneath protection behaviors is always a desperate search for connection. I know that's really hard to believe. You might just have to take my word for it. The bizarre behaviors are actually your child's attempt to avoid feeling something that is not only terrifying but also leaves them feeling trapped, stuck, and helpless.

To say it another way, they are trying to avoid feeling like they are going to die.

The biological drive for connection, both when we are safe and when we are afraid, is always there. You might have a child who has covered up their need for connection underneath layers and layers of protection. I can't promise you that you'll ever see evidence of their need for connection, but I can promise you that it's there somewhere.

There are other reasons to be overwhelmed by and rejecting of connection, including unique neurotypes, sensitive sensory systems, neuroimmune disorders, and more. The experience of connection involves a lot of sensory stimuli. For some children, that sensory experience is overwhelming. Too much sensory data too fast can be neuroceived as dangerous, flipping the nervous system into protection mode. This book focuses on the impact of trauma, as that is the basis of my clinical experience, but please know there are many other reasons why children have a difficult relationship with connection.

If you see your child in this book, then you're probably pretty dysregulated, too. It is highly dysregulating to care for a child with this level of chaos in their nervous system.

I know Sammie has a lot of chaos in her nervous system, and I know Nat is exhausted, confused, and feeling helpless and hopeless.

In a way, Nat is feeling what Sammie is feeling. Sammie's nervous system at times gets so overwhelmed that it engulfs Nat, and Nat ends up feeling the same way.

Then they get stuck together and it feels like there is no way out.

This isn't Nat's fault, and it's definitely not Sammie's fault. Nat needs support so she doesn't get so quickly engulfed by Sammie's energy. Over time, Nat will remain more regulated and more available to offer connection and felt safety, and the tangle of connection and protection in Sammie's nervous system will begin to loosen.

CHAPTER 4

What's Regulation Got to Do with It?

As our weeks together progress, I notice that you are feeling safer in this space, and with me. You get your own coffee now—sometimes you even get mine. The owl mug is your favorite, and you know I love the one with the rainbow. You aren't timid anymore—you plop right down on the couch, kick your shoes off, and tuck your legs up next to you.

When I say something you don't want to hear, you give me your trademark raised eyebrows with a smirk, and we both laugh. You've shown me your rage over your daughter's behaviors, and the hopelessness you sometimes feel. You've sobbed that you can't see how this can ever get better.

Yet you keep coming back.

"Okay wait," you say, halfway through our next session. "You keep using the word 'dysregulated.' Like, you probably say it 25 times every time I come here. But what does that actually mean?"

"Ha! Fair enough! I do use that word a lot. It's such a normal part of my vocabulary that I forget to define it."

I reach for my white board and draw this wavy line again.

"Remember how I drew this during our first appointment?" You nod.

"So, this is regulation. Energy in our body goes up," I point to the line that goes from bottom to top, "and energy in our body comes down." I point to the line coming down. "Up and down, up and down, all day long."

I hold the marker and look back at you. "Sometimes my energy goes up because I gotta get ready for work. Sometimes it goes up because something really funny happens. Or because I'm exercising. Or scared, or even mad. But inevitably my energy comes down. I'm hustling around getting ready for work, but once I get in the car, I take a breath and my energy comes down. Or I get mad at my kid because he forgot to take out the trash and we missed trash day! But then the mad eventually goes away. What goes up eventually comes down, right?"

"Yeah," you say. "Sure, that makes sense."

I continue. "Okay, well if that happens in this nice, even, up-and-down motion inside my window of tolerance," I draw a line on top and a line on the bottom, "then I'm pretty regulated. I'm managing the stress of life without freaking out. Make sense?"

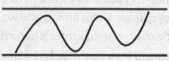

You nod. Excellent. I rub out the drawing with the side of my hand and start again. This time I make a jagged line.

"Sometimes—and for some people it's a lot of the time—energy doesn't have that nice up and down motion. It looks more like this. Like Sammie!"

"Oh yes, that's Sammie for sure."

"Right. It's a fast 0–60 UP, and then it crashes down, and then it gets stuck at the bottom, then ZOOM back to the top. Sometimes it's like both the accelerator and the brake are going at the same time."

"YES!"

"Okay, that's dysregulated. The energy and arousal isn't in balance. And I don't mean sexual arousal! Arousal just means energy. It's all over the place. It's too fast, too slow, and doesn't seem to match the situation. When I'm dysregulated, I'm totally freaking out. I can't think straight, I'm not paying attention to what I'm doing or to anyone else. I'm just spinning out."

I furiously draw a swirling motion and lock eyes with you.

"That's dysregulated," I reiterate.

"Okay yeah, I remember this now from our first session. You said we were going to help Sammie's body feel less like that jagged line and more like the smooth one."

"Exactly. Can you imagine what kinds of behaviors you'd see in a kid who has a nervous system that is regulated and looks more like this?"

"Normal ones?"

I laugh. "Yeah, I guess that's one way to look at it. I mean, she'll still be a kid with normal ups and downs and certainly nowhere close to perfect behavior. But it will be the kind of behavior you can help her with, and it won't leave you feeling like you've been hit by a bus."

"Okay, great. But how do we get there?"

"Let's look at how regulation develops in the first place." I reach for my always-nearby baby doll and cradle her. "When this baby cries, her energy goes up. As the caregiver, my energy also goes up a little as my body notices that the baby is crying. This little burst of energy means I'll do something—I'll move my body to get to her and pick her up. That burst of energy is also important because this sweet baby can feel our nervous systems match up, and then she gets the experience of feeling seen and known. Once I pick her up, though, I soothe myself so I can soothe the baby. The brakes of my energy and nervous system engage so I can start to settle. I make calming 'shhhhh' noises and sway back and forth. And eventually, the baby borrows my regulation and her brakes grow stronger. Babies have strong accelerators but not very strong brakes. We help make their brakes stronger by doing this for them about a billion times in that first year.

"What do you think would happen if, when I picked up the baby, my accelerator stayed on? If I was really anxious or even angry? If I tried to say soothing words, but they came out all worried or scary? Would the baby be soothed?" You shake your head no. "Right, she wouldn't. And what if I just didn't do anything? If I left the baby alone, maybe said soothing things from a distance like 'Hey you're fine.' Would the baby be soothed? Nope. A baby needs a regulated caregiver to soothe them when their accelerator is going, because their brakes aren't very strong. They don't have a lot of balance yet."

"But Sammie isn't a baby anymore," you say.

"No," I agree, "but her brakes are weak and her accelerator is pedal to the metal, and before you know it, she is whizzing out of control! We might say it's bad behavior, or she's rude, or defiant, or give her all sorts of other labels. But really what she is, is dysregulated. And to strengthen her regulation circuits, we have to do exactly what the caregiver does for a baby. First, we match their energy. Then, we make sure that even if our energy is high, we are in connection mode. We are regulated. Then we step in to help. With a baby, that means we rock them and give them a bottle."

"I'm not giving Sammie a bottle!" you say, with a confused laugh.

"Definitely not! With Sammie it's going to look a little different, though honestly, not that much. Rocking and a drink are two of the primary things I suggest for dysregulated humans of all ages! Anyway, we stay regulated—not necessarily calm, but regulated. And we focus on this process of co-regulation. With a baby, if I'm regulated, I'm not really thinking about getting the baby to stop crying. I'm thinking about soothing her and helping her feel better. Eventually I might get dysregulated and start to focus on how I can just make her stop crying. Ironically enough, as soon as I focus on that, it becomes less likely I'll be successful.

"It's the same with Sammie. If we stay focused on providing regulation, connection, and felt safety, eventually her nervous system will shift and the negative behaviors will decrease."

You look puzzled. "Other kids Sammie's age don't need all that. Why does she?"

I shrug. "My best guess is that Sammie didn't get quite enough co-regulation when she was tiny, so her nervous system didn't have what it needed to get strong and healthy. So now her nervous system is sensitized. She has huge reactions to what seem like small problems. That's because her stress response system isn't very strong. She had too much stress as a baby and not enough co-regulation.

"The cool thing, though, is that we can repair this system. We do it by giving her the experiences she needed when she was tiny—co-regulation when she is dysregulated. That means we, the grown-ups, stay regulated, and we focus not on her behavior, but on how to help her feel safe and then soothed."

I pause to let it sink in, then say, "Easy, right?"

You actually roll your eyes at me and I think that's the moment my affection for you turns into pure delighted adoration. It always comes. I adore all my people. "All true selves are loveable" (a quote from one of my early mentors, Candyce Ossefort-Russell). Your delightful true core self comes bursting to the surface with just one little eye roll.

"Okay, not easy," I agree with your eye roll. "But I'll help you."

Regulation, Regulate, and Regulated

In the past few years, I've seen the word "regulation" in more and more parenting books, educational resources, and social media posts. It's exciting to watch adults begin to shift away from a behavior-based model toward a regulation-based model.

But there's still a lot of confusion about what it means to be regulated. Sometimes when I ask a kid what regulation means, they sit cross-legged on the floor, close their eyes, put their thumb to middle finger, and say, "Ohmmmm." Or they strike a yoga pose. In other words, they think regulated means calm.

Regulated does not equal calm. (Lisa Dion)[1]

Regulation:

Keeping the accelerator and the brakes (of energy and arousal) in balance. (Dan Siegel and Mary Hartzell)[2]

Managing the ebb and flow of the energy and arousal in my nervous system without freaking out. (Robyn Gobbel)

Regulate:

To monitor and modify the change of something across time. Monitoring involves the capacity to sense a process; modifying involves the modulation and shaping of that process over time. (Dan Siegel)[3]

Regulated:

To be mindful, aware of, and connected to ourselves. (Lisa Dion)[4]

In his definition of *regulate*, Dan Siegel calls our attention to the fact that regulation involves some mindful awareness.[5] To regulate something, I have to first be mindful enough to monitor (notice and pay attention to) it and then be capable of modifying (changing) it.

Self-regulation, then, means that we have the ability to notice and change the energy in our own bodies. I notice I'm starting to get stressed out so I take a break and go for a walk. (Or let's be real, I eat some candy.)

For our children who haven't yet developed self-regulation, they need a present, regulated adult to help with this "monitor and modify" process. The adult notices that the child needs help and steps in to help the child "modify" the energy and arousal of their nervous system.

You'll notice that none of these definitions includes "feeling" words. Regulated doesn't mean calm. Regulated doesn't mean happy. A person can be regulated and also be sad, mad, happy, and all sorts of other feelings.

Can I be angry while still being connected to myself, with the ability to shift the energy in my body if I want or need to? Absolutely.

This book talks a lot about the importance of a parent staying regulated. Again, regulated does not mean calm! It doesn't mean acting like everything's fine with a fake smile, or ignoring behavior that simply isn't working for anyone.

Regulated means you can still use your thinking brain to make choices about what to do next. Your accelerator could be engaged, you could actually even be slightly in protection mode, but you can still be regulated.

You might be peering at this book with the narrowed eyes of skepticism. Maybe just trust me on this one for now. Regulated does not equal calm.

Attachment Theory Is a Regulation Theory

In 2000, psychologist and researcher Dr Allan Schore published a paper in the journal of *Attachment & Human Development*.[6] He proposed the idea that attachment theory is fundamentally a regulation theory. The attachment cycle described in Chapter 3 is, at its core, a theory of how two people come together and impact—regulate—each other's physiology. The baby's stress undoubtedly impacts the caregiver's stress. The caregiver does their best to regulate their own stress response so that they can, in turn, co-regulate and soothe the baby's stress response. This mutual, dyadic exchange of energy that goes up and down while the caregiver and baby come in and out of connection is the foundation for the development of regulation in the baby's autonomic nervous system.

The Accelerator and the Brakes

Dan Siegel defines regulation as keeping the accelerator and the brakes in balance.[7] This concept applies to all sorts of things. The thermostat regulates the temperature in my home by monitoring and then modifying it by either pressing the accelerator (turning on the air conditioning or the heater) or pressing the brakes (turning off the air conditioning or the heater).

Behaviors are just what we see on the outside that give us clues about what's happening on the inside, specifically with regard to the energy and arousal of the autonomic nervous system. Changing our children's big, baffling behaviors means we have to look at what's happening in the energy and arousal of their autonomic nervous system. If we balance the accelerator ("go-go-go" energy) and the brakes ("slow down" energy), those big, baffling behaviors will begin to disappear.

Attachment and Regulation

The regulation of the autonomic nervous system is cultivated within the attachment cycle. A baby has a need. The accelerator of their nervous system engages and they voice their distress. It's like pressing on the gas pedal of the car. Babies have nice, strong accelerators that work great the moment they are born.

What goes up must come down, but babies can't come down without the help of a caregiver. Babies need to borrow the energy of their caregiver's brake.

Chapter 3 discussed that when the baby's accelerator is pressed (the baby has a need), the caregiver gets a little burst of their own accelerator. They realize "Oh! The baby is crying!" which gives them the energy they need to go to the baby. It also gives the baby the experience of being matched energetically, which creates the experience of being seen. The caregiver has just enough energy in their body to go to and match the baby, but not too much energy that they startle or cause more distress in the baby.

Once the caregiver connects with the baby, the caregiver's brake engages so that they can soothe the baby. A caregiver with their accelerator to the floor isn't going to soothe the baby very well. In fact, this usually leaves the baby with their accelerator engaged and creates an increasingly frustrated caregiver.

With the caregiver's brake engaged, their own nervous system soothes. They can now meet the baby's need and offer their soothing to the baby. Eventually, the baby is soothed. Wash, rinse, repeat one bajillion times in the first year of life.

If this cycle happens enough—and enough is shown to be about 30 percent of the time[8]—then this child is likely to develop secure attachment and age-appropriate regulation. I say "age-appropriate" because of course a three-year-old's capacity for regulation is a lot different than a 43-year-old's—though they both benefit from a drink and a snack when they're dysregulated.

As the baby and caregiver move through the attachment cycle over and over again, an important cell called myelin begins to grow in the baby's brain. Myelin wraps itself around the nerves that create the "brake" side of the autonomic nervous system and helps the brakes work better and faster. Myelin growth is supported by co-regulation. More myelin means more regulation and a wider window of stress tolerance. Isn't it just wild how co-regulation creates the development of neurons that lead to self-regulation? I think it's amazing!

Self-Regulation Isn't the Goal

Hang with me for just a few moments before you reject this premise. Not only is self-regulation not the goal, sometimes I wonder if it actually even exists.

The development of myelin during the co-regulation process is amazing, but so is the creation of neural nets. In his seminal text *The Developing Mind*, Dan Siegel describes neural nets as patterns of neurons that fire at the same time.[9]

I like to think of neural nets like constellations. There are billions of stars and billions of neurons. Some stars are linked together to form constellations. Some stars are in more than one constellation. Same with neurons. When your child has an experience, their brain lights up a particular pattern of neurons. If that experience is repeated enough times and that pattern of neurons lights up enough times, those neurons begin to wire together and eventually they create a neural net. Neurobiologist Carla Shatz even came up with a catchy phrase to describe this phenomenon: "Neurons that fire together wire together."[10]

When a baby receives sufficient experiences of co-regulation, they develop a neural net that represents that co-regulation. That neural net gets stronger and stronger, and eventually that neural pattern of co-regulation can fire even without the caregiver being present!

Chapter 3 introduced the idea that we build mental frameworks for connection with our attachment figures. If something distressing happens, I almost immediately think of my husband and want to reach out to him. Neurobiologically, the neural net in my mind that represents my husband is activated. It's like he's there, even when he isn't.

Remember how one of the three core attachment behaviors is to turn toward connection when the "danger-danger" circuitry gets activated? When my nervous system tips into protection mode, I turn toward the representation of my safe, secure attachment figure that now lives in my mind. This happens because over the last 20 years, my brain has connected the neurons that represent comfort and connection with the neurons that represent my husband.

I've created a neural net of my husband in my mind due to what psychologist Louis Cozolino aptly named the *resonance circuitry*.[11]

Resonance Circuitry

Fully diving into resonance circuitry goes beyond what we need in a book about parenting dysregulated kids, but here's just a quick overview of this system:

> *Resonance*: The mutual influence of interacting systems on each other that allows two or more entities to become a part of one functional whole. (Dan Siegel)[12]

Relational resonance happens when two people come together, impact one another, and create something new—a "we" instead of just a "me." There's a space in between us where our energies seem to touch, resonate, and impact each other. This resonance is how we know whether someone is really paying attention to us, or just nodding along. Your kids know when they are in resonance with you and when they aren't, and they'll work pretty hard to get back into resonance. This is why they suddenly have a lot of needs when you're distracted by a phone call or in the bathroom. They don't just want you nearby; they want to feel you nearby.

It's suggested that our mirror neurons are partially responsible for this experience of resonance.[13] Mirror neurons are neurons that help us simulate in our own mind what is happening in someone else's mind.[14]

Imagine this. You're strolling through the grocery store when you see a young toddler suddenly erupt with a deep, belly-rumbling laugh. You can't help but smile, and probably laugh, too! The toddler's brain had their "belly laugh" neurons light up. And so did your brain! Your brain activated the same belly laugh neurons just seeing that toddler belly laugh! Then you smiled or maybe laughed, too.

Mirror neurons make therapy work! In all the thousands of hours I've spent sitting with people in emotional pain, my resonance circuitry allowed me to feel in my own body what my client was feeling in theirs by creating a corresponding neural firing. Of course, it's not good to get confused and lose sight of whose feelings are whose, so a portion of mirror neurons ensures that we don't resonate *too* much.[15] Still, my brain would literally fire neurons in the same pattern that my client's brain was firing neurons! Wild, huh?

When a caregiver offers co-regulation to their baby, the baby is creating a neural net of what it feels like to receive the co-regulation. At the same time, their mirror neurons are creating a neural net of the caregiver who is offering that co-regulation. As the baby grows and develops, both neural nets strengthen, and this combination of being co-regulated and internalizing the regulation of their caregiver leads to the development of what is commonly called self-regulation. Eventually, instead of literally turning toward their caregiver for co-regulation, children and teenagers turn toward the internalization of their caregiver that lives in their mind.

This process allows babies to move farther and farther away from their caregiver. By the time they're toddlers, they can tolerate their caregiver leaving the room for a bit. Later, they can go to preschool and be away from their caregiver all morning. Eventually they become teenagers who need nothing more than a text message and a case of energy drinks once a week. As children grow and develop, the internalization of co-regulation grows stronger and allows the child to demonstrate what we typically call self-regulation.

Can't Teach Self-Regulation

Self-regulation isn't something we can teach with lessons on taking deep breaths and making lists of things that help us feel calm. Don't get me wrong—it's important to help children understand their brains and bodies and learn the things that help them access a felt sense of regulation.

For some kids, a hug and a sip of cold water might help; for others, a cozy corner with their headphones on. But there needs to be an existing internal model for regulation before a child can understand what they're aiming for, and they only get that via co-regulation.

I've learned that if I'm getting stressed, I need to lace up my tennis shoes and find a way to hit the ground hard. I like to do jump squats or burpees, or I go for a run. I have no natural athleticism. But I know that hitting the ground hard stops me from going completely bananas, and I know how to connect the dots from "Wow, I'm feeling stressed!" to "Oh! I'll go for a run."

That's the key point, though—I have enough internalized co-regulation that there is enough time and space between "everything's fine!" and "I'm going bananas!" for me to stop and think, "Oh, I should go for a run." My stress accelerator can slow down because of all the co-regulation I've internalized. Without solid internalized co-regulation, I could know all the coping skills on earth but be unable to access them. I would get too dysregulated too fast.

This might sound familiar. You may have a child who knows a lot of coping skills but doesn't use them. It might even feel like they purposefully refuse to use them, almost as though they prefer to feel dysregulated.

I get it. It really does feel that way. But actually what's happening is that they don't yet have enough internalized co-regulation. The stress accelerator in their autonomic nervous system goes pedal to the metal, and they are so dysregulated so quickly that they can't use any of those skills. It's not that they don't want to; it's that they can't. They haven't yet internalized enough co-regulation to tolerate small amounts of stress without freaking out.

Trauma and Toxic Stress

When babies don't get the co-regulation they need or have caregivers who are mean, weak, or gone (as discussed in Chapter 3), they end up experiencing way more stress than their bodies can process.

Remember—stress isn't inherently bad. Stress is required for any kind of growth, including the growth of our stress response system! If I wanted to run a marathon or bench press 400 pounds, I'd have to stress my muscles a bit to build them big and strong, right? But I'd need the right amount of stress. Too little and I wouldn't grow any muscle. Too much and I also wouldn't grow any muscle because I'd constantly just be getting hurt.

Same with regulation and the stress response system. Too much stress without enough co-regulation means the stress response system develops in a sensitized and vulnerable manner. This creates the classic "mountain out of a molehill" phenomenon, when a teeny tiny stressor (from our perspective) causes a huge response. It feels like such an overreaction when your child flips over a chair because dinner is in five minutes instead of right now. The stress of waiting overloads his sensitized stress response system, and the next thing you know, the table's upside down.

Mean, Weak, or Gone

Let's look at the impact of the baby's unmet need through the lens of both regulation and attachment. The image below shows a baby whose need is continually unmet, no matter how long or loud they cry. This baby will not learn what it feels like to be safe, seen, soothed, and secure, and their attachment pattern will reflect that.

From a regulation standpoint, instead of balance between the accelerator and brakes of the autonomic nervous system, the baby develops an extreme imbalance of chaotic and unpredictable energy.

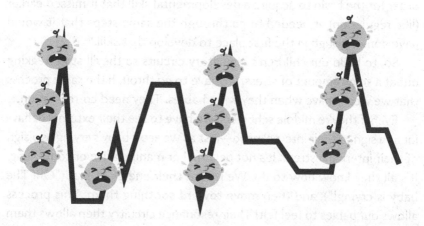

All Behavior Makes Sense

Your child's reactions always match, in some way, their internal experience. Always.

Perhaps their mind gets flooded by memories of being shoved by an abusive caregiver in the past, so they turn around and punch the kid who tagged them during a game at recess.

Perhaps their pounding heart and fast breathing while they were pumping their legs hard on the swing reminded their body of when they were scared and alone. When a peer asks for a turn, your kid screams in their face and runs off.

Perhaps their stress response system is so fragile that the pressure of getting their shoes on and heading out the door to school on time is so much that they collapse like a super-scared possum, and they can't move at all.

From the outside looking in, these seem like huge overreactions.

But from the inside looking out, we can see how all these behaviors could make sense to a sensitized nervous system.

"Recovery of Function Recapitulates the Development of Function"

Well isn't that a mouthful. I heard it first from Karyn Purvis, psychologist and co-author of *The Connected Child* and *Trust-Based Relational Intervention*, at an Empowered to Connect conference. She taught us that in order for the brain to acquire a developmental skill that it missed earlier (like regulation), it needed to go through the same steps that it would have gone through in the first place to develop that skill.[16]

So, to build our children's regulatory circuits so they'll stop freaking out at a small amount of stress, we have to go through the same process that we would have when they were babies. They need co-regulation.

Even if they're middle schoolers, we have to see their external behavior as a sign of their internal need—just as we see a baby's crying as a sign of their internal distress. It's not personal or manipulative or controlling. It's all they know how to do. We match their energy at first ("Oh! The baby is crying!"), and then move toward soothing them. This process allows our babies to feel felt! Their resonance circuitry then allows them to internalize our co-regulation. The brakes of the autonomic nervous system get wrapped in myelin, and they begin to develop age-appropriate regulation skills.

We just gotta figure out how to do that with a five-year-old who is peeing in weird places or spitting in our face. Or a 10-year-old who is calling us mean and fat and ugly. Or the 12-year-old who won't go to school. Or the 15-year-old who is cussing us out and trashing their room when given a limit on screen time.

Can we see each of those kids as a child who is showing us on the outside the way their nervous system feels on the inside? Can we put on our X-ray vision goggles to look past the behaviors and into the depths of their nervous system? Can we see their out-of-control accelerator or their weak brakes?

What if I help you do it through a playful metaphor? What if I keep decoding for you what their behavior really is? And then give you very practical tools for how to change it?

I'm going to do all of those things in Section 2, and we'll start by asking our friends Dorothy, the Scarecrow, the Tin Man, and the Cowardly Lion to teach us a song: "Owls, Watchdogs, and Possums—OH MY!"

NOW LET'S "FIX" THOSE BEHAVIORS

CHAPTER 5

Owls, Watchdogs, and Possums—OH MY!

I close my laptop, push away from my desk, and head toward the waiting room. I stop at the coffee station so I can greet you in our familiar way, but the moment our eyes connect, I see that a part of you has come to the office that I haven't yet had the privilege of meeting.

You're mad. At me.

I notice your crossed arms and the slight narrowing of your eyes. Our eyes meet briefly as you stand up and walk past me without even a hello.

I take a breath and notice a slight flutter in my heart and some heat rise in my chest. I remind myself to pause and invite in a long, deliberate exhale. I close the door gently behind us and set our coffee on the table next to the couch.

"You look mad." Might as well just put it right out in the open. I see you. I welcome all of you, including your mad feelings. Even when they are directed at me.

"These behaviors," you say, "are they really all because of what she experienced before she came to us? I mean—isn't she just a disobedient kid sometimes who needs a consequence?"

"Great question. You want to know how to tell the difference between behaviors that are trauma-related and behaviors that are normal kid behaviors."

"Right! I mean," you shake your head with a confused scowl, "why are we assuming all these behaviors are trauma behaviors?"

Ah, yes. This question comes up a lot. There's fear underneath this question. Fear that if we assume all behaviors are trauma behaviors and we respond in a brain-based way with regulation, connection, felt safety, and, of course, boundaries, that somehow kids are getting away with bad behavior and they won't learn anything.

Hoping that my use of curiosity-based language will help you feel invited into connection and safety, I say, "I wonder what would feel helpful about being able to tell the difference between a trauma behavior and a regular kid behavior?"

"Well, I need to know if she needs help or if she needs a consequence."

"Ohhh, okay. You want to know how to respond. Of course. You love Sammie and you want to respond in the way that is going to help her the most. Am I getting that right?"

"Yes!" Your arms unfold so you can pick up your coffee cup and take a sip. I realize that I've been sitting up straight and leaning in toward you, and I feel tension in my back. As you raise your coffee cup to your mouth, I relax my posture just a little.

"Okay, yeah, that makes sense. But what if I make it a little easier? You'll tie yourself in knots trying to decide if a behavior is about trauma or not, and actually, it really doesn't even matter."

"It doesn't matter?"

"Nope, not really. All we really want to know is how dysregulated her watchdog brain is. Is her owl brain still around at all? Or has the watchdog brain—or maybe the possum brain—totally taken over?"

You raise a skeptical eyebrow at me but I can tell I've piqued your curiosity. I reach for my binder and laugh slightly as I say, "Yup, owls, watchdogs, and possums."

"Oh my," you say as you now fully lean back into the couch. We're back in connection.

"Exactly." I flip to the page with a simple drawing of the brain and a bright, cheerful owl.

The Wise Owl Brain

When Nat wants Sammie's behaviors to change, what she really wants is for Sammie's owl brain to be stronger and in charge more often. Kids with resilient stress response systems have strong owl brains. The wise owl brain is in charge of things like reading and taking a spelling test, but it's also in charge of remembering all the steps involved in getting ready for bed or cleaning up after ourselves. The wise owl brain also knows that social connection is just as important as remembering facts and  carrying out tasks. Social behavior like sharing, cooperating, and caring about someone else's feelings are all part of the owl brain's job. The owl brain helps your child pause before they scribble all over the math sheet they don't want to do and ask for help instead. The owl brain is okay with slightly uncomfortable feelings, the kind of feelings that come up when your child needs to apologize for something, admit they did something they weren't supposed to do, or power through doing a super-unfun chore like cleaning their bedroom or emptying the dishwasher. The wise owl brain is open to connection so it behaves in ways that invite connection.

When your child is neuroceiving safety, their owl brain will take charge and lead the way. That means our number one goal with our kids is to help them feel safe. The owl brain lives in the cortex—that's the highest part of the brain that starts to really flourish somewhere between 18 and 36 months of age, but isn't done developing until the mid to late 20s (see Chapter 1). Just like your child keeps growing and getting stronger when they get to develop in a safe environment, so does the owl brain.

I can almost guarantee that the kinds of behaviors you want from your child are all owl brain behaviors. You want your child to feel safe enough to be honest and remember that lying just creates more problems? Those are all owl brain thoughts. You want your child to be able to play unsupervised with their friends without melting down or getting into a fist-fight? Owl brain behavior! You want your child to be able to clean their room in 30 minutes instead of turning it into an all-weekend-long ordeal? Yup, owl brain.

Big, baffling behavior comes out when the owl brain flies away.

We can't always stop the owl brain from flying away, but as it grows stronger, it won't fly away as often or as abruptly.

We're going to replace the question "Is this a trauma behavior or a regular kid behavior?" with "Is my child's owl brain in charge right now?" We know that kids with a history of trauma (or those who have vulnerable nervous systems for any reason) have less resilient owl brains that fly away a lot. We also know that everyone's owl brain flies away sometimes. In the moment of navigating a tough behavior, it really doesn't matter why our child's owl brain flew away. All that matters is figuring out how to help the owl feel safe enough to return.

How do you know if your child's owl brain is in charge? One way is to ask yourself, "Is this behavior making me want to be in connection with my child?" If the answer is "no," you can be pretty darn certain their owl brain isn't in charge. The owl brain wants to be connected—to themselves and to you!

The owl brain emerges from a nervous system that is regulated, connected, and experiencing felt safety. That's why regulated, connected kids (and parents) who feel safe behave well.

I like to picture the owl brain perched at the very top of the brain, in the cortex, like this.

Here are some cues and clues that your child's owl brain is in charge:

- Logic
- Cooperation
- Curiosity

- Empathy
- Self-reflection
- The ability to "pause" before reacting
- Learning from—and caring about—consequences (not punishments)
- Taking responsibility for their actions
- Asking permission.

When your child's owl brain is in charge, you might see:

- Relaxed eyes and muscles around the mouth
- Relaxed, not collapsed, shoulders, neck, and head
- Even and paced breathing that seems appropriate for the situation
- "Mom, may I..." instead of demanding
- "I'm sorry I..." instead of denying blame or responsibility
- "I need help" instead of throwing their pencil across the room.

While the owl brain comes from connection mode, this does not necessarily mean the owl brain always wants to play or connect! The amount of connection your child seeks or enjoys is based on many different factors, including their unique temperament. Being open to connection is not the same as desiring connection. Your child could decline a playdate or make a choice to spend time alone instead of playing a game with you and they could still be in their owl brain. The owl brain sets compassionate boundaries that might sound like "I don't want to play that game" or even "No thanks, I don't like Brussels sprouts." Some owl brains have more easy-going temperaments and are very flexible. Some owl brains have a stronger need for autonomy and independence.

The Watchdog Brain and the Possum Brain

What happens, though, when neuroception gets more cues of danger than cues of safety and flips into a state of protection? The watchdog brain or the possum brain emerges, ready to keep us safe!

Meet the Watchdog

With much gratitude to all the children who have been vulnerable enough to let me meet and take care of their fiercely protective watchdog brains, it is my greatest pleasure to introduce you to the watchdog brain.

Nestled below the cortex in the limbic regions and brainstem are two different energy pathways. One pathway activates the accelerator of the nervous system and creates an increase in energy. When your child is neuroceiving danger, this pathway fuels what we would typically think of as fight or flight behaviors. This is the watchdog brain!

Like real-life watchdogs, the watchdog that lives in your child's nervous system really just wants to keep your child safe. Also like real-life watchdogs, the watchdog that lives in your child's nervous system sometimes has a small behavior that is protective but not dangerous, like perking up their ears and opening their eyes wide. Sometimes the watchdog has a huge behavior, like biting or attacking. Knowing how scared the watchdog is helps us know the best and safest way to respond. Let's look at some of the behaviors, cues, and clues you will see when your child is in their watchdog brain that will help you know how scared your child really is.

The *I'm Safe!* Watchdog

When the watchdog feels safe—when it detects more cues of safety than cues of danger coming from the 11 million bits of data per second—the watchdog relaxes in the sun and lets the owl brain take charge. This watchdog stays aware of the possibility of danger, but mostly just chills out.

Sometimes, the calm watchdog borrows a little energy from the accelerator, while still feeling safe and connected. This watchdog has the zoomies! It runs and plays and yips joyfully. I like to picture the watchdog and the owl playing together. That helps me remember that the owl brain is in charge even though there is a lot of energy.

The watchdog is always there! But when the watchdog and the owl together feel safe, the watchdog can focus on connecting, playing, and resting while the owl handles everything else. The owl brain can have a fun social exchange with a friend before math class, use logic to do a multiplication worksheet, tolerate the disappointment of not getting all the answers right, and follow the rules of the kickball game during recess.

The *What's Up?* Watchdog

When something happens that causes the watchdog concern, maybe just the sun disappearing behind a cloud, it flips into a very low level of protection mode. This watchdog is asking, "What's up?" Your child's *What's Up?* watchdog wants to protect your child from anything unsafe. It isn't attacking yet or really even getting ready to attack; it's still sniffing the air and checking things out. Your child's owl brain is still around, helping the *What's Up?* watchdog take in more information to decide, "Am I really in danger?"

See how this watchdog's head is lifted up? That's so it can look and listen in every direction in order to decide: safe or unsafe?

Here are some cues and clues that your child might demonstrate when their *What's Up?* watchdog brain is active:

- An increase in body movement, maybe becoming restless or even wandering around
- Slight increase in the intensity in their facial expression, especially around the eyes and maybe mouth. Their face muscles are getting tighter, which communicates to others that they aren't feeling quite as social or as friendly
- Wider eyes that are moving around so they can see things better
- A change in their voice:
  - Whiney and/or edgier intonation
  - Louder
  - Faster
- Decrease in cooperation and flexibility:
  - Sassiness
  - Mild disrespect
  - Increase in "no" response or "I can do it myself" response.

The *Ready-for-Action!* Watchdog

If the watchdog starts to feel like things are indeed dangerous, the watchdog gets *ready for action* and prepares to punch, kick, or run away. See how this watchdog has energy in its limbs? Its body is increasing in energy and arousal, specifically sending more blood and oxygen to its limbs to run or fight. The *Ready-for-Action!* watchdog is focused on becoming "ready for action." Its energy is right on the surface but not mobilized for fight or flight...yet!

The owl has flown away! It's afraid of the *Ready-for-Action!* watchdog and flies off for safety. This watchdog doesn't have any owl brain characteristics and, as you'll learn in Chapter 7, we can't rely on the owl brain anymore to help the watchdog calm down.

Here are some cues and clues that your child might demonstrate when their *Ready-for-Action!* watchdog brain is active:

- Aggressive and/or defensive body language. The energy in this posture prepares your child to punch, kick, or run, but this energy is still in preparation mode, and isn't yet being released:
  - Balled fists
  - Tight and constricted shoulders
  - Making themselves "bigger"
  - Increased energy in legs/thighs
- Increased body movement/activity level:
  - Pacing
  - If sitting, increased movement in legs/feet (kicking, flexing)
  - Standing up from sitting down
- Body movements are less fluid; jerkier and quicker
- Language becomes more difficult. Sentences get shorter, possibly more hostile, and maybe don't make sense
- Overly silly that isn't fun:
  - Maniacal laughing
- Significant increase in oppositionality

- Limited ability to "pause" before behavior (remember, the owl brain has flown away)
- Illogical or unreasonable.

The *Back Off!* Watchdog

As neuroception of fear and danger increases, the watchdog springs into action. Now the watchdog is ready to use all that energy it prepared. This watchdog is very afraid and uses scary behaviors to protect itself. It's trying to get you to *back off!* Think of your child as a barking, growling, or snarling watchdog. Their behavior is scary, but it's really because they are scared and using the best protective skills they have.

This watchdog may also engage the flight response and just turn tail and leave. This may feel very disrespectful or as if they are maintaining control of the situation by choosing to leave. They are! Remember that controlling and disrespectful behavior is about fear and trying to find safety.

The owl brain is loooooooooong gone. In Chapter 7, you'll learn to think about this watchdog as holding up a big stop sign, reminding you to stop and focus only on safety and regulation.

Here are some cues and clues that your child might demonstrate when their *Back Off!* watchdog brain is active:

- Aggressive facial expression, body language, and words:
  - "Air" punching or other provocative and threatening body language and gestures
  - Verbal aggression, "I HATE YOU!," threatening, swearing
- Continued increase in intensity in the body/muscles:
  - Bigger, faster, and more intense body movement
  - This increased energy could be brewing beneath the surface like a volcano. Pay attention to extremely tense muscles even if there is little movement. This watchdog is ready to explode
- Heavier and faster breathing (and heart rate, if you can notice that)

- Louder voice that is raising in pitch
- Fleeing/flight behavior—stomping out of the room, running out of the house, or even just turning their back to you
- Language gets "younger"—fewer words, repeating words
- A "tantrum"—intense expression of energy that feels unstoppable and unreasonable.

The *Attack* Watchdog

The *Attack* watchdog believes it is experiencing immediate danger and will do anything to protect itself. *Attack* watchdogs are physically aggressive and you might see punching, kicking, spitting, and throwing things.

Sometimes watchdogs learn that having threatening movements without really attacking is an effective way to get people to back off. I've seen children "throw" objects that aren't dangerous (pillows or light objects), or kick with energy that is pretty wimpy. The lack of intensity lets you know they aren't attacking. This is good! Remember—behaviors are just cues and clues. Over time, you'll learn to track your child's energy and activation.

The watchdog brain is only going to truly attack if they believe they are in immediate danger. There is no other reason for a human to become physically aggressive. Humans are the most dangerous predator to other humans, so while we are driven to be in connection with other humans, we are also acutely aware of the need to protect ourselves from other humans.

Here are some cues and clues that your child might demonstrate when their *Attack* watchdog brain is active:

- Dangerous behavior
- Physical aggression (fight!):
  - Kicking, hitting, punching, pinching, throwing, spitting.

If you are parenting a child who is regularly displaying terror-level watchdog behaviors, your family needs more support. This book will help you find ways to offer regulation, connection, and felt safety, but will likely not be sufficient to bring safety to your family. Please contact your local community mental health agency for treatment options in your community.

I also want you to know that I know that advice borders on being ridiculous. If your local community mental health agency could help you, they probably would have already. There are simply not enough options for families with kids who live in chronic *Attack* watchdog mode. This book may be one part of the equation but I know it's not enough. I wish it was. I wish what your family needed was easier to access.

The Watchdog Brain (in Protection Mode) at a Glance

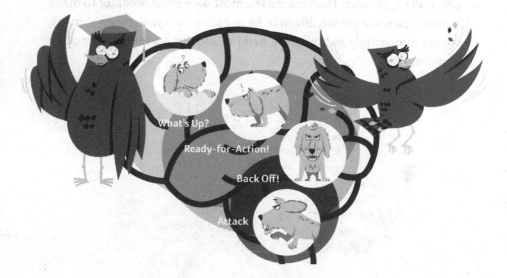

Once the watchdog detects anything that could be dangerous, it flips into protection mode. As fear and energy intensify, your child moves through different levels of their watchdog brain, and their behavior escalates. The *What's Up?* watchdog smells trouble and shifts into a *Ready-for-Action!* and then a *Back Off!* watchdog. Finally, the *Attack* watchdog comes out, fangs bared and ready to bite. Dr Perry's theory of state-dependent functioning[1] explains that as these shifts happen, lower and more primitive levels of the brain start to take charge. See how the *What's Up?* watchdog lives in both the limbic regions and the cortex? The *What's Up?* watchdog still has a bit of connection to the cortex—the owl brain. But the *Ready-for-Action!* watchdog has moved completely into the limbic regions and is no longer connected to the cortex/owl brain at all. The *Back Off!* watchdog moves even lower, and the *Attack* watchdog lives completely in the brainstem.

The lower your child is in their brain, the younger they act. Remember how the brain develops from the bottom up and the inside out?[2] The *Ready-for-Action!* watchdog is kinda like a preschooler, the *Back Off!* watchdog like a toddler, and the *Attack* watchdog like an infant. Those are the parts of the brain that were developing when they were that age—which helps explain why your 10-year-old is saying "milk, milk, milk, milk" over and over again instead of just asking for a cup of milk or getting it themselves.

These shifts happen for all of us when we feel threatened. When my watchdog brain takes over, I tantrum like a toddler. Sometimes logic helps me act reasonably again, but generally it doesn't. Usually I just need to take a break. I might have a snack or go for a jog or even just go outside in the sunshine. Sometimes I just need to get away from whatever is causing my watchdog to freak out.

Understanding this concept—that the further your child is in their watchdog pathway, the lower in the brain they are and the younger they become—is important when we start to consider the types of interventions your child's watchdog needs to feel safe.

Meet the Possum

Dear Reader. It is simply my greatest honor to introduce you to *the possum brain*.

Oh how I love the possum brain. Possums are so heroic. I am filled with gratitude not only for the children who have shared their watchdog brain with me, but also those who have been willing to bring their possum brain to my office. They are so brave.

Remember I told you that when the nervous system flips into

protection mode, there are two pathways it could take? One is the watchdog pathway. It's fueled by a significant increase in energy, which we just explored above.

The other pathway is the possum pathway, which involves a significant *decrease* in energy. The brilliant possum is world-famous for its life-saving behavior of playing dead. Collapsing. The possum is conserving energy, while the watchdog uses a lot of energy. The watchdog's heart rate increases to pump blood and oxygen to the farthest parts of the body (fists and feet!), but the possum takes all that energy and brings it into the torso.

This strategy is so brilliant! Even though the possum believes there is a life threat, it still maintains a small amount of hope. Your child's possum brain is listening to ancient, evolutionary wisdom that says: "Conserve your energy so if the saber-toothed tiger gets you, you don't bleed to death!"

The possum's posture is one of collapse: the shoulders fold inward, the chin flops toward the chest, and sometimes the hands, arms, and even legs squish in toward the torso. If you look closely, you realize that the wise possum is protecting the head and torso. When your child is in the possum pathway, they might fold their arms across their chest and let their head hang down, or curl into a ball and tuck themselves into a corner of the bed or couch, or sit with their arms wrapped around their bent knees, chin resting on kneecaps.

Just like the watchdog, the possum has five different ways of responding, depending on the level of neuroceived danger. Similarly, a parent's response will be most effective when adjusted for each changing level of possum brain. One difference between watchdog and possum brains is that most possum brain interventions work for all levels of possum brain. We'll get to that in Chapter 8.

It's very common for possums to fly under the radar. Sometimes possum behavior isn't perceived as "bad," so it doesn't always get the recognition it needs as being very, very afraid. This is especially true in families or classrooms where there are both watchdogs and possums. It's easy to give a lot of energy to watchdog kids because they seem more dangerous while the possum brain kids get overlooked.

The truth is that even if possum behavior doesn't seem as destructive as watchdog behavior, a nervous system that moves into the possum pathway is letting us know that this person is very, very afraid. Sometimes, this is the nervous system of a child who has experienced extreme levels of terror in the past and was unable to use their arms and legs to stay safe—by running or fighting. The only way to stay safe was to get smaller, protect the vital organs, and try to disappear. In many very young children, if this pathway gets exercised frequently, it becomes the chosen pathway in the future, even in situations that aren't life-threatening.

Interacting with someone in the possum brain can be frustrating—so frustrating that sometimes parenting a possum brain child can wake up that parent's watchdog brain! One of the most important things to keep in mind when you are trying to connect with a possum brain is that they are actually very, very scared. Remembering this often helps your owl brain stick around a little bit longer. As you can imagine, watchdogs are pretty scary to possums.

The *I'm Safe!* Possum

When the possum neuroceives more cues of safety than cues of danger coming in from those 11 million bits of data per second, it can stay calm and connected. The owl brain is in charge! The possum gets to live a nice, happy, relaxing life. I imagine this *I'm Safe!* possum lounging on a beach chair, sunglasses on and drink in hand. This possum is living their best life.

The *I'm Safe!* possum can borrow a little bit of energy from the emergency brake and become a peaceful possum. These peaceful possums love snuggling on the couch watching a movie, or listening to a bedtime story as they drift into sleep. This peaceful possum likes lots of connection with lots and lots of stillness.

It's possible that you have never met this peaceful possum. So many of the families I know raise their eyebrows at me when I suggest this possum helps their child drift into sleep. There is no drifting off to sleep in those families! Just a loud crash of exhaustion.

I know what they mean! Just like the *I'm Safe!* watchdog needs a lot of practice being playful (safe, with energy), the *I'm Safe!* possum needs a lot of practice being peaceful (safe, with stillness)—like snuggling or drifting into sleep. A lot of the kids I work with didn't get many of those safe experiences. Some kids may avoid stillness at all cost because it feels too scary. At the most extreme end of the spectrum, kids with overactive possum brains get stuck in collapse. They sleep all the time or else they fight sleep until their bodies just crash.

In Chapter 6, we'll dive deep into growing the owl brain. You might find that growing the owl brain helps you see parts of your child you didn't even know existed! Like the ability to play tag in the playground without it escalating into violence or a tantrum, or more capacity to snuggle peacefully with their stuffed toy animal before gently drifting off to sleep.

The *La-La Land* Possum

When something potentially dangerous catches their attention, like a slight rustle in the grass that just might be a hungry fox, the possum brain drifts off into la-la land. When the possum is in la-la land, the neuroceived threat is still pretty low and the possum can communicate with the owl brain. This possum brain is starting down the slippery slope of protective shut-down, but might also be open to owl brain interventions to help bring back safety, connection, and regulation (see Chapter 8).

Here are some cues and clues that your child might demonstrate when the *La-La Land* possum is in charge:

- Staring off into space ("la-la land")
- Flat facial expressions:
  - Lack of expression
  - Facial muscles become looser around the eyes and mouth
- Disconnected from you
- Looking bored or even saying they are bored
- Avoidance of connection, play, or work, including "work avoidance"
- Seems distracted, unfocused, and off-task.

As we get to know the possum brain more intimately, you'll discover that knowing *your* child's level of possum brain relies on your experience of being with them. In order to truly feel your child's energy, you have to be in your own owl brain with a clear sense of your own energy. That will help you feel the difference between yours and theirs.

The *Trickster* Possum

The behaviors, cues, and clues we see from this possum are often surprising! Instead of behaviors that reflect the need to protect and disconnect, this *Trickster* possum can appear to be in connection mode if we aren't paying close attention. A trickster indeed!

The *Trickster* possum relies on behaviors of overcompliance and false connection. That's because this possum is disconnected, even from itself! It doesn't feel safe enough to be real and authentic, so instead, it tries to make everyone else happy. After all, happy people aren't usually angry, threatening, or otherwise dangerous. It's almost like this possum has a mask on. This possum might say "YES!" when you know they don't agree or maybe didn't even hear the question. They might say "I don't know" to avoid having a thought or feeling that might be considered "wrong."

Having a very compliant child can feel like such a relief. Especially if you have other non-compliant watchdogs or possums in your family. Some of us learned that compliance is a sign of love and respect, so we might even reward or encourage that behavior. But compliance is different from cooperation. Cooperation is about meeting the needs of both people involved, but compliance is typically more fear-based and involves the needs and desires of the more powerful person.

Sometimes, this *Trickster* possum acts sorta robotic. Its voice and movements can seem overly rigid or automatic. These kids sometimes remind me of Data from *Star Trek*.

Here are some cues and clues that your child might demonstrate when their *Trickster* possum brain is in charge:

- Robotic change to their vocal tone or inflection
- Extreme people-pleasing behavior:
  - Lots of "YES!"
  - Lots of "I don't know"
- Movements and body may get extremely slow—almost like they are moving through molasses and cannot concentrate on what they are doing
- They don't always make sense, and it's easy not to notice! It seems like you're having a perfectly reasonable conversation and then you realize you're actually very confused.

The *Shut-Down* Possum

Eventually, the possum starts to shut down. This is different from the dreamy *La-La Land* possum. As the possum starts to shut down, their body begins to collapse and movement becomes difficult. Their body posture curls inward to protect their head, neck, and torso. A possum could survive an arm being ripped off by a saber-toothed tiger, but they are much less likely to survive a torso or head injury.

Remember! Possums aren't just afraid of danger; they are afraid of death. The possum brain emerges when it neuroceives life-threatening danger. When the possum starts shutting down, it believes that death is imminent. I know it doesn't make sense. But we have to remember that our present reality is created by our experience of what's happening right now combined with our memory of everything that has happened in the past. When the response doesn't seem to match reality, we are likely dealing with a mind being flooded by the past. A child with an active possum pathway has a very sensitized stress response system and has had too many experiences using their possum pathway to stay safe.

Here are some cues and clues that your child might demonstrate when their possum brain is starting to shut down:

- Significant lack of eye contact; eyes looking down as the head is also angled down
- Body collapses inward, making a "c" shape. Knees might come to chest. Arms and hands are in front of head and torso
- Extremely slow and sluggish; maybe refusing or unable to move (like get out of bed!)
- "Doe-eyed"—disconnected eyes that seem alert but don't seem to be responding to what's happening in the moment
- Stops speaking

- Losing significant coloring in the cheeks
- Could have uncontrolled crying that feels despondent as opposed to the intensity of a watchdog "tantrum."

The *Play Dead* Possum

Playing dead is the possum's last-ditch effort at staying alive. This strategy works because a lot of predators will walk away from dead prey. The dissociation that appears as playing dead also helps protect the possum from painful feelings or sensations.

Yes, I know: the child in your life who plays dead is almost certainly not at risk of actual death. But all behavior makes sense, and *this* behavior tells us that this child is neuroceiving extreme danger and life threat. This situation is overwhelming, frustrating, extremely sad, and exhausting for parents, who must continually keep in mind the sensitized stress response system of their child.

If your child has "playing dead" behaviors a lot of the time, please seek specialized mental healthcare immediately. While everything you learn from this book will help you create safety for your very scared possum child, this level of dysregulation in the nervous system needs professional medical and mental healthcare.

Here are some cues and clues that your child might demonstrate when their possum brain is playing dead:

- Completely non-responsive
- Fainting (or falling asleep suddenly that isn't due to narcolepsy)
- Dissociation that causes a complete disconnect from reality.

The Possum Brain (in Protection Mode) at a Glance

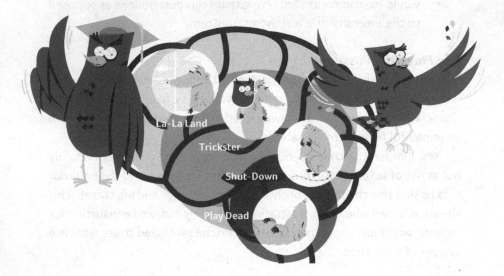

Once the possum detects anything that could be dangerous, it flips into protection mode. As fear increases, the possum collapses more and more. It goes from la-la land, to acting like a trickster, to shutting down, to playing dead. Let's again turn to Dr Perry's theory of state-dependent functioning.[3] As the energy in the possum brain continues to decrease, lower and lower parts of the brain start to be in charge. See how the *La-La Land* possum lives in both the limbic regions and the cortex? This possum still has some connection to the cortex, where the owl brain lives. Once the possum puts its mask on and becomes the *Trickster* possum, it has moved completely into the limbic brain and is no longer connected to the cortex/owl brain at all. The *Shut-Down* possum is moving down into the brainstem and the *Play Dead* possum is completely in the brainstem.

As the possum collapses, it becomes more and more disconnected— from itself and from you. When your child is in their possum pathway, they aren't thinking about anything except getting as small as possible; in a way, they want to be invisible. They start to act younger and younger, and have needs like those of a younger child. *Shut-Down* and *Play Dead* possums need help doing almost everything—just like an infant or toddler.

Here's the deal. I have an overactive possum pathway. My current life is extremely safe. We live in a safe home, are financially stable, and have a lot of support. Even still, sometimes my possum brain takes over.

When it does, there is absolutely nothing you could say to me that would help my owl brain come back. Logic and words and, in a way, even reality becomes completely irrelevant. Since I've worked very hard to learn about my possum brain, I now know that what my possum brain needs isn't reassuring words. My possum brain needs to rest. And then it needs to have experiences that help me feel my body again. A hot bath, a hot cup of coffee, or a walk in the woods. Think about how we soothe infants and toddlers. Not with reassuring words, but with things that help their body feel better, like a bath, a bottle, or a walk in the stroller.

Knowing my possum pathway behaviors has helped me recognize when I'm in the possum pathway and it helps me know what to do. That's exactly why you are going to start paying very close attention to your child's owl, watchdog, and possum brain behaviors.

Tracking the Owl, Watchdog, and Possum Brains

Getting to the end of this chapter has likely already impacted how you see your child's behaviors. I invite you to simply pay close attention and bring your most curious owl brain to situations where your child's behavior doesn't seem to be inviting connection. Is that a watchdog behavior with increased energy? Or a possum behavior with decreased energy? Some behaviors will start to make more sense right away.

Maybe you have a child who seems to say "I don't know" to almost every question. Maybe you have a child who seems stuck in oppositional-ity, responding "no" to everything, even an invitation to do something fun!

Maybe you're now seeing your child's intense foot tapping or leg swinging in a new light. You're noticing key phrases they say a lot when they get to a certain level of dysregulation, and most of the time it feels like the things they say don't make any sense! Like "You hate me" or "You're being mean to me" or "You always tell me I'm doing everything wrong" when all you did is remind them it's trash night.

You'll start to sometimes see these behaviors more as clues about their watchdog and possum brains, and less about being disrespectful or controlling.

If your owl brain likes a lot of structure, you can start making lists of your child's owl, watchdog, and possum brain behaviors. The character-istics I gave here in this chapter are just general cues and clues. Every watchdog and possum is a little different! With practice, you'll be able to stay focused on how to work with the energy underneath challenging behaviors, rather than on changing the behaviors themselves.

I also encourage you to start noticing *your* owl, watchdog, and possum brain behavior. If you can be aware of your own cues and clues, you can usually hang on to your owl brain a little bit longer. That's good for both you and your child!

CHAPTER 6

Parenting Strategies that Grow the Owl Brain

Something has shifted since the session when you came in angry with me. For so long, you've had to be the co-regulator for the people around you. But that day, you got to be the dysregulated one, and to feel the safety of my co-regulation. Our work together has deepened since then, and now there is more trust in our relationship. This result is what I want for you and for Sammie, too.

I start today with a question. "What does Sammie need," I ask you, "so that her only option is to be successful?"

You stare at me. Blink.

"Isn't that what I'm paying you to tell me?" you ask, with just enough petulance for a pang of delight to emerge from my heart. You hide your teasing smile behind a long sip of coffee.

"Well yeah, kinda," I say with a grin. "I mean sure, you're here because I know a lot about the science of behavior. But you know a lot about Sammie. So I can give you some good ideas because I've walked this road before. But you're the only one who can take those ideas and make them work for Sammie."

"Wait," you say, as you set down your mug on the side table. "You aren't going to just tell me what to do?"

"Do you want me to?"

"Yes!" You're surprised. Of course this is what you want.

"Is that what other parent coaches and therapists have done?" I ask.

You shrug, like it should be obvious. "Yeah!"

"Huh," I say, considering. "And has that been helpful?"

"Well," you say, then pause. "I guess so. I mean, it's helpful at first."

"Okay," I agree. "Giving you structure and clear instructions is a great way to calm your watchdog and possum brains! That's definitely really important—and it's good that it's been helpful. So, sure! I can do a little bit of just telling you what to do."

You look at me quizzically. You know there's a catch.

"But you actually know Sammie way better than I do," I say. "Nobody knows her better than you—except Sammie of course, she's the real expert. But given what you know, what does Sammie need so that there is really no option except for her to be successful?"

"Well…" You pause and reflect on this for a moment. "A lot more supervision, that's for sure. It's like the instant I look away, she misbehaves. On purpose! I really can't trust her."

"Oh yeah, that's the worst feeling! Like, as long as you watch her like a hawk, she'll behave. But the second you turn away, she breaks all the rules." I feel pretty confident that Sammie's behavior isn't about trust, but I know that it feels that way. I make a point to validate your feeling, without validating your conclusion.

"Yes! Does she think I'm stupid or something? Like I won't find out? And she won't get in trouble?"

"Good question! I think you're talking about Sammie's owl brain here, right? Sammie's owl brain definitely knows the rules." You nod. "Okay. And Sammie's owl brain also knows the consequences?" You nod again. "And Sammie's owl brain is pretty darn sure you'll always find out."

"Yes!"

"Okay great—we're on the same page there. So, if Sammie's owl brain knows all those things, why does she do things that will get her in trouble?"

"She doesn't care about the rules or consequences?"

"Well, maybe. There is some truth to the fact that given what Sammie experienced in life before she came to your family, very little punishment could ever come close to making her feel as bad as she's felt in the past. But I'm not sure that's the real reason, if we believe that regulated, connected kids who feel safe behave well."

"Hmm. Okay, yeah I see your point there. So is the answer to everything that she isn't regulated or connected or feeling safe?"

"Well, maybe not to everything. But generally speaking, you're right. We can always start there."

Attunement first. Always. If I match you, there's an opportunity for connection. If we connect, we have the opportunity to fall in step with each other, in the follow-lead-follow dance of resonance. The resonance we cultivate together will make it easier for you to offer the same to Sammie.

You look genuinely confused now. "But what changes? She follows the rules when I'm watching or when I'm nearby."

"Let's think," I say. "What changes?"

"I guess I stop watching?"

"Right," I agree. "And if we assume this is about regulation, connection, or felt safety—and not about Sammie maliciously plotting how to break all the rules as soon as you look away—how can we make sense of that?"

"Something about me not watching her," you puzzle it out, "changes her regulation, connection, or felt safety...?"

"Exactly. Co-regulation is sometimes a very active process where you give Sammie a lot of scaffolding. Maybe you're tending to a need like hunger or a movement break, or you're offering a lot of emotional attunement and presence. But co-regulation also happens passively, kinda like this energy field that keeps you two connected, even when you aren't actively engaged with her.

"Co-regulation requires a lot of physical closeness until it becomes more internalized. Even when you don't say or do anything, just being physically nearby provides connection, co-regulation, and felt safety. When the distance increases, even if it's just energetic distance because you get distracted or turn your attention to something else, the watchdog brain perks up a little. And as the watchdog gets more and more active..."

"The owl brain flies away," you finish my sentence.

"Yup," I say. "Sammie's regulatory circuits are a little developmentally delayed, so to speak, and she needs more co-regulation than other kids her age—both active and passive. So one way to help her be successful is to literally decrease the distance between her and a regulated, present adult she trusts." I laugh a little.

"What?" you ask.

"Well, now I'm thinking of a story a friend recently told me. To help their son be successful on the soccer team, dad was on the field, running right next to their son. All the time! When their son felt safe enough to be out on the field alone, dad started running up and down the sidelines. Finally dad could just stand in one place on the sidelines. Then eventually, he could sit. Except he never actually got to sit, because the league asked if he just wanted to coach, since he was on the field the whole time anyway!" We both laugh—loudly but wearily.

"Before I see you again next week, start making a list of all the times Sammie struggles. Recess? Gym class? School bus? Chores? Let's see if those are times when there is more distance between Sammie and a regulated, present adult. I'm guessing that will almost always be the case."

"Then what?" you ask.

"Then we'll try to get Sammie closer to a regulated, present adult during those times. She might not be able to ride the school bus. She might not be able to go into her room and get it picked up without you. If we're asking Sammie to do things that exceed her regulatory capacity, no wonder her owl brain is flying away. We can't do anything except strengthen her owl brain—and one way is by decreasing the distance she has with a regulated, present adult."

You sigh. Deeply.

"That was a big sigh," I say, feeling tenderness for you. "Tell me what's coming up for you."

"I'm tired." You sound tired. "I'm so, so tired. And you're telling me the way out is by being even closer to Sammie? Spending even more time with her?"

"I know," I say, empathetically. "It's not fair. Parents expect their job to get easier as their kid gets older. It's one of those unspoken expectations. It feels like the payoff for all those years of very active parenting. It's exhausting that Sammie still needs that level of involvement from you. There's probably a lot of grief there for you. Probably for Sammie, too.

"If Sammie broke her arm, you'd have to go back to doing things for her like you did when she was little. Help her get dressed, maybe even feed her? It's a similar idea. Sammie's regulatory circuits function like those of a much, much younger child, so we have to offer more support to help her owl brain grow big and strong. She may always need more help than other kids her age staying regulated, I don't really know. But I do know that building her owl brain will help her be successful."

You sigh, but you look a little more hopeful. You're starting to trust this process.

I speak a little more brightly now, reflecting back the hope in your eyes. "And that isn't the only idea I have about strengthening Sammie's owl brain, I promise! We'll also look at adding structure and predictability, and infusing more attunement and connection into her life. And my favorite? We'll pretend Sammie's a houseplant! We'll make sure to keep her fed and watered, to move her when she needs it, and to give her lots of sunlight. You know, like a houseplant."

I give you a big cheesy grin. You aren't that impressed with my joke. That's okay. No one ever is.

Parenting with Co-Regulation

Co-regulation was needed to grow our children's owl brain when they were babies, and co-regulation is what is needed to grow their owl brain now!

Co-regulation inherently involves felt safety and connection, right? In order to truly offer co-regulation, we have to be regulated ourselves; our nervous system needs to be in connection mode. "Parenting with felt safety, connection, and co-regulation" is a little clunky to write out (and read!), so I'll summarize by simply writing "parenting with co-regulation."

For whatever reason, your child has an overactive watchdog or possum brain. Their stress response system is sensitized, so they have huge reactions to what seem like small stressors.

When your precious little one was a teeny tiny baby, they would express their distress by crying. Now they are big, loud, and maybe smelly (depending on just how big they are and how well they use deodorant), and they express their stress in different ways: screaming, cussing, throwing things, spitting, lying, stealing, saying hurtful things, or peeing in really weird places.

These behaviors are so big and baffling—and sometimes even dangerous—that it is very, very difficult to respond with co-regulation.

But parenting with co-regulation means remembering to see these behaviors as dysregulation, and not just your kid being bad. Co-regulation-based parenting means meeting the need while staying regulated (not calm).

What's the Need?
Regulation. Connection. Felt safety.

Your child may also need to learn some new skills. Dysregulated behavior can emerge when we have expectations for our children that they simply can't meet due to a lack of skills. But skills are best taught to the owl brain. So first, focus on regulation, connection, and felt safety, and then look at what skills your child needs for their success to be inevitable.

Increasing co-regulation when your child is in their owl brain is pretty easy. Responding to your child's dysregulation—their watchdog or possum brain—with co-regulation will feel like holding on to a ball of fire instead of reaching for the fire extinguisher and putting it out. You're going to wonder how this could possibly be the right way to respond. It's going to feel confusing.

You'll have to be brave and just take a leap of faith with me.

Let's start with increasing co-regulation when you aren't responding to watchdog or possum brain behavior. If we focus on these "outside the moments of bad behavior" ways of growing the owl brain, you'll eventually see fewer watchdog and possum brain moments. You'll also have grown your own co-regulation muscles (and owl brain!), and it'll be easier to respond with co-regulation to your child's watchdog and possum brains (see Chapters 7 and 8).

You're going to get to a point where you'll be asking yourself (or screaming to the sky wishing you could ask me directly) how this way of parenting will possibly teach your child not to behave this way. You'll wonder: "If I don't make my child STOP this behavior, am I just teaching them that acting this way is okay?" Let me just go ahead and answer that question now: No. The watchdog and possum brains are not connected enough to the owl brain for *any* learning to occur, including that "acting this way is okay."

Generally speaking, children are not confused about what's appropriate behavior and what isn't. Your child's dysregulated behavior isn't happening because they "think it's okay to act that way." They know it's not okay to act that way. They are doing it anyway.

Teaching them it's not okay to act that way isn't solving the real problem. The real problem lies somewhere within their regulation, connection, or felt safety. Let's solve that!

This chapter outlines six specific tools for parenting with co-regulation:

- Decrease the distance
- Pretend they are houseplants (food, water, movement)
- Structure, routine, and predictability
- Attunement
- Scaffolding
- Increase connection.

Decrease the Distance

If you're parenting a child who you feel can't be trusted, one who is regularly breaking rules or creating chaos, you're parenting a child who doesn't yet have enough internalized co-regulation. Their regulatory circuits are underdeveloped. This isn't about trust; it's about co-regulation, felt safety, and connection.

The most effective intervention you can implement right now is to decrease the distance between your child and a regulated adult. Decrease the distance as often as possible by as much as needed.

You know how puppies need constant supervision so that you notice the moment they start sniffing around and can quickly get them outside before they pee on your rug? Or so that you can quickly replace the legs of your couch with a chew toy? If you weren't right there with your puppy, you wouldn't be able to intervene quickly and they'd develop neural pathways for peeing on your favorite rug and chomping on your couch.

As a puppy owner, your responsibility is to create an environment for them in which success is the only option. Pee outside! Chew on chew toys!

The same theory applies to your child. That means continually asking what your child needs so that success is the only option.

Just like I asked Nat to do, make a list of the times your child typically struggles. Then ask yourself how close they are to a regulated adult at those times.

Parents often tell me their child gets into trouble at recess. They can't drop their child at a friend's house to play, and they certainly can't drop their teen off at the movies or the mall. Parents tell me that their child has been banned from the school bus due to out-of-control behavior. Most of the parents I know can't even let their kids play in a different room of the house without direct supervision.

Regulated, connected kids who feel safe do well. When our kids aren't doing well, they need more regulation, connection, and felt safety.

We can't give regulation, connection, and felt safety from a distance until our kids have internalized enough co-regulation into their own minds and nervous system. If you're reading this book, I'll assume you know a child who simply doesn't have enough internalized co-regulation in their own minds and nervous system.

Misbehavior is not about a lack of trust. It's a lack of internalized co-regulation.

There is a lot of righteous grief that you deserve to feel as you realize that you must parent more actively and for much longer than you expected. Feel it. Give yourself a lot of compassion. Maybe skip ahead to Section 3 where I help you grow *your* owl brain so challenging behaviors are a little more tolerable for you.

And then decrease the distance.

When They Protest

Believe it or not, I have known some kids who were relieved when their parents started to make their world smaller. More often than not, though, kids aren't exactly grateful for your newly discovered tactics that will help their success become inevitable.

Decreasing the distance can feel like a punishment, especially if these new boundaries are put into place after your child struggled with their behavior. This reaction makes perfect sense and is a valid way for your child to feel.

Your job is to make sure you aren't implementing new boundaries as a punishment. Your intention might not change the end result (no more riding the bus), but it changes how you tell your child about the new boundary.

Implement the boundary with rock-solid commitment to your child's success and a willingness to do the hard thing in service of helping them be more successful.

When they protest, remember that they are allowed to have their feelings. They'll possibly flip into their watchdog or possum brain. That's okay, because by the end of Chapter 9, you'll know how to respond to watchdog and possum brain behavior.

Pretend They Are Houseplants

I'm a fan of interventions that are both easy and powerful, and this one ticks both boxes! When we tend to houseplants, especially if they aren't doing well, we make sure the soil is nutrient-rich—we feed them. We check their hydration—we water them. We think about their environment, and if they've been stuck for too long in a dusty corner or a crowded shelf—we move them. Finally, we make sure to give them sunlight. Humans have needs that are remarkably similar to houseplants. Thinking of your kids as houseplants is an easy way to support their sense of felt safety and ultimately grow their owl brain.

Feed Them

Food is a complex issue for children with vulnerable nervous systems, and particularly for children with a history of relational trauma. We aren't going to solve those problems in this book, but there are some simple steps we can take to increase your child's felt safety through the lens of food and feeding. Please refer to Dr Katja Rowell's *Love Me, Feed Me* book if you have a child who struggles with extreme picky eating or food preoccupation.[1] You can also search my podcast archives for an interview with Dr Rowell.[2]

EVERY TWO HOURS

Is your child getting a snack or meal with enough regularity? If you have a chronically dysregulated child, consider increasing the frequency (and quality) of snacks and meals. Kids with a history of relational trauma often need concrete reminders that there is always enough food for them. Offering a snack sends that message clearly.

Children with vulnerable nervous systems may be extra sensitive to the small physiological changes that occur in their bodies when they go for a few hours without eating. Preventing fluctuations in blood sugar through regular, nutrient-dense, and protein-heavy snacks can be helpful.

It's also very common for kids with vulnerable nervous systems to struggle with something called interoception, which is the sense that monitors and transmits signals from inside our body. Interoception tells our brains when our stomachs are hungry. You may have a child who doesn't "tune in" to these cues, and will go too long without eating if not offered food.

KEEP FOOD VISIBLE

I met a mom during the pandemic who started storing non-perishable groceries outside the cupboards. She had food stashed above the cabinets, on countertops, everywhere but behind a closed door. This is so brilliant! You already know that owl brains and watchdog brains don't always talk to each other. Owl brains can absolutely know there is lots of food in the pantry, but watchdog brains might need to see it to know it.

KEEP FOOD ACCESSIBLE

Create a place in your house that is filled with food your child likes and can eat whenever they want, without asking, even if it's five minutes before dinner. This could be a specific drawer in your refrigerator, a basket in your pantry, or a large bowl on the counter. One family I knew used a dorm-size fridge as their child's "take any time, eat any time" fridge. Another family put a fanny pack on their child and stuffed it full of snacks. As your child's felt safety increases, especially as related to food, you can implement more structure around eating and snacking. But until then, focus on sending the message that food is always available.

EXTREME PICKY EATING AND FOOD PREOCCUPATION

Food is a huge source of stress in almost every family I work with. Delving into the nuances of food-specific challenges goes outside the scope of this book. Again, I encourage you to read Dr Katja Rowell's *Love Me, Feed Me*—or have a listen to her interview on my podcast.[3]

Water Them

Dehydration can happen quickly and without a lot of warning. Usually by the time we realize we're thirsty, some level of dehydration has already set it. Dehydration can tip your child's felt safety to "danger-danger" since survival is literally dependent on having enough water to drink.

Ideally, water is the best thing for your child to drink. But I live here in the real world with you, and I know that lots of kids (and adults) don't drink enough water because they don't like water. Give your child unlimited access to whatever liquid they will drink that is as nutritious as possible. I've known kids who prefer sparkling water or flavored sparkling water, which usually doesn't contain any added sweetener. Some kids like water flavored with fruit. Drop in an orange wedge, a couple of strawberries, a cucumber slice, or even a piece of lemon.

If your child refuses any liquid that isn't juice or soda, see if you can water it down. You could even try watering it down with sparkling water, which might make it feel more like soda. But if they simply won't drink anything besides juice or soda, then give them juice or soda. If we don't create felt safety from the inside, every other parenting strategy will be like bailing water from the Titanic.

Remember to experiment with hot drinks! Many children will drink and feel comforted by tea or hot cocoa.

PUT THEIR BODY IN WATER

When my son was small, sometimes the only thing we could do for his out-of-control watchdog brain was get him into the bathtub. There are many reasons why water seems to have magical properties, but let's just go with that one—it's magic.

Try offering a shower or a bath when your child is showing that their owl brain is about to fly away. Make bathtime nourishing with special toys, bath bombs, or bubbles, or even bring them a snack or a cup of hot chocolate or tea while they soak!

I lived in Texas for 15 years and it was basically swimming weather year-round. Getting to the pool as often as possible was life-changing for some of the families I worked with. A small backyard pool could be just what your child needs to keep their owl brain around. Playing with the hose or a sprinkler, or even just playing with water in the sink, can offer up those magical water properties and strengthen the owl brain.

Consider making bathtime not about getting ready for bed or getting clean, which could be a sure invitation to the watchdog brain. Instead, offer baths at unusual times of the day, and make them only about having fun. No need to even use soap! Get creative and look for ways to increase your child's time in, around, and drinking water.

Move Them

Many of our kids don't move their bodies as often or as hard as they really need to. Movement gives our bodies the feeling of "I exist! I'm solid here in the world." When our bodies don't get enough movement, our inside world starts to send cues of danger to our owl brain, making it easier for the watchdog or possum brain to emerge.

Our bodies need movement basically all the time. As I'm writing this book, I have to remind myself to stand up and stretch. I sit in an office chair that rocks and swivels. Sometimes I work at my treadmill desk.

Advocate for your child to get their movement needs met at school, and advocate extra fiercely for your child to never, *ever, ever (ever, EVER!)* lose recess as a consequence. I work really collaboratively with schools and teachers, but when a school insists that losing recess is a reasonable consequence I give myself permission to set a clear, firm boundary. This is one issue I will not budge on.

Take your kid to the park immediately from school pick-up. Have them walk or ride their bike to or from school if possible. Reframe how you see fidgety behavior and reconsider the circumstances your child needs to do homework. Definitely make sure they get in a good amount of movement after school and before homework. Bonus points if they can get out in the sun—sunlight and nature don't get the credit they deserve for how quickly they can offer our bodies and minds felt safety.

I could write a whole book about tending to your child's movement and sensory needs, but I don't have to because my dear friend and colleague Marti Smith, OTR, wrote an amazing book, *The Connected Therapist*, where you can get practical ideas for how to support your child's body.[4]

Structure, Routine, and Predictability

One of the primary ways our brain helps keep us safe is to predict and prepare us for what's going to happen next, based on our past experience. When the brain isn't sure what's going to happen next, that's a cue of danger. And for people with vulnerable nervous systems, their brain will often fill in the blank with something much more dangerous than what really is about to happen next.

You can help prevent that feeling of danger by providing as much structure, routine, and predictability for your child as possible, without becoming overly rigid. Good structure isn't rigid and, in fact, it allows for flexibility.

Take a look at your child's schedule. Is it predictable? Do they usually know what's happening next? Is the schedule posted somewhere? It can be as simple as hanging up a dry-erase board calendar. In my house, we have two. The weekly calendar contains a lot of details about the schedule for each person in our family. The monthly calendar gives a great "month at a glance" overview.

If your child isn't reading yet, you can easily make a picture-calendar. I promise, you don't have to have any craft skills or make it Pinterest-worthy. Do a Google image search for things like "wake up," "take medicine," "brush teeth," "hang up backpack." Copy, paste, and print. If you wanted to get really fancy, you can laminate them so your child could cross off their completed tasks with a wet-erase marker. Laminators aren't very expensive and provide shocking amounts of fun. You'll be surprised at how suddenly you feel compelled to laminate the reminder postcard you get from the dentist's office.

When you're doing something new, even something as mundane as going to a new restaurant, get as much information about it as possible. Check out pictures of the restaurant online and look up the menu. Your child could choose what they want to eat before you even get to the restaurant. Almost every business has a website these days. You can look up the movie theater, amusement park, and eye doctor's office. Going to a new therapist? Ask them to send a photo of their office. I've done this for many new clients and even sent photos of my newly decorated office to a couple of long-term clients with especially vulnerable nervous systems.

It might be really challenging to give your child the amount of structure they need, especially if you're like me and not particularly structured in your own life. If you love spontaneity and are parenting a child who needs structure for felt safety, be sure to find places in your adult life that have room for the spontaneity you need.

Wild Cards

When I trained in Trust-Based Relational Intervention (TBRI), the late Dr Karyn Purvis recommended that families have "wild cards." This is literally a physical card that a parent can pick up and hand to a child to signal a temporary change in routine. When your child knows that wild cards exist, using one can put structure in place even when their routine is upended.

Keep wild cards with you in your purse, wallet, or glove compartment. If you usually go right to the playground after picking up your child from school, but today you have to pick up a prescription instead, you can give your child the wild card as you explain what's happening.

I'm not promising this will eliminate your child's watchdog or possum brain getting involved in this routine disruption, but it will likely decrease the intensity of the watchdog or possum brain response. Over time, wild cards might help your child's owl brain stay online when faced with the inevitable disruptions in routine.

Attunement

In *Parenting from the Inside Out*, Dan Siegel and Mary Hartzell define attunement as "Aligning your own internal state with those of your children. Often accomplished by the contingent sharing of nonverbal signals."[5]

Attunement is when we step into our child's world and communicate, "I feel you. I feel what you're feeling. I'm here with you right now, even if what you're feeling is uncomfortable."

Attunement is pretty easy when our kids are feeling good and behaving well, but we often have to be more intentional about offering attunement when our kids are feeling bad or not behaving well. Attunement could sound like "You're so mad that you can't go to Sergio's house," or "I get it, it feels like we are being really unfair." Attunement could sound like "You feel like you hate me!"

Attunement does not send the message "Your behavior is okay." Attunement sends the message "All of your feelings matter to me, even the huge ones, even the uncomfortable ones, and even the ones I don't agree with."

As Dan Siegel and Mary Hartzell say, attunement has a lot to do with our non-verbal communication and body language. We communicate our attunement through our eyes, body posture, energy, and tone of voice.

Look for ways to increase attunement, even when your child is rude. When they grumble "This dinner is disgusting" before they've even tasted it, it would be so easy to respond with annoyance. "I've been cooking for an hour and all you have to say is that it looks disgusting?" Your feelings are valid! An attuned response might sound more like "Just by looking at it you're sure you won't like this dinner!"

Attunement doesn't mean ignoring rude behavior. Follow up your attuned response with "Your dad spent a lot of time making dinner for our family. It's okay not to like dinner. It's not okay to be rude. Next time, try something like 'I don't care for this. Can I make a peanut butter sandwich instead?'"

Attunement also means attuning to your child's reaction to your attunement. If your child rejects your verbal attunement by telling you to shut up or that you're wrong, or they become more dysregulated instead of less, focus on non-verbal attunement. Maybe make a face that communicates "Yeah, I get it." If your child is extremely committed to rejecting all attempts at attunement, shift your focus back to yourself so you can stay in your owl brain. It's very hard to parent a child who continually rejects your attempts at connection and co-regulation.

Scaffolding

Scaffolding is a parenting technique that we often do implicitly—without even thinking about it—when we slowly decrease the amount of support our kids need as they grow in skill and regulation.

As parents, we scaffold everything. We scaffold our child's ability to eat lasagna by first feeding them liquid only; then moving to purees; then chunkier food; then lasagna cut up really small; and then finally, a full piece of lasagna that we put on their plate with a fork, so they can eat it all by themselves.

Think about how you have scaffolded your child with riding a bike, or doing homework independently. When my son was 15 and then 16, we actively scaffolded his eventual ability to drive a car without a parent in the passenger seat.

Scaffolding is very active and deliberate co-regulation, and kids with vulnerable nervous systems and big, baffling behaviors need a lot of it. Your child might need scaffolding before they can successfully be dropped off at a birthday party. Maybe first, you attend the birthday party with them, staying involved and close by. Next, you attend the birthday party, but hang out in the kitchen with the birthday kid's family. After that, you sit in your car in front of the birthday kid's house. Next you drop your kid off but go to the neighborhood grocery store so you can return quickly if needed. Finally, one day, you can drop them off at the party, make sure they have a ride home, then have a couple hours to yourself.

Your child might need scaffolding to play alone in their bedroom without supervision, or to play a game with their siblings without it ending in tears, tantrums, and somebody getting hurt.

If your child isn't behaving correctly, I can almost guarantee that they need more scaffolding and more co-regulation (decrease the distance). You might have to get creative and think about challenging behaviors through a slightly different lens. The child who declares that "Dinner is disgusting" needs help building the skills to express their honest feelings without being rude and insensitive. If we approach this rude behavior as skill building, we have the opportunity to honor their bodily autonomy and teach that their preferences matter.

And scaffolding means you follow through the way you told your child you would. So when they sit down and say "I don't care for this dinner, can I make a peanut butter sandwich instead?" you say, "Yes! Thanks for expressing your feelings so respectfully."

Increase Connection

Connection is an inherent aspect of co-regulation, so it makes sense that increasing connection between you and your child will strengthen their owl brain. Connecting with a growling watchdog or a super-scared possum is tricky! It can feel overwhelming to just be told: *offer more connection.* So here are four concrete ways you can grow the owl brain through small moments of connection.

Express Interest and Curiosity

I know, I know. You aren't interested in Pokémon or Minecraft or watching another squishy video.

See if you can try. Find something your child is interested in and do it with them. Play a video game with them or just watch while they play. Ask them to show you the TikTok they are laughing at. Better yet? Ask them to teach you something that interests them. Kids love to feel competent and it might make hearing about Minecraft for the third hour of the day a little less mind-numbing.

Does it feel like your child isn't interested in anything? You'll have to look really hard! I recently connected with a family who were really struggling to identify anything their child was interested in. They mentioned that she would only wear one pair of leggings. Knowing that most families find it stressful when their child is so rigid, I suggested that they instead treat that rigidity as an interest. I encouraged them to wash the leggings every day so they'd always be clean and ready to go, and to make comments like "You really love those leggings!" or "I wonder if you love how those leggings feel on your legs." Responding to a child's interest—even one expressed with rigidity—sends a clear message of "I see you" and "Your preferences matter to me."

Delight

In their book *The Circle of Security Intervention*, Bert Powell, Glen Cooper, Kent Hoffman, and Bob Marvin describe delight as "taking joy *in* your child for who they are rather than enjoying an activity *with* your child."[6] They also note that delight isn't about expressing approval or joy over specific accomplishments; it's that spontaneous look on your face and the feeling that bursts from your heart when your child does something so precious you can't even stand it. Delight says "I adore you just because of who you are, and it's easy for me to see it."

One hot Texas day, I watched my colleague Katie prep to make finger-paint footprints with one of our mutual clients. Like a lot of the kids we work with, this child struggled with bathing. I remember thinking how brave Katie was to do an activity that meant taking off this child's shoes and socks.

Katie wasn't brave. She didn't have to be, because she felt genuine, pure delight toward this child, stinky feet and all. This was a child who didn't get the message "you're delightful" from many adults, and wow, did he melt. Katie taught me about the power of delight. We all want to know we delight others simply because we exist. If delighting in your child feels like a distant memory, see what happens if you pay close attention for any subtle moment of delight. Sometimes all we have to do is look for something for it to appear. Delighting in your child is good for your kid, and it's good for you, too.

Welcome!

I noticed one day that my therapist always greeted me the same way when our eyes first met before each appointment. "Welcome!" she would say.

This is so different than *hello*. It almost feels like a hello that is mashed together with delight.

Welcome says "I'm so glad to see you." Look for ways to communicate welcome even without the word "welcome." Pay attention to those first five seconds when you and your child come into contact with each other—first thing in the morning, or after school. It can be so easy to launch right into "It's time to get dressed" or "Time to do your homework." Sometimes we're already on edge anticipating reconnecting with our child, because it feels like it always goes poorly and within moments someone is yelling. It can be powerful to experiment with offering nothing but a smile and your soft, sparkly eyes that communicate non-verbally "I'm so glad you are here."

Playfulness

Remember how sometimes the owl brain gets a burst of energy and will dance and play with the watchdog brain while still feeling safe and connected?

Kids with vulnerable stress response systems and overactive watchdog or possum brains need playful moments to help grow their owl brain. So many of the parents I work with feel exhausted by the idea of playfulness. They can't remember the last time they felt playful, and often they feel a little resentful when I suggest it. It feels like one more impossible and exhausting chore.

I'm including it here anyway because I think playfulness is actually that powerful. The research behind the benefits of playfulness is staggering. I'll summarize it by saying that playfulness decreases stress, increases resilience, and makes hard things easier.[7] In short, playfulness grows the owl brain.

Playfulness does not involve you doing anything extra, I promise. Playfulness is most impactful if you can infuse it into everyday moments, like making lunches, clearing the table, or brushing teeth. Put on 80s dance music or Google "laughing toddler." Both will infuse a moment of playfulness into your nervous system and make it easier for you to bring playful energy to your child.

Don't be discouraged if your grumpy watchdog or possum child rolls their eyes or otherwise rejects your playfulness. Even if they don't join in, playfulness is good for your soul.

Let's Pause Before We Go On

I'm guessing that you've reached the end of this chapter with a variety of feelings.

You are already exhausted. If you weren't, you likely wouldn't have picked up this book. I just gave you a chapter full of strategies that require a lot of energy. It makes sense to me, if you feel like you just can't, that you don't have one more ounce of energy to give. If that's how you're feeling in this moment, consider skipping ahead to Chapter 11. Before you change how you relate to your child, you might need to grow your own owl brain. I offer a lot of ideas in Chapter 11 and I promise—no bubble baths or golf outings required (though by all means, if those fill your cup and you can do them, go for it).

But maybe you're feeling inspired. Finally! Someone has given you a list of very practical things you can actually do that will help your child feel more safe, regulated, and connected.

Or maybe you feel really let down. Maybe your child is way too dysregulated for any of those strategies to be helpful. I get it. I know you. You might be a family that needs case management and actual services, not another parenting book. You might even be a family that needs services that frankly don't even exist, or if they do, that aren't accessible.

You might be ready to just put this book down. Or you might be ready to skip ahead to Section 3.

Ultimately, we cannot change anyone else's behavior or nervous system. We can make a lot of offers of connection, felt safety, and co-regulation, but we are not responsible for those offers being received.

Sometimes, the very best thing we can do is care for our own owl brain. Offer support to our own watchdog and possum brains. We'll do that in Section 3.

If you're ready to keep moving forward with caring for your child's owl, watchdog, and possum brains, Chapter 7 is all about offering safety and connection for your child's watchdog brain. Chapter 8 is all about offering safety and connection for your child's possum brain.

Ready? Nat sure is.

CHAPTER 7

Parenting Strategies for the Watchdog Brain

"This isn't working," you tell me. I can't see your face because I'm straggling behind you, closing the door to my office as you make your way to the couch.

"Tell me," I say as the door clicks closed. You toss your keys on the side table while I land in my office chair, rolling it toward you with my feet since I'm already sitting in it. "What's not working?"

"None of it!!! This weekend was a disaster. She punched a kid at the playground! And you'd think that would be the worst part, but it was just the start of everything. All weekend long, she just refused to comply with even the simplest of instructions. It took her four hours to clean her room and I swear she did that on purpose just so she wouldn't have to do the rest of her chores. THEN last night when I went to put clean towels away in the bathroom, I see that she has used every last drop of shampoo, conditioner, soap, AND TOOTHPASTE! It's all gone! Just squeezed right down the drain, I guess! I only restocked all those things last week!!!"

"Oh wow, that is a terrible week! What a complete waste of money—literally money down the drain. And all that after she punched a kid at the playground? That must have been the icing on the cake at the end of a hard weekend."

"I know we are supposed to try to see what's underneath the behavior, but the only thing underneath that behavior is that she hurts kids for no reason. She can't be trusted and wants to waste all our money."

"It's really hard to see any reason at all for these behaviors!"

I notice a little increase in my heart rate as I'm pulled into resonance with you. I'm feeling frustration, irritation, a little bit of overwhelm, and even a tiny touch of hopelessness. You're feeling those things, and for a moment, I do, too. Frustration that after all our work together, it's still so easy to conflate trust with ability. I feel irritated that after all our work together, it's still so easy to just go right to taking Sammie's behavior personally. Overwhelmed that after all our work together, we're still here. A tiny touch of hopelessness that maybe I can't help you, after all.

Ahhhhhh, old friend, I whisper to these parts that are trying to elbow their way to the front of the class. There you are! Thank you. Thank you for helping me feel, for just one moment, what Nat is feeling.

With a breath and some compassion sent to both you and me, I can see more clearly again. You are in your watchdog brain!

"It's ridiculous. She's 10 years old. Why is she dumping shampoo like a toddler?"

"Great question! I wonder if it could be helpful, though, for just a moment, to notice what you just said. It's behavior like a toddler." I increase the energy in my voice a little, to be closer to the energy you have, but without the anger. I want you to know I'm hearing you and I'm taking you seriously. I want you to feel matched and seen and known.

"I don't want to parent a toddler! I already did that! She knows better!"

"I absolutely agree with you that her owl brain knows exactly how much toothpaste, shampoo, and conditioner to use. I bet her owl brain even understands that all those things cost money and she knows exactly how much shampoo to put in her hand."

"Exactly. She knows these things!!"

I'm noticing that you are still really angry—and rightfully so—but the intensity in your voice has come down just a notch. You shift your body from the edge of the couch where you'd been perched since arriving, and you sink back just a little bit.

I take a breath and sink back ever-so-slightly into my chair, too.

A long time ago a client asked me if they teach us that in therapy school.

"Teach us what?" I'd asked.

"To shift your body to mirror your client's body."

I'd realized she was right, and we'd laughed together. It's something I still catch myself doing frequently.

Mirroring helps us both. It helps you feel seen, even if unconsciously. And it helps me embody—literally feel in my body—what you might be experiencing.

I feel my shoulders come down, my jaw unclench, and my back relax. I start to feel a bit more grounded and regulated. I consider the possibility that you do, too.

"I know she knows all these things," I tell you. "She knows these things because you've taught her these things. Gosh, I wish this journey was just about teaching her things. But if that's all it was, you wouldn't even be here, would you? Because you're good at that. You know how to teach her things and she can learn them."

"So why isn't she DOING THEM?" Your intensity increases a notch.

"Well, this is a great question. I love that you're open to being curious about that question."

Your question lets me know you've moved out of the assumption that the shampoo dumping is about trust and wasting your money on purpose.

I also make a note that you're focused on the shampoo dumping. This surprises me, since you also told me she punched a kid at the playground and I would have thought you'd feel that was a bigger problem. I wonder if something about the shampoo dumping feels very personal and therefore a little harder to see beneath.

"I'll bet after all the dysregulation from the weekend, finding the wasted shampoo and toothpaste just put you over the edge."

"Oh, I was already over the edge. I'd basically fallen off the cliff and was sitting there dazed at the bottom!"

"Right!" I agree. "And that's when the empty shampoo bottle dropped on your head!"

We both laugh a little. Playfulness. A sign of connection.

I invite you to tell me a little more about the playground punching and you heave a heavy sigh.

The exhaustion of raising a child with so much fight in their nervous system leads to a bone-deep weariness that is almost impossible to describe with words. Your sigh says it all.

"I guess it was my fault. She was having a good day and I thought she could play hide and seek with the other kids. She wants to do things the other kids do and I want that for her, too. But it never goes well."

"I know. It's so exhausting and so unfair. For both of you."

We both take a breath. You glance at my face, and I see you register my expression, which says: "This sucks and I'm sorry."

"Punching is realllllly high on the fear factor in the watchdog brain," I remind you. "What do you think was happening?"

"NOTHING was happening. She was playing hide and seek. She was hiding and I guess having a hard time finding a hiding spot? Because when the other girl opened her eyes and said 'Ready or not, here I come!' Sammie wasn't hiding and instead just started running. The IT girl chased her and tagged her. And then Sammie punched her."

"Ahhhh. Great information. This is super-helpful. Would it be okay if we slowed this down a little and looked at it moment by moment?"

"Yes, please! I need to understand this. Why does she have to punch people? It's so embarrassing."

"So, punching people is definitely a behavior from the protection brain, yes?"

"Well, I guess so, but come on! They were just playing hide and seek! And everything was fine. It literally came completely out of nowhere."

I grab my binder of page-protected important handouts, find the page that describes the behaviors you might see from all the different watchdogs, and turn it around to show you.

It's usually easy to see that aggressive behaviors are behaviors of protection; it's often much harder to see why the child's brain flipped into that mode.

"Do you remember which watchdog is the only one that punches people?"

"Yes, the *Attack* watchdog. And she certainly attacked!"

"Yup, sure sounds like it. So, what do you think that tells us about her brain?"

"Well, you're saying that punching and aggression only come from a terrified brain. But why was she terrified?"

I explain my thinking to you: my best guess is that Sammie was playing hide and seek with kids about her same age. Kids with nine-year-old social skills. Sammie's brain was working hard, trying to figure out nine-year-old social behavior and blend in. Up until the punching happened, it seemed like she was doing a pretty good job staying in her connection brain, blending in, and playing with friends. They were running around and laughing while their hearts were beating harder and their lungs were breathing faster to be able to fuel their bodies through the running and laughing.

They were playing. Playfulness is connection mode with lots of energy.

Punching is protection mode with lots of energy.

When the seeker yelled out "Ready or not, here I come!" Sammie was still running around, trying to find a place to hide. Her heart rate was high. She didn't get any moments of rest while hiding. She was likely starting to move into protection brain when she heard the seeker say "5! 4! 3! 2! 1!" and she realized she was running out of time.

As her protection brain came more fully online, it used all that energy to keep her safe—safe from losing the game, safe from feeling embarrassed. She used the energy in her legs to run from the seeker, but ultimately, she was tagged.

When she stopped running, she was still brimming over with high levels of energy. Now she felt disappointed she'd been tagged, and maybe embarrassed or just plain mad. That sky-high energy combined with her protection brain fueled her arms instead of her legs, and she punched the seeker.

The look in your eyes lets me know you understand and are maybe shifting a bit into hopelessness.

"This is just so hard," I say. "So hard for both of you. You just want to take your daughter to the park and not hover like she's a wobbly toddler. She just wants to play with kids and be a normal girl. Her body must be so exhausted from always working so hard to protect itself from all this danger she feels in the world. You're exhausted, too."

I watch you take a deep breath and sink even deeper into the couch.

"Sometimes, this all just feels hopeless," I say.

"You're telling me." You pick up your warm mug of coffee with cream that has become our ever-present anchor of safety, bring it to your lips, and take a sip.

You tell me that Sammie was mostly cooperative with leaving the park and starting to head home, which was a relief. You were worried she'd refuse to cooperate and that her aggression would get even worse. Sammie was angry, yelling, and tearful, and you did a great job reassuring her she wasn't in trouble and she was safe. You offered her a break from the game and a drink. Brilliant! These are all great strategies we've gone over for the fear and terror-level watchdog brain.

Finally home, Sammie agreed to take a quick shower (great thought, Mama!!! Just add water!) and you were hopeful that the weekend could continue without more aggression—which it did—but Sammie just seemed to coast along at a lower level of protection brain.

"She was just rude and mouthy all weekend long. For no reason! It's like she doesn't even want to feel better. She just keeps herself in this pissy place, says nasty things to all of us, and doesn't do her chores."

"She just couldn't get regulated and back into connection brain, huh?"

"Well, I guess you could say that but it didn't seem dysregulated. It just seemed rude and controlling."

Ah yes. Controlling behavior always goes along with opposi-tional behavior. Oppositional behavior that persists is a classic sign of the *Ready-for-Action!* watchdog. Control means the brain is trying to find felt safety again. Sassy, mouthiness, and just general discontentedness are all common behaviors of the *Ready-for-Action!* watchdog.

"It's hard to see oppositional and controlling behavior as dysregulation, isn't it?" I say.

"Yeah. It doesn't seem dysregulated at all. It seems manipulative and intentional and totally within her control to stop."

"I get that," I say. "It's easier to see punching and kicking and hitting as signs of dysregulation. Those big behaviors are just more obvious signs of protection brain, aren't they? But, think of it this way. Do you think oppositional behavior comes from connection brain or protection brain?"

"Well," you say, considering the question. "It certainly doesn't make me want to be connected with her."

"Exactly," I say.

You heave a big sigh and open your eyes wide. "I know, I know. It's protection behavior. It just feels so intentional!"

"And I'll bet that makes you flip right into protection mode yourself!"

Our nervous system states are contagious. Our brains are designed to match each other. This is a good thing, except for when we live with someone who is protecting themselves a lot.

But here's the thing. If we think about Sammie's oppositional behavior as her watchdog being ready for action, we can get some ideas about how to intervene—for all of our sakes.

First, we have to remember that once the watchdog gets ready for action, the owl brain has flown away. I like to think about how the watchdog scares the owl away. This approach helps us stay focused on calming and soothing the watchdog so that the owl feels safe enough to return. Once the owl brain is back, we usually find the behaviors we were hoping for in the first place. If not, we can teach and practice those behaviors. But try as we might, teaching, explaining, and reasoning with a *Ready-for-Action!* watchdog just isn't useful or impactful, and often makes the watchdog more scared.

I flip my three-ring binder over to the "Characteristics of the *Ready-for-Action!* watchdog" page as we continue talking.

First, we look at what was happening for Sammie:

- Oppositional and unreasonable behavior
- Difficulty staying on task and completing a chore that we both know she can do (picking up her room)
- Increased physical activity and sensory seeking (which I suspect is behind the toiletry dumping).

We agree that these behaviors came from a *Ready-for-Action!* watchdog. I flip to the page of possible interventions, including easy movement activities that even watchdog brain kids might be enticed into, including:

- Arm wrestling
- Running around the house
- Pillow fight
- Dance party
- Cooking and baking
- Sensory play like finger painting or shaving cream.

"These are good reminders," you say, "but I'm pretty sure Sammie would have rejected every single one of these ideas." I see your eyes pause on the last item. "But you know what I think she would have loved if I'd thought of it?" you ask. "A can of shaving cream in the bathtub."

Yes! I hadn't thought of that, but I totally agree. You are your child's expert, so it makes sense that you saw something I didn't. Sammie was showing you what she needed to regulate her nervous system by squeezing and dumping the toiletries. But wasting four months' worth of toiletries doesn't work for the family budget. Cheap shaving cream in the bathtub might have helped her regulate by fulfilling the sensory experience she was seeking (squeezing, squishing, and slip-sliding in the bathtub) without causing more dysregulation from getting caught doing something she shouldn't.

Meet the need, decrease the fear, and allow her innate drive for sensory seeking to actually help her regulate.

You sound more puzzled than frustrated now. "It is just so hard to see the shampoo and toothpaste wasting as anything other than outright defiance, but I know, I know. Nothing is ever quite that simple."

"I'm not saying she wasn't being defiant," I admit. "She was in protection mode after all. But there are so many ways to express defiance, right? Why squeezing a bottle of shampoo? So yeah, I think chasing the why can lead to some helpful answers. When she's dysregulated, she likes to squeeze things, squish things between her fingers. Good thing to remember for next time. Shaving cream is cheap at the dollar store!!!"

You take the binder from me, flip to the next page, and read the title aloud: "Increase co-regulation and decrease the stressor." Then you look at me. "She really needed me to help her with cleaning her room, huh?"

"Yeah, I think so. She can do it when she's regulated, but she probably can't think, plan, or sequence when she's dysregulated. So I think she needed some scaffolding. She was probably too overwhelmed and to come up with the steps needed to get the job done. Kinda like..."

"A toddler," we both say.

You sigh.

"You're doing so well," I add. "When things go south, you're willing to pause, reflect, and get curious about her behavior. The next time you see Sammie, you'll look at her with eyes that see her for who she really is...a precious child who struggles sometimes. She'll look at you and see that in your eyes."

I watch your chest swell as you take a huge breath and then exhale. You feel it too. Hope.

"I'll see you next week," I say.

Interventions to Invite Safety, Regulation, and Connection with the Watchdog Brain

It's helpful to learn about the interventions through Nat and Sammie's story, but there's so much more that can be done to support the watchdog brain. In the rest of this chapter, we'll learn more about interventions that might be helpful for different watchdog levels. Whether your child's watchdog is asking "what's up?," is "ready-for-action!," needs you to "back off," or is "attacking," there are things you can do to help.

Back in Chapter 5, you got really good at noticing your child's behavior and reminding yourself that what you see isn't really what you get. You learned about the owl, watchdog, and possum brains. You learned that the owl brain is in connection mode, and that watchdog and possum brains are in protection mode. You spent time tracking and observing your child's behavior in Chapter 5, asking yourself, "What does this behavior really mean about my child's nervous system?" Now you can more accurately figure out if your child is in their owl, watchdog, or possum brain. That information helps you choose the right intervention at the right time.

The watchdog pathway is what Dr Perry refers to as the arousal continuum.[1] For those readers familiar with polyvagal theory,[2] you can equate the watchdog pathway with the sympathetic nervous system. When we believe we are in danger, the sympathetic nervous system provides power and energy to the body so that we can "fight or flight" to protect ourselves.

Maybe your child uses a lot of energy and power in the face of problems that seem very small to you—like having to turn in their homework or wait an extra five minutes for you to pick them up from school because of traffic. Their stress response system is sensitized and their watchdog works overtime, which means it activates a very big reaction to a very small amount of stress.

Before we go any further, let's quickly remember each of the different watchdogs.

Remember that as the watchdog gets increasingly active, fear and energy are increasing.

I'm Safe!	• Owl brain is in charge • Social behavior • Could be playful • Could be energetic
What's Up?	• Increased body movements • Change in voice (whiney, louder, faster) • Irritated, sassy, mild disrespect • "No" and "I can do it myself"
Ready-for-Action!	• Aggressive or defensive body language (preparing to fight or flee) • Hostile, oppositional • Illogical, unreasonable • Maniacal laughing or overly silly
Back Off!	• Aggressive or provocative movement (posturing, air punching) • Verbal aggression • Leaving or fleeing • "Volcano"—energy bubbles below surface
Attack	• Dangerous behavior • Physical aggression

In the rest of this chapter, I'm going to offer you specific interventions that might help your child's watchdog brain feel more safe and less dysregulated. Each watchdog needs something a little different. The *What's Up?* watchdog needs something different than the *Ready-for-Action!* watchdog, who needs something different than the *Back Off!* and *Attack* watchdogs. For each different watchdog, I'll suggest three different interventions.

Three Interventions

What's Up?	• Yes and... • Invite the owl brain • Compromise
Ready-for-Action!	• Give clear signals of "You're safe and I won't hurt you!" • Connect them to their senses • Remove the stressor—temporarily
Back Off!	• Clearly state "I am safe!" • Keep the environment safe • Stay regulated (not calm!)
Attack	• Keep yourself safe • Keep your child safe • Stay close, but not too close

I'm also going to share three common things to watch out for with each different watchdog so that when they inevitably happen, you can make sense of them and know what to do.

Three Things to Watch Out For

What's Up?	• Expecting obedience • Fear they are "getting away with bad behavior" • "This doesn't work!"
Ready-for-Action!	• Activating YOUR watchdog brain! • Fear you are "rewarding" bad behavior • "I have to do SOMETHING!"
Back Off!	• Not noticing when the Back Off! watchdog becomes "ready-for-action!" • Trying to engage the owl brain • Not sticking with it long enough
Attack	• Flying objects • Your child's arms, legs, and spit • Anything that could hurt your child

Don't worry—we're going to go through each intervention and each pitfall more closely in this chapter.

But first remember...

Safety Is Always the #1 Goal

Regardless of which watchdog you are dealing with, the most important thing for you to remember is that the watchdog brain believes it's in danger. This might seem completely ridiculous in the moment, as it did for Nat, when she saw Sammie punch her playmate in the hide and seek game.

Every person in the whole world—including you and including your child—determines how safe they are in any moment in a completely unique and individual-to-them way. Sometimes we have to just trust the message of their outward protective behaviors (opposition, defiance, and aggression) telling us they feel unsafe—even if we think they shouldn't—mean a brain in protection mode and a nervous system that feels unsafe.

It's important to always keep the following questions in mind, regardless of your child's level of arousal:

- How does my child know I'm not a threat? Am I in protection mode or connection mode? Do my inside feelings match my words, behaviors, facial expression, and body posture? Am I regulated, but not necessarily calm? Are my words and behaviors communicating safety?
- Does my child's internal physiology feel safe to them? Are they hungry or tired or are their sensory needs met? Are their medications adjusted appropriately?
- How does my child know this place they are in is safe? School, playground, their bedroom?

If you need a refresher on how your child is determining felt safety from inside, outside, and between, head back to Chapter 2. If you need help remembering how to help children feel safe when they are safe, refer to Chapter 6.

The *What's Up?* Watchdog

Safe or not safe?
- Still communicating with owl brain
- Orienting and gathering more information
- Not attacking or even preparing to attack

When you're dealing with your child's *What's Up?* watchdog, you'll be asking yourself the question "How can I help my child's owl brain feel confident that they are not in danger?"

#1 *What's Up?* Watchdog Intervention: Yes and...
The owl brain feels safer when it hears "yes." The watchdog brain feels less safe when it hears "no." This is true about your brain, too.

When your child asks for something that you want to say "yes" to but you're triggered because they've asked in a disrespectful, demanding, or sassy manner, give the "yes" first so that the *What's Up?* watchdog doesn't become "ready-for-action." Then simply show or tell your child a more respectful way to ask for what they need and want. For example:

Child: "Give me milk!"
Adult: "You bet! [With a light tone and while walking to get the milk] While I'm grabbing the milk, how about we have a Take 2 and ask again using your owl brain."

There's a lot happening in this one five-second interaction!

1. The child's fear is calmed because you are clearly stating that you will meet the need
2. The child feels that you saw them and not their behavior
3. You stay connected to your owl brain, which sends cues of safety through neuroception, while using a playful and light-hearted tone.

When you can't give a "yes" to the immediate request, see if you can say "no" without saying "no." For example:

Child: "I'm going to Sarah's house!"
Adult: "Oh, that sounds fun. Sarah is such a neat friend. Let's look at the calendar and see when we can schedule a time to go to Sarah's house."

Be sure you aren't expecting your child to respond in a way that robs them of their valid feelings of disappointment. It's okay for children to express disappointment or even anger that they can't do or have what they want.

Tolerating the frustration of disappointment is an owl brain skill that grows as your child's brain develops. Providing co-regulation through valid feelings of disappointment grows your child's owl brain and teaches them that their feelings matter. Kids who believe their feelings matter and that they'll get support with those feelings have stronger owl brains.

#2 *What's Up?* Watchdog Intervention: Invite Owl Brain Behavior
As I write this chapter, I'm looking out my office window into our newly planted garden. It's unusually hot and the plants are looking droopy, wilted, and even a little sunburned.

The plants are stressed and not getting exactly what they need. I'm asking myself "How can I help nurture these plants so they can grow to be the best plants they can be?" I'm not mad at the plants for responding to their environment.

I wonder what would happen if we took a similar approach to our children. When the watchdog is asking "What's up?" it's just a clue that the owl brain needs a little help. For example:

> Child: "I hate this homework. I'm not doing it."
> Adult: "Ah! You need a break from homework. For sure—sometimes we all need breaks when our brain is working hard. We'll definitely take a brain break. Let me know you need a brain break with owl brain words, please!"

I could stay focused on the disrespectful tone, the disobedience, and their mindset that isn't going to help them succeed at school.

Or I could just notice all of this as cues that their owl brain needs help. Homework is stressful, especially after a long day at school. Your child's owl brain deserves as much support as the wilted tomato plants in my backyard. You can offer your child the support they need and keep your boundary about how members of your family communicate with each other (with respect). For example:

> Child: "I'm going to Samira's house."
> Adult: "Oh sure! You can go. Can your owl brain ask me about Samira's house and then let me know when you'll be home?"

In my family, it's considered respectful and caring for us to all keep each other informed about where we are, and to check in with each other first rather than just doing whatever we want. It helps for me to stay focused on why our family values certain behavior, or else I can fall down the "Because I said so!" rabbit hole, too!

#3 *What's Up?* Watchdog Intervention: Compromising

Teaching kids how to compromise is my favorite strategy for a watchdog that is asking "What's up?" Compromising is like doing little bicep curls for the brain. Each attempt at a compromise strengthens the connection between the owl brain and the watchdog brain just a tiny bit.

Compromising is an extremely important life skill and helps the owl brain keep the other person's experience and perspective in mind. Creating a mind map of the other person is a key component in empathy, and indicates increased regulation and integration in the brain.

Compromising teaches kids so many important things, including:

- They have a voice
- Their needs and wants matter to you
- You will take their experience into consideration.

When kids feel empowered to use their voice, they'll:

- Begin to use their words instead of behaviors to negotiate getting their needs met
- Learn to tolerate frustration as they see that you aren't mean or punitive, but are actively on their side and part of their team.

For example, you've just asked your child to turn off the video game and come to dinner.

Child: "No!"

Adult: "Ah! I think I hear you saying that you aren't ready to turn off your video game or maybe that you need more time! Remember—you can definitely ask for a compromise. How about 'Dad, can I please have five more minutes and then I'll come to dinner?'"

If your child doesn't follow through with the compromise, they need help getting their owl brain back. Head back to Chapter 6 to review ways to grow your child's owl brain.

#1 Thing to Watch Out For: Focusing on Obedience and Compliance

I get it! Life would be so much easier if our kids just did what we wanted when we wanted it. My life would be easier if everyone I knew just did what I wanted, when I wanted it! I've also come to realize over the years that when I'm focused on expecting compliance and obedience from my child, my own *Ready-for-Action!* watchdog is usually getting involved. My owl brain doesn't expect my child to joyfully do things they don't want to do. I sure don't always joyfully do the laundry, but over the years I've grown my owl brain enough to regulate through the frustration of sometimes having to do chores instead of more fun things.

Remember that cooperation is a characteristic of the owl brain. As your child's owl brain grows, they will get better at managing frustration without saying mean things or stomping through the house.

Your child is entitled to their own feelings, thoughts, likes, and dislikes. They also need scaffolding to develop the skills to express those feelings, thoughts, likes, and dislikes in a way that works in relationship. As with any new skill, there are times when your child just can't do it. That doesn't mean they aren't trying or that they'll never learn. It just means they can't do it yet.

#2 Thing to Watch Out For: Being Afraid that Your Child Is Learning They Can Be Disrespectful and Still "Get What They Want"

Ooooh, this one can really get a parent's watchdog brain going, and understandably so. Many of us parents have learned that our kids should be respectful, and that we should teach them to be afraid of what will happen if they aren't.

Remember: *regulated, connected kids who feel safe behave well.*

If you use strategies focused on regulation, connection, and felt safety while also expecting behavior that matches your child's ability, they will not learn that they can be rude and get whatever they want. They will learn that they can expect to be seen for their true selves and that they deserve to receive support, not judgment or punishment. Relationships are satisfying and rewarding to the owl brain.

When you start to feel like your child needs a punishment in order to learn they can't "act that way," that is a clue you are in your watchdog brain. Don't worry! Section 3 of this book is all about how to help you stay more connected to your owl brain!

#3 Thing to Watch Out For: Feeling Like "This Isn't Working!"

When the interventions aimed at the *What's Up?* watchdog don't lead to increased connection and more regulated behavior from your child, or it seems like your child would never cooperate or respond the way the examples suggest, it doesn't mean those strategies aren't working. It may mean that your child isn't:

- Connected enough to you to prioritize cooperation
- Experiencing enough felt safety that they trust their words matter and that you'll consistently live up to your word
- Really asking "what's up?" but is instead "ready-for-action!" or even telling you to "back off!" No problem! You just misjudged their arousal level—or maybe it increased. Try shifting your approach to match a more activated watchdog.

Then head back to Chapter 6.

REAL-LIFE EXAMPLE

The late Dr Karyn Purvis, co-author of *The Connected Child* and co-developer of the Trust-Based Relational Intervention (TBRI), taught me about the power of Dubble Bubble (bubble gum).

I can get a bucket of 300 pieces delivered right to my door in 48 hours for only about $15, thanks to the convenience of online shopping.

Chewing offers proprioception to the mouth and jaw. Proprioception is almost always regulating.

Dr Purvis had two bubble gum rules:

1. The gum stays in your mouth or in the trash.
2. Ask with respect and I'll always say yes.

The giant tub of Dubble Bubble lived in my cabinet, behind a closed door, and the use of it as a way to create trust, connection, and co-regulation was mentioned in my informed consent paperwork. I never had a parent decline.

Hillot, a sweet, precious, and extremely irritable six-year-old, knew the rules: ask for bubble gum with respect and I'll always say yes.

One day, as we were getting ready to transition to the end of session, instead of asking for one or two pieces of Dubble Bubble, Hillot flashed a big smile and asked for 60.

I took a breath and thought fast. He'd started a dance of trust and asked me to join.

"Yes!" I said.

On one condition. We'd count out 60 pieces together and I'd give the baggie of Dubble Bubble to his parents. Over the week, he could ask his parents for the gum and the same rules would apply. In your mouth or in the trash. Always ask with respect and the answer will be yes.

We counted Dubble Bubble one at a time. All the way to 60.

My first job, before a compromise, was to prove trust. I had to prove to Hillot that if he used his words to ask for what he needed, I'd say yes. I had explicitly told him this. By asking for 60 pieces, he took me to task to see if I could put my money where my bubble gum was.

Hillot wasn't really asking for bubble gum. He was asking if I was true to my word.

I was committed to proving that I was.

For weeks, Hillot asked for 60 pieces of gum. For weeks, I said yes.

His parents confirmed that much to their surprise, Hillot was following all the bubble gum rules.

One week, I decided to explore if he was ready to move on to the next brain skill: compromise.

"I'm low on bubble gum this week. How about today we do 20?" I chose a low number on purpose so there was lots of room to compromise.

"NO!!!" he said, but playfully, so I knew we had his owl brain. "50!!!"

I shrugged my shoulders nonchalantly and said "Fine."

Over several weeks, I occasionally challenged his compromising skills until eventually we were down to 20. I decided this was a perfectly reasonable amount of Dubble Bubble to get him until our next session, and never tried to decrease the number again.

Every week, we counted out 20 pieces of Dubble Bubble one by one. Every week I handed the baggie to his parents, and every week they confirmed Hillot was having no problem following the bubble gum rules.

One week, we were running a little late at the end of a session. Without even thinking, I just grabbed a fistful of Dubble Bubble and tossed it in the bag.

"Do you want me to count them?" I asked, secretly hoping he'd say no.

"Yes!"

I counted the Dubble Bubble one by one.

20.

We locked eyes. He winked. I smiled.

This little one learned over weeks and weeks of hard work and patience (on both our parts!) that his voice mattered. That I could be trusted. If my fistful of bubble gum hadn't equaled 20 that last day, I would have ponied up. He knew that. The fact that there were exactly 20 pieces in the bag when I'd just grabbed a fistful was icing on the trust cake.

The *Ready-for-Action!* Watchdog

Not safe!
- Energy in arms and legs in preparation to fight or flee
- The energy is right at the surface but not mobilized for fight or flight—yet!
- Defiance

The owl has flown away! When your child is "ready-for-action!" try to resist the urge to use logic, reasoning, or even much language. Remember that active watchdogs live in lower places in the brain, places that developed before your child acquired much logic or language. In fact, if the *Ready-for-Action!* watchdog brain is trying to process much language, they might actually get more dysregulated. Processing language is hard and tiring.

#1 *Ready-for-Action!* Watchdog Intervention: "You're Safe and I Won't Hurt You!"

In this level of activation, your child's brain believes they are in danger. Prove that you aren't dangerous or scary!

When your child's *Ready-for-Action!* watchdog is in charge, your child isn't physically dangerous and you don't need to provide containment.

Nobody ever got physically injured from mouthiness, yelling, or your child sauntering away.

Stay focused on the long game; decrease activation so the *Ready-for-Action!* watchdog doesn't escalate to aggression or violence.

STATE VERY CLEARLY *WITH YOUR WORDS* THAT THEY
ARE SAFE AND YOU ARE NOT A THREAT

> "We're on the same team here and I want to help you. You are not in trouble."

> "You are safe. I am not going to hurt you."

ALSO BE VERY CLEAR *WITHOUT USING WORDS* THAT
THEY ARE SAFE AND YOU ARE NOT A THREAT
A couple of ideas:

- Take a step back. Get out of your child's immediate proximity, especially to their legs and arms.
- Release the tension in your body:
  - Relax your fists
  - Lower your shoulders
  - Unclench your thighs
  - Relax any defensive posturing.

Bonus!!! Changing your body tells YOUR watchdog brain that things are okay, too! This will help keep your owl brain nearby, even as the energy in your body increases.

ASK YOURSELF: "AM I STAYING IN CONNECTION MODE?"
Your child is relying on neuroception right now and they are acutely aware of whether your nervous system is in connection mode or protection mode. Remember that you don't have to stay calm. Think about staying mindfully present and aware of your sensations, feelings, and behaviors.

Remain clear, confident, and firm without being scary.

**#2 *Ready-for-Action!* Watchdog Intervention:
Connect Them to Their Senses**

The watchdog mostly lives in the feeling and sensing part of the brain. To connect with the watchdog brain, don't use a lot of words and instead focus on helping your child's body feel safe by offering sensory experiences.

What do I mean by sensory experiences?

We have five external senses—smell, sight, touch, taste, and hearing—as well as the senses that are involved in moving our bodies (proprioception and vestibular). Once you start to pay attention, you'll notice how you often help yourself feel better by connecting to your senses. For me, I like realllllly hot coffee, the smell of coconut, and moving my body by running or going to boot camp workout classes. All these things help me feel better.

Not sure what kind of sensory experiences help your child's body feel better? Start by paying attention to the things they like, and then use trial and error.

Remember how Sammie squeezed the bottle of shampoo and the toothpaste until they were gone? That was likely a sensory experience for Sammie that helped her body feel better. That prompted Nat to think of how she might give Sammie a similar sensory experience without her wasting money or items needed by other members of the family.

The *Ready-for-Action!* watchdog might like some of these sensory experiences. No guarantees, though! You'll have to experiment.

Drink	Snack	Move	Water
Hot	Chewy	Jump	Bath/shower
Cold	Crunchy	Run	Swimming
Thick	Sour	Wiggle	Sprinkler
Sweet	Sucking	Upside down	Drinks

Back in Chapter 6, I recommended my colleague Marti Smith's book, *The Connected Therapist*, for more practical ideas on how to offer sensory experiences to your child that will support their felt safety and regulation. I'm mentioning it again because it really is that good!

#3 *Ready-for-Action!* Watchdog Intervention: Remove the Stressor—Temporarily

Sometimes the best way to send cues of safety is to remove the stressor—homework, chores, mealtime, the discussion you are having, etc.

One of the most powerful lessons I've learned from children is that we adults need to listen to what they are telling us, and *believe* them. We also have to get over insisting that they use words to tell us. If they could, they would. They are telling us what they need and what they can and can't do all the time...with their behavior.

If your child is refusing to do math worksheets and being rude to their teacher, consider the very real possibility they don't have access in that moment to the part of their brain that would allow them to tolerate the frustration of working on a math problem.

Remove the expectation that they do the math worksheet—temporarily—and focus instead on regulation, connection, and felt safety.

Trust that your child's owl brain wants to grow and learn things—including math.

#1 Thing to Watch Out For: Activating Your Watchdog Brain

Your watchdog brain wants to get ready for action when your child's watchdog brain is ready for action! By design, watchdog brains aren't very self-aware. As the adult, it's your job to prioritize and practice noticing signs that you are in your watchdog brain. Remember in Chapter 5 when we focused on getting to know your child's owl, watchdog, and possum brains? Be sure to get to know your own owl, watchdog, and possum brains too! If you skipped that, maybe take a break and head to Chapter 5 now.

What are your watchdog cues? My voice gets squeakier and faster. My eyes get bigger. I have a tightening in my chest. When I notice these signs, I take a breath. I deliberately talk a little slower (or stop talking!). Since my watchdog is only "ready-for-action!" and the situation I'm in with my child isn't physically dangerous, I have time and the safety to notice my own response.

#2 Thing to Watch Out For: Being Afraid You Are Rewarding "Bad Behavior"

This is a normal and common fear of the watchdog brain, especially because the strategies in this section feel like rewards: drink, snacks, movement. Your owl brain knows that your child isn't "just acting bad." Your child's challenging behavior is happening because of their level of activation and lack of felt safety. Your child's watchdog brain might need more structure and boundaries in order to feel safe. If you want to try that strategy, head to Chapters 6 and 9 for ideas on increasing structure and boundaries.

Giving your child what they need in order to feel regulated, connected, and safe isn't a "reward." It's loving and respectful.

#3 Thing to Watch Out For: Believing You Have to Do Something

Sometimes your child's watchdog misinterprets your attempts to help it feel safe. Your child might actually feel like you are trying to change them or trick them, and this could make their watchdog brain more afraid!

Since your child isn't being physically dangerous or aggressive and is only "ready-for-action!" consider disengaging.

Stop talking.

Stay close enough that they don't feel abandoned but far enough away that you've removed yourself as a threat. Even if you aren't being threatening, your hope and expectation that they "change" can be experienced as a threat. It's important to stay close enough that when your child starts to feel more regulated, you're right there to help them.

When I'm with a *Ready-for-Action!* watchdog, I occasionally offer a drink or a snack or a movement break. This is something to try! When your child finally says "yes" or is willing to receive your offer, you'll know that arousal is decreasing and the owl brain is on the horizon. Continue to stay focused on connection and co-regulation (not teaching) until your child is solidly back in their owl brain. This could take a while. Chapter 9 covers what to do when the owl brain returns.

REAL-LIFE EXAMPLE

Children are telling us exactly what they need. We have to listen and believe them.

My sweet bubble gum guy was a child with academic aptitude but very little frustration tolerance. His watchdog quickly became "ready-for-action!" at school, and he was oppositional, defiant, rude, and "work avoidant." Due to his lagging reading skills, Hillot was pulled out of class for a special small group where his behavior would escalate quickly. The reading support specialist was baffled and easily flustered by his behaviors. She didn't understand his brain or have the tools to support him. Some days he did well in reading group. Other days, he'd sit with his arms crossed, grunt, glare, and refuse to do anything. On his most stressed days, he'd flee from the reading room or even the school building.

Luckily, the staff at the school he attended was fiercely committed to learning how to support him. The school counselor walked around with Dubble Bubble in her pocket in an attempt to build trust the same way I did!

One afternoon in session, mom and I were exploring how to support Hillot and his reading teacher. Looking back, what we were really doing was trying to find a way to coerce Hillot into behaving better. In what felt like a lightning strike moment, I looked at mom and said, "He is telling us exactly what he can and can't handle. Clearly, in the moment he rolls his eyes at the reading teacher and calls her stupid, what he is really saying is 'I can't do this today! The mental skill required to figure this out is too much. It's stressing my already stressed body and I cannot do it.'" Eyes wide, mom slowly nodded as she considered this explanation and realized it was completely true.

When children tell us what the problem is, it's our job to listen—even if they don't use perfect sentences. Which they won't because watchdogs don't speak in sentences!

As a team, we created a plan to more easily identify Hillot's behavioral cues. When he behaved in a way that communicated "I am too stressed," the adults responded by decreasing the demand, increasing connection and co-regulation, and offering movement. He was allowed to go to the sensory space that his guidance counselor had created. Sometimes Hillot regulated enough to return to reading group; sometimes he didn't. The adults in his life learned that soothing his stress and strengthening his owl brain was more important than reading worksheets. They trusted that as Hillot's owl brain got stronger, his natural desire to explore, learn, and cooperate would emerge.

This doesn't mean that the adults were never frustrated. Hillot's nervous system was particularly vulnerable, and sometimes his watchdog behaviors felt a little bit like he was giving all the adults the middle finger. Hillot's mom and I would chuckle a little, wondering what would happen when he actually learned that gesture. Hillot's parents and teachers sometimes had their own watchdog brain moments in response to his behavior. They were only human, after all.

Over time, the severity of Hillot's behaviors decreased. He stopped fleeing from the building, which was a serious safety threat, and instead started fleeing to the sensory room. His sassiness decreased (a little) and he would even sometimes use sassiness in playfully appropriate ways. His ability to receive cues of safety increased because his brain was less stressed and he began to trust that the adults at school were on his team. This shift led to increased socially appropriate behavior because he was in connection mode more often.

Hillot continued to struggle at school both academically and behaviorally because his brain-based disability left a gap between his intelligence and his academic performance. He struggled with processing and therefore often experienced frustration. More often than not, his nervous system was tipped toward protection mode and the adults in his life learned to take it a little less personally. Part of working with Hillot's family was helping everyone create appropriate expectations for Hillot and grieve for what they thought raising him would be like. Hillot began to experience being seen for exactly who he is, instead of who all the adults hoped he would be.

The *Back Off!* Watchdog

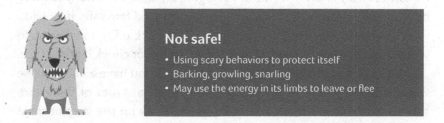

Not safe!
- Using scary behaviors to protect itself
- Barking, growling, snarling
- May use the energy in its limbs to leave or flee

The *Back Off!* watchdog is barking, growling, or acting scary. It may decide that instead of getting you to back off, they'll back off themselves by leaving the situation, either physically or energetically. They shut you out, ignore you, and refuse to answer.

If you see physically aggressive behavior in this level of arousal, it's not truly dangerous. It's a behavior that says "back off!" but this watchdog isn't actually in "attack" mode.

The owl brain is looooong gone. Think about your child's *Back Off!* watchdog as holding a big stop sign. Don't do anything except create safety.

#1 *Back Off!* Watchdog Intervention: Clearly Communicate "I'm Not Going to Hurt You!"

The only words you'll want to use while your child is focused on getting you to back off will sound something like "I'm safe," "I understand," "I am not a threat."

Your child's watchdog is paying attention to what you do, not what you say. Pay very close attention to your tone of voice and your body language.

Shift your body so you are physically lower than your child. Sit, squat, or just back up.

#2 *Back Off!* Watchdog Intervention: Keep the Environment Safe

A lot of kids with very active watchdog brains came to my office in the past, and I was very strategic and purposeful about toys, decorations, and furniture. Other therapists have beautiful decor, expensive couches and pillows, and meaningful knickknacks.

I never wanted anything in my office that would prompt me to have more concern over the item than the child. This means low-budget items that are easy to replace, fix, or wash. If my couch gets peed on, I need to be able to easily clean it. If glue or paint gets spilled, I don't want to focus on the carpet—I want to focus on helping the child feel safe. If a child's watchdog gets activated and is telling me to back off, I don't want to worry that they will break my favorite knickknack or chuck it at my face.

I highly suggest you think of similar things if you have a child whose watchdog is regularly telling you to back off. What types of things are safe to have in their room—or in any room? Pack up the irreplaceable dishes you inherited when your grandmother passed away. Keep decorations sparse. This isn't the time to splurge on the couch you've been dreaming about.

#3 *Back Off!* Watchdog Intervention: Keep Yourself Regulated

How on earth do you keep your cool when the chaos is just too much?

This is such a great question that there's an entire chapter devoted to the answer—Chapter 12.

It is possible. You'll never be able to keep your cool all the time because you're going to continue to be a real person who reacts to chaos sometimes, no matter how much you grow your own owl brain. If you live with a child whose watchdog brain is almost always telling you to back off, you might want to skip ahead to Chapters 11 and 12.

#1 Thing to Watch Out For: Not Noticing When Your Child Goes from "Back Off!" to "Ready-for-Action!"

The most important thing to watch for when you are engaging with the *Back Off!* watchdog is their back down to the *Ready-for-Action!* watchdog level. All of our children have different cues and clues that they are coming down. Be patient with yourself as you figure out those of your child.

Maybe the pitch of their voice changes. Maybe the intensity of their cry changes. Maybe you notice their eyes change or the things that they are saying changes just a little.

When your child is focused on getting you to back off, your primary goal should be simply not to escalate them. As they eventually come down in activation, you can use the interventions that work for those lower arousal levels, like drinks or snacks, movement, or compromising.

#2 Thing to Watch Out For: Trying to Engage the Owl Brain

When your child is focused on getting you to "back off!" they aren't being reasonable at all. They might say things that don't make sense or accuse you of things that aren't true.

Things like "You hate me!!!"

You are going to be tempted to respond to these *Back Off!* watchdog behaviors with owl brain interventions like logic and reasoning.

Don't be fooled! There is no reasoning with this watchdog. Don't try to convince them they are wrong, that you don't hate them. Ironically, attempting to do so usually just makes things worse. The owl brain is nowhere nearby so you can't reason with this child. But don't worry. Not arguing with things like "You hate me!!!" doesn't mean you agree with them.

You might say "It feels like I hate you!" or maybe you just say nothing at all.

#3 Thing to Watch Out For: Not Sticking With It All the Way Until the Owl Brain Has Returned

Parenting a watchdog is exhausting. Sometimes parents are so eager for the owl to return that they misread cues and start engaging with their child as if the owl is back.

Luckily, your child will make it clear that they aren't fully connected to their owl brain because their behavior will escalate again.

Notice your own triggers, which might be things like feeling you are pressed for time, or that you've given in long enough, or that it's simply just time for this to all be over. While those are all very valid feelings for you to have, your child's owl brain doesn't necessarily agree.

I know this is exhausting and not what you signed up for. I also know it truly is possible to become more tolerant of the most bizarre and chaotic behavior so that you get better at keeping your cool. Section 3 will give you concrete steps that will grow your own owl brain without adding more work to your already extremely stressful life.

REAL-LIFE EXAMPLE

Jasmine, a spunky 10-year-old with a particularly vulnerable nervous system, was getting ready to leave our therapy session when she asked her dad if they could stop at a gas station for a drink. This child commonly regulated with food, as well as with things she perceived as a treat or a gift. Often, her parents would respond with a yes, and this became a lovely therapy day ritual.

This particular afternoon, they were in a hurry to get home due to another commitment and they did not have time to stop. Dad gave a sympathetic "no" and attuned to her feelings by saying "I know this is disappointing, but we don't have time to stop today."

Despite dad's attunement, Jasmine immediately escalated. She screamed "You hate me!" and tossed a stuffed animal in dad's direction. "I never get what I want!"

Her irrationality and intensity let me know how dysregulated she had become. Her behavior was mildly physically aggressive (throwing) but didn't have the intensity of an *Attack* watchdog, so I knew the tossed stuffed animal was more about getting us to "back off!"

The first thing I did was take a breath.

Honestly, I was frustrated. It was time for her to go. Her dad definitely didn't hate her and she almost always got a treat after therapy; this was a very unusual exception. I knew I had a client waiting in the waiting room, not to mention three other therapists in the building who were with their clients while mine was screaming. Screaming was of course normal and expected when choosing to do therapy in our little blue house, but I often felt a pang of regret when my clients escalated to the point of disrupting someone else's therapy session.

I noticed my frustration and reminded myself that this was a place for dysregulation. I knew that, my colleagues knew that, and our other clients knew that.

As my client climbed into my windowsill, I quickly assessed if there was anything in her reach that could be dangerous. Confident that she was safe in my windowsill, I sat down on the ground with my legs crossed.

Her dad took my cue and sat down on the couch. He said nothing.

"You wanted a treat and dad said no!" I said, with intensity in my voice. I wanted to provide a mirror, let her know I understood.

"He hates me!!!"

Dad still said nothing. Perfect. Arguing with a watchdog is a losing battle and increases dysregulation.

"Do you want me to get you a drink?" We had a watercooler in the waiting room and I kept juice boxes in our little dorm-style fridge.

"SHUT UP!!!!"

Attunement means attuning to *all* our children's feelings, even if they are expressed with disrespect. When the watchdog is focused on getting me to back off, it isn't going to be respectful. We could deal with respect when the owl brain returned.

So, I shut up.

For the next five or so minutes (it seemed like longer!) she growled, bared her teeth, and screamed "You hate me!" and "Dad hates me" and "I never get what I want." She was not physically aggressive.

Occasionally, I'd say something like "Wow, your body is probably getting so tired and thirsty. Can I get you a drink?"

To which she'd scream "NO!!!!!!!!!!!!!!!"

Whenever I'd start to lose my patience and feel tempted to say something decidedly unhelpful ("It's time to go," "You get treats all the time," "Nobody hates you!" etc.) I'd take a breath and picture a scared owl hiding in the corner of the room. The owl can't hear me, I'd remind myself. Arguing and getting frustrated with the watchdog will only increase its growl.

Finally, she received one of my feeble attempts at offering a sensory experience and some nurturing care. "Okay," she said, she'd take a drink.

"Dad," I asked, "would you grab a juice box from the fridge?"

Dad said, "Yes, absolutely." When he came back, he popped the straw in the juice box, handed it to his sweaty daughter still perched in the windowsill, and sat back down on the couch.

"I'll bet you are so thirsty and tired," I said. "Your watchdog brain worked hard to keep you safe!!!"

After sucking the juice box dry, she climbed down from the windowsill and glanced her eyes toward her dad.

"You ready to go?" he said.

She nodded and grabbed his extended hand.

"I'll see you next week sweet girl. I can't wait to be with you again."

The *Attack* Watchdog

Not safe!
- Believes it is in immediate danger
- Hitting, pushing, spitting, kicking

The *Attack* watchdog believes danger is imminent and will do anything to protect itself.

Remember! The only reason for your child, or anyone else, to be physically aggressive toward another human is because they believe they are in life-threatening danger. Humans are the most dangerous predator of humans, and our watchdog brain evolved to keep us safe from danger.

#1 *Attack* Watchdog Intervention: Keep Yourself Safe

If you do not need to provide physical containment for your child in order to ensure safety, stay out of arm's reach and put your hands behind your back. Next, quickly glance around the environment. Are there any items or objects you need to quickly and safely move out of reach of your child?

#2 *Attack* Watchdog Intervention: Keep Your Child Safe

When our children's *Attack* watchdog is in charge, we are at risk for our own *Attack* watchdogs to get activated, and from there, we might unintentionally use our hands in ways that are not safe.

If you are parenting a child who occasionally requires physical containment, protect yourself and your child by getting appropriate and approved training. Physical containment should only be used if it's the only way to keep you or your child safe. Physical containment is never a strategy—it's only protective.

#3 *Attack* Watchdog Intervention: Stay Close, But Not Too Close

If you are regulated (not calm!), stay close enough to provide physical safety, and containment if necessary, but far enough away to communicate clearly "I will not hurt you."

Staying close allows you to notice very subtle cues that the *Attack* watchdog is starting to decrease their activation. Then you can use parenting strategies that are appropriate for the *Back Off!* or *Ready-for-Action!* watchdog.

#1 Thing to Watch Out For: Flying Objects

Be sure to duck! In all seriousness, watch out for anything that could hurt you or your child.

#2 Thing to Watch Out For: Flailing Arms, Legs, and Well-Aimed Spit

If you get hit, you're too close. Physically take a step back from your child. If they pursue you and continue to hurt you, do what you need to do to keep both of you safe.

#3 Thing to Watch Out For: Anything that Could Hurt You or Your Child

The only thing you should be thinking about when your child's watchdog is attacking is how you keep everyone safe.

REAL-LIFE EXAMPLE

A crash in the waiting room alerted me that 11-year-old Jackson had arrived for his appointment. I arrived in time to watch Jackson hurl a magazine at his dad, narrowly missing only due to his dad's quick reflex to duck.

I'd love to tell you exactly what I did and said next but I have no idea. I know at one point I moved a lightweight end table out of Jackson's reach because he could have easily picked it up and used it as a weapon. It was easy enough to reach because he had already shoved it toward me.

I know when it was over Jackson was safe, I was safe, his parents were safe, and nothing was broken.

I have written and rewritten this *Real-Life Example*. It's impossible because there is no right way to respond to an *Attack* watchdog. When your child is being physically dangerous, your watchdog brain is going to take over. Let it. The watchdog's job is to act fast and keep you safe.

This Isn't Enough

If you have a child whose watchdog brain is regularly attacking, you are certainly disappointed at how short this section is. You've probably been eagerly, if not desperately, waiting for this section.

You're the family who needs help the most, but unfortunately you need real, live, in-the-trenches-with-you help. There are so many nuances to supporting families with kids with chronically aggressive or dangerous behavior that it simply isn't fair to you to attempt to address that in a book.

The most important thing your family can do to decrease the frequency of how often your child's *Attack* watchdog is activated is to focus on the tools and techniques in Chapter 6, as well as the interventions for the *Ready-for-Action!* watchdog described in this chapter.

What's Next?

In Chapter 9, Nat asks a question that you might be wondering about, too. "But, what about a consequence?"

Calming the watchdog brain might be the hardest part of responding to challenging behavior, but it's not the last part. One important thing that helps children feel safe is having clear and predictable boundaries and expectations. Once your child's owl brain has returned, we can turn our attention to connecting with and teaching the owl brain. Reconnecting with the owl brain with the steps outlined in Chapter 9 makes it clear to your child's watchdog brain that you are not ignoring bad behavior; you are using it as a clue so you can solve the real problem instead. Ignoring bad behavior actually leaves the watchdog brain on alert, and then yup, you guessed it. More watchdog brain behavior.

This is so important that I wrote an entire chapter (Chapter 9) about connecting with and teaching your child's owl brain. If it'll calm your watchdog brain to skip ahead, go for it! You might need to read about strategies to reconnect with the owl brain more than you need to read about strategies to calm the possum brain (Chapter 8).

CHAPTER 8

Parenting Strategies for the Possum Brain

"Would it be okay if I ask you a question about my other child?" you ask.

"Oh of course! You know, we almost never talk about Sammie's brother. Sometimes I forget all about him!"

"Well, Sammie needs so much of our attention and active parenting that I think Morgan gets a little overlooked sometimes. He is so easy compared to Sammie, but I'm actually starting to wonder if that's a problem."

"Tell me about Morgan," I invite you. "What's up?"

"Well, yesterday, Morgan forgot to empty the dishwasher. That's not a big deal and I wasn't upset. Morgan was getting a drink in the kitchen so I just reminded him about the dishwasher. And gosh, by his reaction, you'd have thought I screamed and yelled or something."

"Oh yeah? What'd he do?"

"Nothing! That's just it. Sammie might have thrown her drink at me, but Morgan does nothing. He won't look at me, doesn't even respond to me or acknowledge that I said anything, though he clearly heard me. He just stood there while the fridge hung open, waiting to be closed."

"So then what?"

"Well, I got frustrated and said something like 'Hello? Morgan? Earth to Morgan!'"

"Ah yes, your watchdog brain came out! That happens a lot when dealing with a kid in their possum brain."

You actually roll your eyes at me. It's delightful.

"What?" I ask, feigning a bit of hurt. "You don't like possums?"

"Well, no. Possums are freaky. But I forgot all about the possum brain. I mean, of course there's another animal here. It's like a regular ole zoo."

"Possums are freaky. Have I told you about the time I woke up to one sitting on my printer? In my home office? Yes! True story. I freaked out, it freaked out. It hissed and snarled at me for a couple minutes. The possum had a watchdog brain reaction! But eventually I guess it got scared enough that it just, you know, played dead." I cross my eyes, stick out my tongue, and tilt my head. "You know. Like a possum."

"That did not really happen," you say.

"Oh, it really happened. And actually it was good it finally played dead because then we could move it outside. Five minutes later I went to check on it and, sure enough, it was gone. Playing dead was definitely the safest move for that possum—and for us!

"Remember how protection brain has two pathways? One pathway increases energy—the watchdog pathway? That's the pathway Sammie usually takes. The other pathway decreases energy—the possum pathway. I'm wondering if Morgan's nervous system sometimes takes the possum pathway when he's stressed."

"That makes sense. So what do I do about that?"

"First, notice your own reaction," I say, and your shoulders sag slightly in disappointment. You probably wanted a concrete answer for how to help Morgan, but I continue. "It's easy to jump into watchdog brain when your child goes down the possum pathway. But if you remember that the possum brain is already very, very afraid…"

"…then a watchdog probably scares the possum even more," you finish my thought. The moment of resonance and connection between us is relieving and we both simultaneously take a breath and relax back into our chairs.

"Exactly." I allow for a short pause before going on so you and I can both feel just slightly into our own possum energy. After a moment, I continue with a quieter voice and softer intonation. "After you notice your own reaction, the next important step is to remind yourself that this possum behavior is the behavior of a brain in protection mode. This can be hard to remember, especially compared to Sammie's watchdog brain because possum behavior doesn't seem as 'bad.'" I put air-quotes around "bad."

I go on. "Possum brain kids need us to have low and slow energy. Energy that matches theirs, but without the scared, dazed, and confused thing. You know, kinda like the energy you and I have now. Big energy, even if it's not scary, can really overwhelm possum kids. In a perfect world, when you notice Morgan move into his possum brain, you could take a breath, lower the volume and intensity of your voice, and say 'Oh hey! You're not in trouble, I'm just reminding you about the dishwasher.'

"Then you might say something like 'Finish getting a drink and, you know, I think I'll have one too. You can do the dishwasher after a drink and maybe a snack.'

"You already know drinks and snacks are my go-to ways for connecting with watchdog and possum brains. Kids in the possum pathway are disconnecting their mind from their body, so sensory strategies like drinks, snacks, and low-energy movement or sensory play are great ways to gently pull them back in. Does Morgan like shaving cream play like Sammie does?"

"Morgan hates things squishy on his fingers but loves arts and crafts projects like coloring and sewing."

"That makes sense. Oftentimes kids with stronger possum pathways like quiet, independent activities that have just a little bit of sensory impact, like coloring, sewing, or other arts and crafts projects. Sometimes with possum brain kids, the best thing to do is take a break from whatever's happening—the chore or homework or whatever—and do something quiet that engages the body a little. He can finish the chore later."

I reach for my three-ring binder and flip to "Characteristics of the *La-La Land* possum."

"It sounds like Morgan had a la-la land response...spacey, checked out, and ignoring you. Just like with the *What's Up?* watchdog, the *La-La Land* possum still has a little connection to the owl brain. My guess is you would have been able to reconnect with Morgan's owl brain pretty quickly if you'd slowed down and encouraged the drink. What do you think?"

"Yeah, I think so." Your eyes start to glisten as tears spring up.

"Oh, Nat," I say quietly and slowly, with the slightest tilt of my head. "The tears. What's under those tears?"

"It's so easy to just assume Morgan is doing fine. His behaviors aren't bad, and when I notice them, I usually just feel annoyed. Morgan's getting overlooked and it's not fair."

"Yeah, so much of this isn't fair. It isn't fair that Morgan is that stressed by being reminded to do a chore. It isn't fair both Morgan and Sammie have such vulnerable nervous systems. It's so hard on them—and you. Those tears make a lot of sense." You grab a tissue from the closest-of-many-tissue-boxes and we lock eyes.

Sometimes the only thing we can do is honor the grief by seeing it and acknowledging it.

Interventions to Invite Safety, Regulation, and Connection with the Possum Brain

One of the most important things to keep in mind with kids who have an overactive possum brain is that the owl brain is far away and it may take a lot of time for it to return.

Back in Chapter 5, you got really good at noticing your child's behavior and reminding yourself that what you see isn't really what you get. You learned about the owl, watchdog, and possum brains. You learned that the owl brain is in connection mode, and that watchdog and possum brains are in protection mode. You spent time tracking and observing your child's behavior, asking yourself "What does this behavior really mean about my child's nervous system?" Now you can more accurately figure out if your child is in their owl, watchdog, or possum brain. That information helps you choose the right intervention at the right time.

The possum pathway is what Dr Perry refers to as the dissociation continuum.[1] If you're familiar with polyvagal theory, you can equate the possum pathway with the dorsal vagal complex. The possum pathway activates where there is a neuroception of life threat, not just danger. The watchdog believes in its power to do something about the scary situation.

It can growl, run, or fight. The possum believes it is helpless in a hopeless situation. Instead of expressing energy, the possum pathway conserves energy by collapsing. The dissociation continuum is a last-ditch effort at staying alive but feeling less pain by "vacating the premises."

Before we go any further, let's review the five different levels of dissociation in the possum brain. If you need more than a quick review, flip back to Chapter 5.

I'm Safe!	• Owl brain is in charge • Social behavior • Could be peaceful • Could be very still or resting
La-La Land	• Staring off into space • Disconnected • Looking bored, saying "I'm bored" • Avoidance/work avoidance • Distracted, unfocused, off-task
Trickster	• Robotic voice/inflection • People pleasing—"Yes!" or "I don't know" • Slooooow body movements (taking 45 minutes to tie shoes) • Poor concentration • May feel like they are in their owl brain, but it's a trick
Shut-Down	• Significant lack of eye contact/eyes looking down • Body collapses into a "c" shape, knees may come to chest • Arms may protect head/torso • Extremely slow/sluggish (i.e., not getting out of bed) • Stops speaking
Play Dead	• Completely non-responsive • Fainting or sudden falling asleep (not narcolepsy) • Dissociation that causes a complete disconnect from reality

If you have a child who regularly or even occasionally falls into their possum brain, you might be confused by the fact that this pathway activates in response to a serious life threat. Your child probably doesn't have many (or any!) truly life-threatening experiences in the present.

But maybe they did in the past.

The possum pathway gets well exercised when babies don't receive the co-regulation that they need. For tiny babies, being left alone or without co-regulation is life-threatening and the possum pathway is their only defense. Babies can't run away or fight back.

When the possum pathway gets used a lot, it becomes the default.

This child's stress response system is so oversensitized that later, normal life stressors like having to finish homework or do a simple chore activate a possum brain response.

A Life Threat Even When It's Not

What's important to remember here is that children with possum behaviors are extremely stressed. Their brain is neuroceiving life threat. The possum pathway begins to disconnect their mind from their body. This is smart because who wants to stay connected to their body if they're under that much threat?

Sometimes, possum brain behavior seems like less of an emergency than watchdog brain behavior because it isn't outwardly aggressive. Because so many of us were raised to value compliance over autonomy, we can sometimes overlook the dysregulation and fear that is underneath possum behavior. Despite appearances, when children land in their possum pathway, we can trust that their nervous system is in extreme distress.

Believe it or not, recognizing this is the first strategy.

A Possum Is a Possum Is a Possum

Just like in Chapter 7 on the watchdog brain, in this chapter I'll offer you some interventions for all the different possums: the *La-La Land* possum, the *Trickster* possum, the *Shut-Down* possum, and the *Play-Dead* possum. Unlike the watchdog brain, there isn't much difference in how you might connect with each different possum. Most of my recommended interventions are appropriate for every possum.

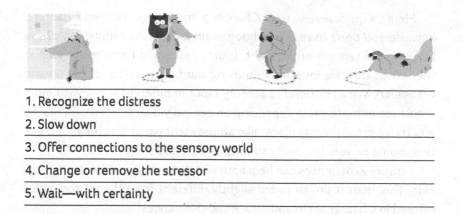

1. Recognize the distress

2. Slow down

3. Offer connections to the sensory world

4. Change or remove the stressor

5. Wait—with certainty

#1 Possum Brain Intervention: Recognize the Distress

Changing how we see people changes people, and it changes you. If you can see possum brain behavior for what it really is, you are much more likely to respond by providing a moment of safety and healing for your child. Recognizing the distress is as simple as creating new meaning out of behaviors we commonly see from our kids. The la-la land, dazed look? Maybe that's a stress response. Not answering? Maybe that's a stress response. When you start to feel agitation in your own body because it seems like your child isn't "there" (like when Nat said "Earth to Morgan!"), you've probably come into contact with your child's possum brain stress response.

#2 Possum Brain Intervention: Slow Down

The possum pathway is the opposite of the watchdog pathway when it comes to energy and activation. Watchdogs get a lot of energy in their arms and legs so they can run or fight. Possums step on the energy brakes. The energy dramatically decreases, draining from their arms and legs. A child in the possum pathway needs us to meet them in this low and slow place. Take a breath and decrease the volume and tone of your voice. Be a little quieter, a little softer, a little gentler, while still staying connected to the confidence of your owl brain.

#3 Possum Brain Intervention: Offer Connections to the Sensory World

Gently help possum kids reconnect with their body by engaging their senses. As your child falls further down the possum pathway, you'll have to be more gentle with the offering of a sensory experience.

Here's a quick review from Chapter 7 (maybe you skipped Chapter 7 because you don't have a watchdog brain kid in your family!). We have five external senses—smell, sight, touch, taste, and hearing—as well as the senses that are involved in moving our bodies (proprioception and vestibular). We all respond to sensory input in different ways, with more regulation or more stress depending on our individual preferences. Maybe you thrive in busy, noisy places like amusement parks, but for your child, that would be way too many sounds, sights, and smells.

Sensory experiences can help *both* watchdog brain and possum brain kids. This chart is similar to but slightly different from the sensory chart offered in Chapter 7. Do you notice the differences?

Drink	Snack	Move	Water
Hot	Chewy	Fidgets	Bath/shower
Cold	Crunchy	Seats that move	Swimming
Thick	Sour	Thumb wrestle	Sprinkler
Sweet	Sucking	Coloring/art/crafts	Drinks

In the "Move" category, look for movement that is small and low energy. Hand fidgets are great to keep around for your possum brain kids because they invite a very small amount of movement. You can experiment with different textures, like a balloon filled with Play-Doh versus a balloon filled with water beads. I also love giving possum brain kids a place to sit that has a tiny bit of movement in it, like a yoga ball (on a base), a wobble cushion, or a chair that gently rocks. Desk chairs that are padded, spin, and rock forward and backward can be a great thing to keep in non-traditional places, like the dining room.

Coloring and other arts and crafts can help a possum brain child connect to their senses. Most arts and crafts activities involve small movement (cutting, coloring, folding, gluing) and many arts and crafts engage other senses, including visual, tactile, and even smell. We all know what a box of crayons smells like! Consider covering tables or flat surfaces with butcher paper and offering crayons or colored pencils. Provide lots of supervision (decrease the distance) if your child tends to color on inappropriate surfaces.

Here are a few other ideas to gently engage the possum brain child.

Pressure	Rhythm	Breathing
Lycra (sheets, body socks, compression clothing) Weighted items (blankets, wraps, scarves) Temporary tattoos	Listen to music Back and forth games, like tossing balloons or rolling a ball Dancing/swaying/rocking	Blow up balloons Blow bubbles Blow cotton balls or craft feathers back and forth

Lycra is an inexpensive fabric with so many uses! My friend Marti Smith, OTR, is the Lycra queen! Check out her book, *The Connected Therapist*, for more ideas about how to use Lycra.[2] Weighted items can be expensive and I've found that some kids love them, some hate them, and some become indifferent after a few days. If you can, borrow a weighted item from a friend before making the investment.

I've had entire sessions with children where we put temporary tattoos all over our arms and legs. Temporary tattoos are cheap and require some gentle pressure to apply. As kids start to get a little more regulated, temporary tattoos can become a cooperative experience where I apply the pressure for putting tattoos on the child's body, and the child applies the pressure for putting tattoos on my body. Don't be afraid to put temporary tattoos all over! Temporary tattoos are easy to wipe off with rubbing alcohol or baby wipes so you don't have to go to work with a mermaid on your forehead. Some kids may even enjoy having matching temporary tattoos with you, putting the same tattoo on the same parts of your body.

Look for ways to invite rhythm into your child's body. Listening to music is an easy way to bring in rhythm if the child enjoys it. I often encourage parents to examine their rules around what music their child is allowed to listen to and when their kids can have earbuds in. It can seem rude for your child to walk around with earbuds in, but it is almost certainly a way they are intuitively bringing regulation into their body. Remember, we all have different sensory needs and preferences. The music your child finds regulating might be the exact opposite of the music you find regulating. It can be tempting to insist that your child can't think clearly enough to do their math homework while listening to that noise (AKA their music!); however, if they are actually doing their homework, then the music is regulating, not distracting.

#4 Possum Brain Intervention: Change or Remove the Stressor

I spend a lot of time acknowledging to parents that, yes, your child should be able to do what you want them to do, based on their age and skills—while also acknowledging that despite what they should be able to do, they simply can't. We have to parent the child in front of us, not the one the development books say we should have or even the child we had five minutes ago.

A huge stress response indicates that the child just doesn't have the stress resilience to do what we want them to do *in that moment*. Sometimes the best thing we can do is eliminate the stressor. Take a break from homework, for five minutes or maybe forever. Take that chore off their list of chores, for today or maybe the whole year. Sometimes we have to reevaluate things that seem non-negotiable, like school, and ask ourselves if it really is non-negotiable.

Writing this book has been hard and stressful! Some days, I have a lot of capacity to regulate through that stress. Some days, I support myself with all my favorite sensory strategies. Coffee and gum and the *Bridgerton* soundtrack. Sometimes I write while slowly walking on the treadmill. Sometimes I take a movement break and go for a run, then go back to writing.

Some days, I simply can't write a word. I just can't. I'm capable of writing, sure. But I can't! The idea of writing makes my brain hurt.

I'm a grown-up and make my own rules, so I don't write on those days. If someone forced me to write when it felt like it was making my brain hurt, my *Trickster* possum brain would first try to help me just comply. Then I'd probably get mad and start saying grouchy things that might even intentionally hurt the feelings of whoever this mystery person is who is making me write. Then I might start trying to negotiate. Then I might just cross my arms and refuse. If someone was still forcing me, I might toss my now lukewarm cup of coffee at them. Who knows what I would do. Anything. Because I just. Can't. Write.

I'll be right back. I need a coffee warm-up.

#5 Possum Brain Intervention: Wait—With Certainty

Sometimes, our possum brain kids need us to just be okay with the fact that they are in their possum brain, and to just be with them. When your child seems unable to reconnect to their owl brain from the possum pathway, take a breath and just be. Be still. Be quiet. Have no agenda except to just be.

I know you have real life to deal with. You might not be able to do this for very long, if at all. You have to get dinner on the table or you have to get to work on time. You have other kids to be with, and they might be in their watchdog brain! When you can't just be with your possum brain kid, it is still helpful to keep your X-ray vision goggles on so you can see what their behavior is really showing you: *a child whose nervous system is responding in exactly the way it believes it needs to, given the safety they are neuroceiving from inside, outside, and between.*

#1 Possum Brain Thing to Watch Out For: Missing It!

It's easy to overlook the dysregulation of the possum brain, especially if you have watchdog kids in your family (or on your caseload or in your classroom). Possum brain kids can look quiet and even compliant (especially when they are being a "trickster").

Sometimes we notice possum brain behaviors but label them as negative personality traits, like lazy or unmotivated. When we label behaviors as negative character traits instead of as behaviors that indicate a stress response, we make very different choices about how to respond.

I am not sure there is any such thing as a lazy person. The human body is supposed to work as efficiently as possible, using as few calories as it can to get done what needs to get done. "Lazy" might just be a nervous system that is conserving precious energy it needs because having an overactive watchdog or possum brain is exhausting. "Lazy" might be a nervous system stuck in possum mode. Their nervous system is dialing back all their energy intentionally as a way to stay safe and alive.

Brilliant.

Children who quickly and regularly activate the possum pathway have a nervous system that is really hurting. Possum kids need help and patience. Possum kids don't make quick progress with parenting or therapy. We have to expect that connecting with possum brain kids can feel slow, boring, or even like a waste of time.

It's not. I promise.

#2 Possum Brain Thing to Watch Out For:
Having a Watchdog Brain Response

Parenting a child in their possum brain is frustrating. It can feel like you're constantly repeating yourself, your child is never listening to you, and nothing is getting better.

Sometimes you are going to be rightfully preoccupied with life. You're feeling the urgency of getting out the door on time so you aren't late for work (again) and your child is just sitting by their shoes, staring at them. Or they are aimlessly wandering around the house despite the fact that you've told them to get their backpack, grab their lunch, and meet you at the door to put shoes on. Things they know how to do and are completely capable of doing on their own some days!

This can feel maddening and it is understandable that your watchdog brain would respond. Try not to let it.

In Section 3, we'll look at ways that you can grow your owl brain so you have more capacity to tolerate frustrating behaviors. For now, simply notice if your watchdog brain is quickly activated by your child's possum brain. If so, tell your watchdog brain that this is normal! Your body doesn't want to fall down the possum pathway with your child, so it responds with protective watchdog energy. Send some gratitude to your watchdog brain for trying to keep you safe, and then reassure it that the owl brain can safely connect to your child's possum brain.

If you just rolled your eyes, that's okay. It does sound a little ridiculous.

It works, though. Trust me.

#3 Possum Brain Thing to Watch Out For:
Pushing Interventions Too Hard

Nobody likes to feel as though someone else is trying to control them, but possum brains are especially sensitive to feeling like you want them to change. In fact, possum brains are going to feel this as more danger.

This is a tricky spot to be in. You want your child's nervous system to heal. You want their behaviors to change. I've given you a lot of practical strategies on how to support that goal. And now I'm telling you that you can't try too hard.

It is so uncomfortable to connect with intense possum brain energy. This makes sense! Our own nervous system wants to keep us out of our possum brain and will often respond with watchdog energy. Sometimes that watchdog energy sounds like Nat did with Morgan—frustrated, irritated, or even punitive. Sometimes it has us frantically and forcefully offering "interventions" to the possum brain that are just scaring it even more! I have found myself doing this even in the therapy room. It's like the ultimate game of whack-a-mole. You want a drink? How about a snack? I know! Let's get in the hammock. Oh not that? How about blowing bubbles? You wanna dance?

This frantic energy is not going to feel safe to anyone, let alone a kid whose possum brain is in charge. It also sends a very clear message to your child: *I want you to be different.*

Think about it like this. Possums want an invitation. They don't want to be yanked, pulled, or prodded.

Working with possum brain kids helped me embody something that was always true whether I liked it or not: I have absolutely no control over someone else's body. Not my client's, not my own child's.

The *La-La Land* Possum

Not safe!
- Starting to shut down
- May still be able to communicate with owl brain

As you read through these interventions for the *La-La Land* possum, as well as the *Trickster* possum, the *Shut-Down* possum, and the *Play Dead* possum, always keep in mind the Five Interventions and Three Things to Look Out For that we have already reviewed for the possum brain.

Just like the *What's Up?* watchdog, the *La-La Land* possum still has a bit of a relationship with the owl brain and you can use owl brain interventions, like logic and language, to help it. When you encounter a *La-La Land* possum, the first thing to do is to pause and take a breath. I can pretty much guarantee that your nervous system is moving faster than theirs and you'll need to deliberately slow down to match them.

For example, you're trying to talk to your child about their grades when it seems like they stop paying attention and stare off into the distance. You want to say "Hey! Pay attention!" but instead you take a breath and recognize this as a sign of distress. Maybe you say, "Oh gosh, I just started doing that mom-talk thing again didn't I?"

Then wait to see what happens next. If your child agrees that you're starting to do that "mom-talk thing again," this means they are back in connection with you. You might say, "Yeah, I noticed your eyes were glazing over and that let me know I needed to change things up a bit. I'm going to get us both a glass of water."

If the conversation about grades really does need to take place, try again with more regulation supports in place. Have the conversation while riding in the car or while mutually sharing a snack. If your child is old enough to participate in written communication, consider having the conversation over text instead, which also encourages you to use fewer words.

REAL-LIFE EXAMPLE

Twelve-year-old Jorge was generally an easygoing and compliant child, especially compared to his extroverted brother who had a strong watchdog pathway. However, his parents were beginning to feel increasingly frustrated that 15 minutes' worth of homework could take three hours. During homework time, Jorge seemed to just waste time by taking a lot of bathroom breaks, doodling, getting snacks, and wandering around the house. His parents said he wasn't exactly oppositional, but seemed to be checked-out and in "la-la land" during homework time. Jorge's parents were growing resentful over the amount of time that they had to spend coaxing and cajoling Jorge to do his homework, especially because "if he would just sit down and do it, it would take only a few minutes!" Their watchdog brains were making it hard for them to address the real problem, and they were unintentionally causing more stress for, and therefore more possum brain behaviors from, Jorge.

First, his parents and I reframed his behavior as *La-La Land* possum behaviors. Making sense of these behaviors helped Jorge's parents stay more connected to their owl brain. Almost immediately, this helped his parents respond differently, though they were still human and would still occasionally get frustrated.

Next, I helped Jorge's parents notice that he was actually doing a lot of things naturally to help his owl brain stay engaged. Doodling, eating snacks, and wandering around the house all have a sensory component. Even though Jorge was still very much living in his possum brain during homework time, it was clear to me that his body was trying to find ways to be safe and regulated. Now that Jorge's parents were more connected to their owl brains, they were able to lean into Jorge's behaviors, making small adjustments in the hopes that Jorge's sensory-seeking behaviors would help him stay more connected to his owl brain.

Jorge's parents explained to him that they noticed he liked to doodle when he was doing homework, and they covered the dining room table with butcher paper, giving him explicit permission to doodle as a sensory regulating strategy. They even bought crayons that were special "homework time" crayons. His parents "beat the need" for a crunchy snack by setting out a bowl of pretzels during homework time. Jorge seemed to prefer crunchy, salty snacks, plus we know that both crunch and salt can be sensory experiences that keep the owl brain connected. I also encouraged his parents to set a timer so Jorge could take a Go Noodle[3] break every 10 minutes. Go Noodle is a website and app with fun, kid-friendly videos and activities that encourage movement and mindfulness. Jorge was already familiar with Go Noodle from school, so this was a great option. His parents worried that 10 minutes was not a very long time to work on homework without a break, but I reminded them that as Jorge's owl brain got stronger, we could decrease the scaffolding and Jorge would probably be able to stay on task for longer than 10 minutes.

Over the course of the semester, homework time became less stressful at home. Some days it would still take way too long, and this would really frustrate Jorge's parents. They learned to take a break and leave the dining room when they started to have a watchdog brain reaction. Some days, they'd just back off from homework completely; it simply wasn't worth the negative impact it was having on their relationship with Jorge. This felt risky to Jorge's parents! They came from backgrounds where they learned that completing your work, whether schoolwork or a job, was more important than anything. But there aren't a lot of hours between afterschool and bedtime, and they were tired of sacrificing those hours to stressful homework. They even started redefining a successful afternoon not as Jorge getting his homework done but as an afternoon where they weren't arguing and frustrated. Decreasing this stress increased felt safety and therefore increased Jorge's frustration tolerance—which actually resulted in Jorge completing more homework, not less.

I worked with Jorge and his family until he was a junior in high school. Jorge got to know himself and knew he wasn't going to be successful taking several honors or Advanced Placement (AP)-level classes. He simply didn't have the nervous system that could regulate through that kind of stress—and that was okay! This self-knowledge allowed Jorge to be purposeful when choosing his classes. Sometimes Jorge's parents felt like he was lazy, but I reminded them we all have different temperaments and stress response systems. Adults make choices, sometimes not as mindfully, about the types of job they have. People with a high tolerance for stress choose high-stress jobs. Other people choose lower stress jobs. Both are valid choices, and the best part is knowing yourself well enough to make those kinds of choices.

Jorge stopped doing homework at the kitchen table but almost always had a crunchy snack while he worked on it in his room. At school, he advocated for himself to be allowed to chew gum. It was really remarkable to watch his owl brain talk to teachers about the things he needed to be successful. His parents came to see that self-advocacy as a life skill was even more important than learning to just push through difficult tasks.

The *Trickster* Possum

Not safe!
- Puts on a disguise and appears to feel safe and connected
- Overly compliant
- Robotic

It can be so tempting to ignore the signs of distress from *Trickster* possums. *Trickster* possums sometimes trick us into thinking they are in their owl brain. They can be so compliant, which is the opposite of all the watchdogs and all the other possum brain behavior. *Trickster* possums say "Yes!" and appear to agree to do what you say. The more we pay attention, though, the more we start to realize that the *Trickster* possum isn't present enough to form an opinion or make a decision about cooperating or not. The "yes" response is an automatic, protective response.

Another tricky behavior I can sometimes see from *Trickster* possums is that they can act like such easygoing, cooperative, and happy-go-lucky kids. Adults often find these children endearing and adorable, with their big smiles, wide eyes, and eagerness to please. The truth is that *Trickster* possums are wearing their adorableness like a mask in an attempt to keep us from seeing their real self, which they believe is bad and yucky.

Life is busy and hard, and you might even have more than one child who is prompting you to read this book. Of course you want to just pretend your overly compliant child is fine, especially if you have another one who is defiant and aggressive and peeing in their closet. Honestly, it takes a lot of bravery to notice and respond to *Trickster* possum behavior because it would be so much easier to just go along with it.

Trickster possums need a lot of permission to have an opinion. They also need a lot of narration about the things you notice about them, kind of like we do with babies. Just be sure that when you narrate things you notice about them, you don't focus only on the things you like. Sometimes this skill is called *sportscasting*. For example:

Adult: "What do you want for dinner tonight?"
Child: "I don't care, whatever. What do you want?"
Adult: "Sometimes it's hard to know what we like. Let's see, when we have hamburgers, you usually ask for two, but when we have grilled cheese, you usually don't finish it. I wonder if that means you like hamburgers more than grilled cheese?"

Or:

Adult: "What do you want for dinner tonight?"
Child: [Quickly scans the kitchen for clues about what answer the adult is hoping for and sees a box of spaghetti on the counter] "Spaghetti!"
Adult: "Ah, you see the box of spaghetti I haven't put away yet. I

wonder if you think that's what I was planning since it was still on the counter. There are a lot of things I could make tonight. Spaghetti is one, or we could have tacos, or hamburgers. Oh! I noticed your eyes perked up just a little when I said tacos were an option. Let's do tacos."

Or:

Person who cuts hair: "What are we doing with your hair today?"
Child: [Looks to adult for their opinion]
Adult: "Good question! Here's a book with different haircuts and colors. Let's look through them together."

As you're looking through the book together, pay close attention to your child. Notice pictures they look at a little longer or subtle changes in their eyes or mouth as they look at different pictures.

Adult: "You're looking a little bit longer at the picture of the kid with purple streaks in their hair. Do you want to try purple today?"

Some *Trickster* possums may easily reconnect to their owl brain and say "Yes, tacos sound great" or "Can I do purple? Is that okay?" Some *Trickster* possums may stay stuck in their possum brain. They'll continue to say things like "I don't know" or "Whatever." Or they keep shrugging their shoulders or you notice they're trying to choose something they think you would like. Remember, *Trickster* possum behavior is coming from a part of the brain that was being developed when your child was really young. Sometimes very young kids just need us to choose for them:

Adult: "Sometimes it's hard to know what we like. Let's see, when we have hamburgers, you usually ask for two, but when we have grilled cheese, you usually don't finish it. I wonder if that means you like hamburgers more than grilled cheese?"
Child: [Shrugs]
Adult: "You're not sure. Well, I'll tell you what. Since it kinda seems to be like you like hamburgers more, we'll have hamburgers tonight."

You might guess wrong. Sometimes guessing wrong will be a big deal and you can repair with your child later (we'll learn about repair in Chapter 9). Your child still has the experience that you were curious about what they wanted, noticed subtle behaviors, and made space for their preferences. These are important experiences for the *Trickster* possum.

A child who spends a lot of time acting like a *Trickster* possum needs help getting to know their own preferences and desires. Give this child a lot of space and encouragement to have preferences, likes, and dislikes. They want to have pink hair? Go for it! Support them when they change their mind. They wanted to play soccer but three weeks in they discover they don't really like soccer? Consider allowing them to quit. This child doesn't need to learn how to stick with something they don't really like. They need to learn how to trust the signals in their body that tell them they like or don't like something, and then be allowed to honor those signals.

REAL-LIFE EXAMPLE

Eight-year-old Sarah was born with low muscle tone and had been in occupational and physical therapy for most of her life. The therapies helped her body grow strong so she could run, skip, and play in the playground with her friends, but the sessions were intense and exhausting. When Sarah was a preschooler, she cried in protest to the therapies. Her parents were told the therapies were non-negotiable to her health, and Sarah was forced to participate. Looking back, her parents now realize that some of Sarah's therapists were coercive and manipulative. Sarah would get chocolates for compliant behavior and have favorite activities withheld when she was "non-compliant."

Sarah came to the office every week with what I called her "jazz hands." I felt like she was always giving me a performance. She would skip in with a huge smile, a high-pitched squeaky voice, and oftentimes wearing a dress-up princess dress. It was easy to see how Sarah managed stress in her life by being super-cute. This seemed to get adults to lower their expectations for her, which, in turn, lowered Sarah's stress. I also wondered if her "jazz hands" behavior kept adults focused on what Sarah looked like, instead of on the struggles her body had due to the low muscle tone. Throughout our work together, I paid attention to noticing parts of Sarah that weren't related to her appearance. I used my sportscaster skill of tracking and commenting on all of her behavior, staying as neutral as possible. "You're getting out the crayons." "You're squeezing the shaving cream." "You're jumping on the couch." I wanted Sarah to experience being seen just as she was, without the focus on pleasing or displeasing an adult. When Sarah knocked over a gallon jug of glue, I didn't try to mask my disappointment or frustration. It was a huge mess and I wanted Sarah to know that my office was a safe place for everyone's real feelings—we didn't have to wear a mask. I also reassured her that I've never been stuck in a feeling, and I could be frustrated at the mess and still love spending time with her.

One session, I challenged Sarah just a bit by playing a game of Uno with a therapeutic twist. There were a couple extra rules:

- Reverse card played = player says one thing they like to do.
- +2 card played = player says one thing they don't like to do.
- +4 card played = player remembers a time they felt mad at someone.

I was hoping we could play a fun game and use playfulness and connection as ways to widen Sarah's window of tolerance so she could feel confident talking about real and honest feelings.

Almost immediately, though, I noticed that Sarah had a big smile on her face. Her face muscles looked tight, like there was a lot of tension behind her smile muscles. Her eyes were looking down except for brief moments when she'd look up at me, nod her head, smile a flashy smile, and then look quickly away.

I thought maybe the rules of the game were confusing her and she was stressed about getting the rules right. To offer some felt safety and scaffolding I said, "Hey, I have an idea. Let's make a key so we can easily remember the rules."

I pulled out a piece of paper and drew the reverse symbol with a smiley face next to it, then a +2 with a sad face next to it, and then a +4 with a mad face next to it.

When Sarah played her first reverse card and had to say something she liked to do, she said "Come to therapy!" and gave me a big toothy smile. "I love spending time with you, too," I said, but

I was starting to feel pretty confident I was playing Uno with a *Trickster* possum who wanted to say things that would make me happy.

I played a +2 card and said that I really don't like to empty the dishwasher. It's my least favorite chore. Sarah grinned and nodded.

After a few more turns, Sarah played a +4 card. She looked at me and said, "Nothing makes me mad! I'm always happy!"

After I sent some silent gratitude for her *Trickster* possum working so hard to protect her, I said, "You know, let's just play regular Uno. Why do we have to answer these silly questions? Let's just play and have fun."

I wish I had said that sooner, maybe even before we started playing. I could sense her stress and thought maybe she was feeling overwhelmed by the rules, so I made her the key to make it easier for her to remember. I was hoping I could give her the scaffolding and structure she needed for her owl brain to feel safe. I wanted to have fun with her, but I also had an agenda: I wanted her to spend time reflecting on who she is. That's a good therapy goal for a child who often becomes a *Trickster* possum. Unfortunately, Sarah was too stressed to think about anything except how she should act that would keep her safe.

It was hard for me to decide that we would just play regular Uno without a therapeutic twist. It's common for both parents and insurance companies to ask a lot of questions about what's happening in therapy. "We play a lot of Uno" isn't usually very satisfying. My own *Trickster* possum wanted to please Sarah's parents and the insurance company. I was worried that if I didn't do something that "looked like therapy" that Sarah's parents wouldn't come any more or maybe the insurance company would deny the claim. Ultimately my owl brain helped me remember that I didn't need to please anyone. My job was to offer Sarah felt safety so she could eventually feel safe taking off her mask.

As the months progressed, Sarah's play became more aggressive. At times, she was mean to me. Behind Sarah's mask was a lot of intense, scary energy. Sarah had a lot to be angry about, including the way she struggled to belong in a world that didn't always accommodate her body's needs and the loss of her body autonomy in years of coercive therapy. For a while, it seemed like

Sarah's behavior outside of therapy was actually getting worse. At home and school, Sarah started to have watchdog behaviors: sassy, rude, and oppositional. Although this was uncomfortable for Sarah's parents, I helped them see this as progress. Sarah was experimenting with being her own person and showing behavior that honored herself and her true feelings, even when it wasn't pleasing to others.

The *Shut-Down* Possum and the *Play Dead* Possum

Not safe!
- Starting to fully collapse
- Protecting head, chest, and stomach
- Beginning to prepare for death

Not safe!
- Dissociation and disconnection from reality
- Believes death is likely

Remember in Chapter 7 when you were left feeling a little dissatisfied with my recommendations for the *Attack* watchdog? You're probably going to feel that way again about my recommendations for the *Shut-Down* and *Play Dead* possums.

Children who regularly collapse into shutting down or playing dead have very dysregulated nervous systems that are preparing for a serious life threat. This undoubtedly feels confusing to you as there is nothing happening in your child's life that is life-threatening.

If your child is shutting down or playing dead, review the Five Interventions and Three Things to Watch Out For, for all possums. This level of nervous system dysregulation needs a lot of patience. Have sensory strategies available or use them yourselves. Sometimes, if you are fidgeting with a stress ball or even just gently swaying back and forth, your child's mirror neurons pick up your regulating movements. Continue to offer opportunities for connection without being intrusive. Track your own nervous system response and focus on keeping your owl brain connected because it can be so easy to join your child's dysregulation without even realizing it. For example:

> Child: [Sleeps through alarm—again—and is making no effort to get out of bed and go to school]
>
> Adult: [Gentle knocking, slowly opens door] "Hey bud, looks like you slept through your alarm again. Here, I brought you some hot chocolate. Take as long as you need getting out of bed and ready for school." [Hands the child hot chocolate in a travel mug with a lid] "I'll be back in a couple minutes." [Leaves, takes a big breath with a long exhale, and uses their owl brain to remember their child is shut down. It was a risk to say "take as long as you need" and they notice some watchdog brain thoughts come up, like "You're just giving them permission to be lazy and do nothing." Another deep breath while they label those thoughts as watchdog thoughts, and remember that a watchdog never helped a possum feel safer. Pours a cup of coffee and in a few minutes walks back into their child's room]
>
> Child: [In bed, but sitting up and holding the hot chocolate]
>
> Adult: [Sits on bed and is quiet for a minute while both drink their hot beverage] "I get it, school is hard. Some days, I mean, even a lot of days, I don't want to go to work either. The judge says you're supposed to go to school. Do you wanna explore other ways you can go to school? Or do we think about other ways to talk to the judge?"

If your child regularly has a "shut-down" or "play dead" response to school, be sure to investigate ways to help school be a safer environment for your child. What academic, social, or behavioral supports do they need? Most teachers and administrators are amazing humans who love children, but unfortunately, I have also encountered more than a few who create stressful, hostile, and even unsafe school environments. A cup of hot cocoa is unlikely to solve your problems with school refusal, but if your child believes that you are on their team, it might help them at least sit up in bed and brainstorm with you what to do next.

It's easy to assume that going to traditional school is non-negotiable. That might be the case for your family, depending on your schedule and available resources. But maybe not. Many schools offer alternative school options, including home-bound schooling. There are many variations on homeschooling that could work for your family, even if you work full time or don't have any interest or aptitude at homeschooling. School is just one example. Look at the stressors that surround your child's *Shut-Down* and *Play Dead* possum behaviors. Is it possible to reevaluate if those stressors really are non-negotiable?

Be tenacious in seeking help for both your child and yourself. The availability of quality mental healthcare was poor for families in crisis before the COVID-19 pandemic; unfortunately, the rise in mental health needs and decrease in mental health therapists has made care even harder to access. I know finding mental healthcare that is actually helpful is much harder than it should be, and I'm sorry. Keep trying. Parenting a chronically possum brain kid can sometimes pull us down that same possum pathway. Stay alert to that possibility.

Don't overlook the need for your own support. Find a therapist or a group of parents who are caring for kids with big, baffling behaviors. The internet has made it easier to connect with parents with similar struggles all over the world. Prioritize getting the support you need.

REAL-LIFE EXAMPLE
I used to dread my sessions with 10-year-old Victoria.

I know that sounds terrible. What kind of therapist dreads seeing their clients? Luckily, I learned early in my career that it didn't do me any good to judge my authentic reactions. I needed to just notice them, have some compassion about how bad it feels to dread a client, and then get curious about why I was feeling dread.

I love kids. Generally speaking, the more dysregulated the better. I earned a reputation for working with the kids with the biggest, most baffling behaviors because I adored working with them.

Victoria's behaviors were the opposite of big, though, and at times, I was definitely baffled. Victoria did nothing. She would wander into my office like she was in a trance. She never greeted me and almost never made eye contact. She'd slump into the couch as if she was melting into it.

And then she'd just sit there. She'd stare past me and rarely say a word.

As I'm writing this, I just took a huge breath and shook my head hard and fast, almost like a dog shaking water off their back. Just thinking about Victoria brings possum energy into my body. One of my own possum brain behaviors is that I shake my head hard and fast, almost like I'm shaking off the cobwebs and fuzzy feeling in my brain.

Before every session with Victoria I would remind myself that connection is a biological imperative. It was so distressing to spend time with someone who made absolutely no "reach" toward connection. Victoria never initiated connection and never volleyed connection back to me. When I imagined connection as a literal ball that I would gently toss at Victoria, it usually felt like that ball would sail past her head. She wouldn't even notice it, let alone catch it and toss it back.

One of my favorite poems (included at the end of this chapter) reminds me that sometimes people just need us to wait with them without any expectation that they change. So I stopped throwing balls, or connection, or anything else at her.

I waited with Victoria. Sometimes I'd just sit there with her, working really hard to stay present with her instead of making my grocery list in my head. Sometimes I'd get antsy and start bouncing a balloon off the tip of my index finger. Every now and again the balloon would get away from me and float toward Victoria. Sometimes she'd toss it back, but more often than not it would just fall at her feet.

Sometimes the silence was more than I could bear, and I'd read a book. I wanted to stay present yet step back from any behavior that Victoria might feel like was a demand for connection. Once, I put out all the slime-making supplies before she arrived. Victoria was intrigued and we made slime that day, but never again. The next week she went back to just melting into the couch.

Victoria and I had these painfully silent sessions for over a year. Some days I would try to regulate myself by sitting in the yoga hammock that hung from my ceiling. It was low enough that I could sit in it like a swing with my feet on the ground, just swaying back and forth. One afternoon, Victoria zombie-walked into my office and, instead of melting into my couch, she silently climbed into the hammock. She wiggled until the hammock was spread out wide, and then she laid down. The hammock completely enveloped her.

Huh. Now what? Now I couldn't even see her eyes so I really had no idea how to attune to her.

I stood next to Victoria in the hammock, wrapped my hands around the edges, and slowly started moving the hammock back and forth.

After a few minutes, I changed the motion so I was moving the hammock front to back.

After another minute or so, I asked Victoria which she liked better—front to back or side to side?

No answer. So I said "Like this?" while rocking her front to back, or "Like this?" as I shifted to side to side.

"Like this," she said.

I waited a year for that. Waited, sometimes patiently, and sometimes not. Sometimes with certainty, and sometimes not.

But I waited.

Over the coming months, Victoria arrived each week and went immediately to the hammock. Sometimes she'd rock; sometimes she'd try other movements. After a few weeks of Victoria exploring the hammock on her own, I asked her if she'd like me to teach her how to hang upside down. She said "yes," and from that week forward, she asked me every session to teach her new poses. Eventually, I pulled out my binder of hammock poses and she would flip through, choosing which pose she wanted to learn next.

Victoria found herself in the fabric of the hammock. The hammock supported her body and sensory system, giving her the safety and structure she needed to explore her body and her preferences. Slowly, extremely slowly, Victoria and I created enough felt safety that she risked feeling her body, discovering her preferences, and even volleying back moments of connection.

Get a Drink or a Snack or Move Your Body

Are you feeling a little low on energy now that you've reached the end of this chapter?

I am. My brain feels a tiny bit fuzzy and I could practically take a nap. Possum energy is contagious, even when we're just thinking about the possum brain!

Before you go on to the next chapter, pause. Go get a drink or a snack. Stretch. Move your body. Connect with your body and invite your owl brain to return. Remind yourself that you're safe. I just opened the windows so I could smell the freshly cut grass, and I think I'll go get the mail. Maybe I'll take giant steps on the way down the driveway and skip on the way back.

After you get reconnected to your own owl brain, we'll go on to Chapter 9, where we explore what to do when your child's owl brain returns.

Lost Together
Nihar Sharma[4]

If I am lost, find me
but do not ask me to
come back just yet.
Sit with me in this
lost place and maybe
you will understand
why I come here too
often, what draws me
to my neverland. Find
me, but bring me back
when I am ready. Maybe
you will get to know
me a little better.
Maybe we can get lost
together.

CHAPTER 9

What to Do When the Owl Brain Returns

"But what about a consequence?"

It's been a long week for you. I mean, it's been a long many-years-of-parenting-a-child-with-a-vulnerable-nervous-system! Another week of offering connection, co-regulation, and cues of safety to Sammie and to Morgan, too, now that we have some awareness of the stress that his nervous system is under.

This is not parenting for the faint of heart. This is boots-on-the-ground, always "on," active parenting.

And you are doing amazing.

I know it doesn't feel like it, but you are. You keep showing up. You show up here in my office, you show up for Sammie and Morgan, and most importantly, you keep showing up for yourself. Sammie's behaviors are getting a little less intense. You are seeing them through a new lens and catching her dysregulation a bit lower. You carry an arsenal of crunchy snacks and drink boxes with you for your school-age kids, much like parents carry diaper bags for their infants and toddlers.

"I mean," you continue, "I totally get the need to give her co-regulation in the moment. I can practically see an invisible owl that erupts from her head and flies away scared. But eventually her owl brain does come back—kinda—and then what? We just do nothing? Go on like nothing happened? How is she learning anything?"

I love these questions!

Well, I love these questions now. These questions used to poke at my own watchdog a little bit. I remember how the "but what about a consequence?" question would bring up a moment of irritation in my chest. A voice in my head, with a little more indignation than I'm proud to admit, would ask, "Aren't you listening to anything I'm saying?"

Eventually I learned that this question about consequences almost always comes from a parent who has slipped into protection mode themselves. This question is driven by fear that if we don't give a consequence, our kids are never going to act right.

When we get stressed, we revert back to our old familiar neural pathways. Like the ones that believe humans only act "good" to avoid a punishment that makes them feel bad. It's so brave to consider that something else might be true.

"Great question. Can you give me an example so we can talk about a real-life situation?"

"It's the same thing over and over again. Sammie has a fit and inevitably something, or someone, gets hurt. Either she's really mean, or hits someone, or something gets ruined or destroyed. And yes! I totally agree with you! I can see she's dysregulated and needs help, but what about after?"

I remind myself that the week Sammie pushed a kid at the playground and then wasted all the shampoo, you weren't asking about a consequence. I know that when your owl brain is in charge and you're connected to me, things like consequences or punishments don't even seem to enter your mind.

I focus on that. I want to invite your owl brain back, not convince you I'm right that Sammie doesn't need a consequence. Which is usually just a code word for punishment.

"Okay, great, I gotcha. We've spent a lot of time thinking about how to help Sammie in the moment, but yeah! What do we do after? I know it's been a couple weeks, but can we look at the time Sammie punched that kid at the park?" You nod and I reach again for my binder.

"What are some of the things you see in Sammie that tell you her owl brain has returned?"

"Welllllll..." Your eyeballs shift up as you reach back into your memory to think about the characteristics of Sammie's owl brain. "I don't know, she just feels so different. Like the buzzing uncomfortable energy she carries so often from the watchdog brain is just gone. She feels a little easier, a little less tense..." You trail off as you think of what other words might describe Sammie's owl brain. "I don't know, she's just reasonable again."

"Sure, that makes sense, because the owl brain is the brain in connection mode. Being more reasonable, cooperative, and just less tense." Together our eyes scan the owl brain characteristics from my binder. "So the weekend she hit the girl at the park—when did her owl brain return?"

"Hmmm...well, I think at first I thought it was once we got home. She left the park without too much of a hassle, which was a good sign. But actually, once we got home she was still pretty dysregulated...just a little less dysregulated."

"Yeah, that's what I remember, too. She was just controlling and pissy the whole rest of the weekend. I think I remember we decided that something to try in the future is some sensory play? Like shaving cream in the bathtub?" You nod. It feels like you and I are in sync, so I decide to do a little bit of teaching instead of just focusing on attunement.

"Let's pretend you'd thought of that. Pretend you put Sammie in the bathtub with some shaving cream, and that helped her owl brain come back." I flip forward in the binder to the tab labeled "When owl returns."

"The first step after the owl brain returns is to make a repair. Sometimes when our kids go watchdog or possum brain, we do too! And we parent in ways we regret. And sometimes, it's even us that are in our watchdog or possum brain first. So a repair might sound something like 'Hey Sammie, my watchdog brain took over a little bit today and I couldn't use my owl brain to see that you really needed help cleaning up your bedroom. I think we both had our watchdog brains in charge! I'll keep working on helping my owl brain grow big and strong so it can stay more in charge even when you're in your watchdog brain.'

"Using watchdog and owl brain language is really important.

Repairs are vulnerable for both of you, so it might even be a good idea to offer the repair casually. Maybe when she's sitting at the kitchen counter waiting for a snack so you're not really making eye contact. That way, she could even pretend she's not really listening."

"Okay, yeah, that makes sense. I'm glad you added that last part because I was kinda thinking how Sammie would never let me have a sit-down conversation with her like that. She'd tell me to shut up or ignore me or just walk away."

"Yeah, like I said! Repairs are vulnerable! So sometimes the watchdog brain comes right back out. Think of ways to decrease the vulnerability—like I said, by not requiring eye contact, having the conversation casually, and definitely by keeping your expectations low. Sammie probably isn't going to smile and say 'Oh mother, thank you so much for offering this repair. I'm so grateful.'"

You roll your eyes with a smile and I take that as confirmation.

Looking back at my handy-dandy binder, I see that underneath the word "Repair" are the words "Make success inevitable." "The next step is for you to think about what Sammie needed—or needs in the future—that would make her success inevitable. Meaning— what does she need to be able to play at the park with other kids and not punch them? What does she need so that her owl brain can stay in charge or so that she can better borrow your owl brain? Do you think there's anything you could have done that would have helped her owl brain stay in charge during hide and seek?"

"Well, she needed to hide faster. Maybe I could have helped her hide?" You seem skeptical.

"Yeah, that's one option. When the seeker was counting down, you could have gotten up and helped Sammie find a good hiding spot. That extra co-regulation might have worked—or she would have yelled at you to leave her alone because she can do it by herself."

A little snort of a laugh. "Yeah, that's probably more likely."

"Whenever it seems hard to increase co-regulation, I think instead about finding ways to decrease the amount of time that goes on between moments of connection and co-regulation. How long had y'all been at the playground? I wonder if she needs more built-in breaks? Like you set a timer and every 10 minutes she comes to where you are on the bench to get a drink of water. The hydration, the connection with you, the break from having her heart beat hard while she's playing hard on the playground. All of that would be an owl brain co-regulation booster. That might help her owl brain stick around longer so she can think about a hiding spot more easily?

"Kids who don't have as much regulation as their peers almost always need less distance between themselves and a regulated, connected, present adult. If Sammie was a toddler, you'd hobble around behind her at the playground, never getting more than a few inches from her. That's not super-practical with your nine-year-old, and might even cause more stress in the relationship, not less. Another way to decrease the distance is to increase the frequency of connection and co-regulation, especially if the situation is stressful."

"Yeah, I can definitely help her take more frequent breaks."

"Awesome. While you're in the car on the way to the park, just let her know you'll set the timer and she can come get a quick drink every 10 minutes to help her body stay strong so she can play hard at the playground. And if you're there for a while, snacks, too. Just make it easier on you by bringing drinks and snacks she likes. This isn't a time to hope she'll like the new freeze-dried veggie chips you bought."

"Okay, but still. Where's the consequence? She punched a girl. Then she wasted all the shampoo." There's a hint of impatience in your voice as it's taking us too long to circle back to your original question. That might be leaving you feeling a bit unseen or worried that we're going to run out of time in our session today and you still won't have the answers you're looking for. And that might risk letting down all the hope you're holding that brings you to our sessions each week. Losing hope can feel really scary.

"Yeah, let's talk more about a consequence. What do you want a consequence to do? Like, what's the point of a consequence?"

"To keep her from doing it again in the future." Duh.

"Okay, so give me an example of a consequence." I want to make sure we both have the same definition of consequence.

"No TV time that night? No playing outside the next day?" You hold my gaze with expectation in your eyes.

"Well, sure, if you think TV contributes to her overactive watchdog brain or that her watchdog brain is still too active to play outside the next day, those would all make sense. Those would be ways we would help success become inevitable."

"But if she doesn't lose something she likes, how will she know not to do it again in the future?"

I'm so curious about the way our conversation is going, because I know you know the answer to that.

"Is Sammie confused about whether it's okay to punch people at the playground? Or really, I suppose, anywhere?" I take a little risk, hoping your owl brain is still close enough that my playful tone, slight smile, and curious questions will invite your owl brain back instead of making your watchdog brain more dysregulated. It's a risk I decide is worth taking, knowing our relationship is strong enough at this point that if I cause a rupture, we can repair it.

You do one of those little hard exhales with a slight smile—it's almost a little laugh. "Okay, no, you're right. Sammie is definitely not confused. She knows she shouldn't punch people. I don't have to teach her that."

"So it's not really about her knowing it or not, right? If it's not about that, what is it about?"

With a smirk and a little head shake, you say with a gently teasing tone: "Regulation. Connection. Felt safety. Yeah, yeah, yeah." Our eyes lock and there's a sense of camaraderie that passes between us. We're on the same team.

Playfulness for the win. We're back in the owl brain.

"Okay, one more quick thought before we wrap up for today," I say. "How much have you been teaching Sammie about her owl brain and watchdog brain?" The more Sammie knows about her watchdog brain, the less shame she'll feel about her behavior. If Sammie knows that the behaviors that are getting her in trouble come from an overactive watchdog brain and aren't just because she's a bad kid, she'll be able to soothe her watchdog brain faster and her owl brain will stay in charge longer.

"We talk about watchdog brains a little, but yeah, we could probably do that more."

"Print out the brain pictures—the ones with the watchdog and owl—and put them on your fridge. This week, your only goal is to see how much you can use watchdog, owl, and possum brain language with Sammie. Talk about your own watchdog brain, talk about the watchdog brains of people you see at the grocery store or the characters on TV. We want Sammie to start seeing behavior the same way you do, as just information about how active someone's owl, watchdog, or possum brain is. We also want her to know that she's not the only one with a watchdog brain. Everyone has a watchdog brain! And everyone sometimes struggles with an overactive watchdog brain. Even you."

"Well ain't that the truth." You grab your keys and our eyes connect one last time. I watch you take a breath and exhale. "Thanks."

It's such a relief to be seen. It's such a relief to be with someone who doesn't give up. Someone who sees your behavior for what it really is: your watchdog brain! It's such a relief to be with someone who has the patience to invite and wait for your owl brain to return. The more I do it with you, the more you'll be able to do it with Sammie.

But...What About a Consequence?

I asked my first mentor that same question. Back then, I had absolutely no idea how to work with kids with a history of trauma. I had no idea what was driving behavior or how to help the family I was working with, whose teenager was creating beautiful works of art. With spray paint. On other people's property.

The teen had already been in juvenile detention, and with his 18th birthday drawing near, we were all worried that grown-up jail was on the close horizon.

Also, I wasn't that far past my own 18th birthday. My only experience with teenagers was, you know, my friends.

My mentor, the one who introduced me to the word "dysregulated," gave me all sorts of great things to think about. I don't remember anything about what he said but I do remember looking at him and saying "Yeah, all that makes sense. Cool. But—what about a consequence?"

He laughed.

"I'm pretty sure this isn't about needing a consequence."

Consequences are so appealing because they make us feel like we are doing something. Consequences make it feel like we have control in a situation where we actually have very little. Consequences make perfect sense if we believe that behavior is mostly under our child's control, and that with the right consequence, they'll change their dangerous, scary, or sometimes just annoying behavior.

Re-read that previous paragraph, but this time, let's be honest about what we really mean. Almost always when we talk about consequences, what we really mean is punishment.

Punishments are so appealing because they make us feel like we are doing something. *Punishments* make it feel like we have control in a situation where we actually have very little. *Punishments* make perfect sense if we believe that behavior is mostly under our child's control, and with the right *punishment*, they'll change their dangerous, scary, or sometimes just annoying behavior.

What Is a Consequence?

The definition of "consequence" is simply the thing that happens next. If I switch on a light switch, the consequence is that the light turns on. If I drive my car way too many miles after the bright orange "E" illuminates, the consequence could be that I get stranded on the side of the road and have to walk to a gas station.

In parenting, we'd call this a natural consequence.

The thing is, anytime we move past a natural consequence and create a consequence ourselves, it's no longer a consequence. It's a punishment.

Punishments are intended to make kids feel bad, with the hope that by making them feel bad, they will want to act good. It's harder to see the sense of it when you frame it that way.

Of course, it does make sense that you want to do something to prevent some of the things our kids do, like writing their name on the car with a pointy rock, drilling holes in the screened porch, or flushing their squishy down the toilet again. What a mess!

It makes sense that when we are elbow deep in toilet water, our watchdog brain falls down those well-traveled neural pathways that believe behavior is a choice and that we can change our kid's behavior by making them feel bad. A punishment will motivate them not to flush squishies anymore, right?

Well, maybe. The biggest flaw with this argument is that learned information gets stored in the owl brain. This includes the knowledge that if I do something I'm not supposed to do, something unpleasant will happen to me. But it's rare that our kids' behavior challenges emerge from the owl brain, so it really doesn't help to store that information there.

Also. You're a good parent. This probably isn't the first parenting book you've read. You follow parenting social media accounts. You talk to your friends. If a consequence (punishment) was going to fix your child's behavior, wouldn't that have worked by now?

The squishy went down the toilet because your child wanted to flush the squishy down the toilet, and all the reasons why they shouldn't flush squishies are stored in their owl brain.

Owl brains have the impulse control that helps us not do something we want to do. The owl brain thinks about what will happen later ("The toilet will get clogged, mom will be drenched in toilet water, and I'll get in trouble"). The owl brain doesn't want mom drenched in toilet water because that's gross, and the owl brain cares about that.

If we want our kids to have a nervous system that pauses before flushing squishies down the toilet, then we have to grow their owl brain. That way, they'll stay more regulated, connected, and safe, with behaviors that match.

"But what about a consequence?" is a question that comes from one of two places. Sometimes it's a question that people ask when they don't quite believe that regulated, connected kids who feel safe behave well. They might *think* they believe it, but they also believe in some exceptions. Like "This makes perfect sense, except sometimes my child does something deliberately wrong. That's not about regulation, connection, or felt safety. That's about willfulness. So of course that's one time they need a consequence (punishment)."

Other times, "But what about a consequence?" is a question I hear from a parent's own watchdog or possum brain.

Watchdog brains revert back to things we learned a long time ago. Most of us learned in our childhoods that punishment is the only way to get people to act appropriately. This idea that regulated, connected kids who feel safe do well is a pretty new idea. It's really hard to remember new stuff when we are in our watchdog or possum brain. Frankly, the watchdog or possum just doesn't have the luxury of thinking hard to remember new stuff. It's more concerned with staying safe.

If punishing kids for flushing squishies down the toilet isn't going to solve the problem, what should we do instead?

I know that it's quite possible you're reading this and wishing that your biggest problem was squishies down the toilet. Even if the behaviors in your house are more intense and more dangerous, all of these concepts still apply, once the owl brain returns.

First: Repair

Wait, what? Your kid does something wrong and I tell you that when they (and you) are back in their (and your) owl brain, the first thing you need to do is repair?

Yes. If your child has done something wrong, there has likely been a rupture in your relationship.

When your child hit their sister, maybe you stayed in your owl brain (awesome!), but we know your child's owl brain wasn't in charge. We know their nervous system flipped into protection mode. We know being in protection mode means not feeling safe. Not feeling safe feels bad.

When people feel bad, we offer our regrets. It's a way of reconnecting and coming back into attunement with them.

When my husband works hard all day to make beautiful, tasty home-made pizza (homemade dough, homemade sauce, the whole shebang!) and then the dog eats the entire thing, I express my regret for how bad he feels.

I might even say "Ugh, I'm so, so sorry. You worked hard all day and were moments away from the reward. It is so disappointing."

Expressing regret isn't agreeing that it's my fault. It's letting my husband know I see and understand his pain. I can't fix it. I certainly can't make a new pizza (and I promise, you don't want me to try). But I can connect with him in his disappointment and express regret.

A nervous system that is in protection mode feels bad.

A repair with a child who just hit their sister might sound something like: "Wow, your watchdog brain really took over and then you hit your sister. It feels crummy to have our watchdog brain take over. I'm sorry that happened."

Sometimes, when my kid ends up in their watchdog or possum brain, I do too! Sometimes, I'm even the one who is in my watchdog or possum brain first.

My watchdog brain can make me short-tempered, snappy, and irritable. I have zero patience and am easily overwhelmed. If I say something rude or unkind to my son during one of these watchdog moments, it's my responsibility to initiate a repair later.

"I'm really sorry my watchdog brain took over and I said that. It's never okay for me to talk to you that way. I'm working hard to keep my owl brain more in charge even when I'm irritable so that I don't say things I don't really mean and hurt your feelings."

It's my job to take responsibility for what I did. It's important to be clear that what I did wasn't okay and even more important not to make any excuses. An attuned repair also involves being ferociously committed to doing whatever work I need to do to keep from flipping my lid in the future. Since I'm human, I'll probably be snappy to my child again in the future, but I work really hard on growing my owl brain so it doesn't happen very often.

Initiating a repair with our children does a few important things. Repairs help our kids feel seen. Repairs communicate to our kids that our relationship is important enough to regulate through vulnerable feelings because repairs are vulnerable! Repairs teach our kids that relationships aren't perfect and they can be repaired.

All of those things grow the owl brain, which is exactly what both you and your child need so that negative behavior happens less frequently in the future.

"I'm sorry I said your squishies are a stupid waste of money. I know you love squishies and that probably felt bad. My watchdog brain was totally in charge. I'll keep exercising my owl brain so that even when I'm very frustrated, my watchdog brain doesn't take over and say mean things."

When Repair Feels Too Hard

Initiating a repair can feel too vulnerable, and maybe right now it feels like you could never apologize to your child.

Remember this is "no shame, no blame" parenting. If you're struggling to make a vulnerable and connected repair it just means your owl brain needs some help regulating through uncomfortable feelings.

Maybe you need to give yourself some scaffolding. Can you send a text to your child so the vulnerability isn't so intense?

Maybe you need some more co-regulation. Can your partner come with you while you go into your child's room to make the repair? Can you text your best friend, ask for words of encouragement, and then repeat those words in your head while you go into your child's room to make the repair?

If you're struggling, remind yourself that you need exactly what your child needs when they are struggling: more regulation, connection, and felt safety.

What about when your child rejects the apology? Or twists your apology into "See? You are the worst mom ever!"

A repair is an offering. Once we make an offer, we have no control over how the offer is received.

When you offer a repair and your child doesn't receive it and says something hurtful in response, it's very painful.

You have every right to grieve that.

Second: Make Success Inevitable

After everyone's (well, at least your) owl brain is back in charge, ask yourself: "What does my child need in order for their success to be inevitable?" "What does my child need so that they never flush squishies down the toilet ever again?"

Maybe all your child needed was to see the damage that happened. They didn't know it would overflow the toilet!

Maybe your child absolutely knew what would happen and flushed the squishy anyway. Maybe they just couldn't regulate through the desire to see the squishy swirl down the toilet bowl. Maybe they flushed the squishy because they were mad at you.

Maybe what your child needs in order to never flush a squishy down the toilet again is no more squishies.

Wait, this is confusing! I just said kids don't learn from consequences or punishments.

Removing the squishy isn't a punishment unless you deliver it as one. Removing the squishy is removing the temptation. Removing the squishy is toddler-proofing for your nine-year-old. Removing the squishy is a respectful way of recognizing that their owl brain is not strong enough for them to resist the delight of watching a squishy swirl down the drain, even if it ends with a flooded bathroom.

If they flushed the squishy because they were mad, then what you've learned is their mad feelings were much more powerful than their feelings of connection to you in the moment. Head back to Chapters 5 and 6 to help you grow your child's feelings of felt safety and connection. Until their owl brain can tolerate mad feelings and express them in ways that don't ruin your plumbing, no more squishies.

Now, what if your child just picks something else to flush?

If the situation became extreme and your child was flushing anything and everything down the toilet, you might have to consider even more steps toward what I would call environmental co-regulation, otherwise known as "toddler-proofing."

I wouldn't recommend these actions unless absolutely nothing else was working, but you could adjust your toilet so it doesn't flush. After your child leaves the bathroom, you can go in and flush the toilet. You could do a quick check with your child every time they go into the bathroom to make sure they have nothing harmful to flush down the toilet, and remove everything from the bathroom that could get flushed. You could even provide just the right amount of toilet paper each time your child goes to the bathroom if absolutely needed.

This level of setting your child up for success is pretty extreme. If you are at this point, make sure you are really emphasizing the ideas from Chapters 5 and 6. Also, consider whether your child needs additional assessments and supports in place, including neuropsychological assessments and cognitive assessments.

You may have a child whose "danger-danger" circuitry is so tangled with their connection circuitry that these types of behaviors are related to a commitment to staying out of connection. This is an exhausting and demoralizing situation. Be sure to seek the support you need, whether that be from a therapist, peer community, or a virtual community like The Club.[1] When our kids have this level of entanglement between their connection and protection circuitry, we are more likely to live in our watchdog brains and respond to our children the way they are expecting (with our own dysregulation) instead of the way they are hoping (with regulation and boundaries).

My point here is that instead of doling out a punishment, you can instead consider what your child needs in order for their success to be inevitable. Like taking away all the squishies.

Yes, I know it's the same action, but it's delivered with a different energy and with a different intention. One communicates to your child "I know you are an amazing kid who simply doesn't have in place what you need for that amazingness to shine through. You need help and support, and it's my job to give it to you." The other communicates to your child "I believe the only way you will stop doing something you're not supposed to do is if I create pain in your life, because at your core, you're a bad kid who does bad things."

Changing how we see people changes people.

Develop New Supports and Boundaries

Together, if possible. I understand that until your child has a stronger owl brain, they might not be able to participate in this discussion. They'll feel too much shame and/or their owl brain won't yet be strong enough to look back at what happened without their watchdog or possum brain becoming active again.

Even if your child can't participate in this process with you, be sure your own owl brain is back before you spend a lot of time thinking about this. Otherwise, you'll just come up with punishments. This is normal. You aren't doing anything wrong! Just wait a little longer for your owl brain to come back.

You can apply this kind of problem-solving to any situations that are challenging. Your child may need:

- Scaffolding through the transition of getting off the school bus by having you meet them right at the bus door, to help prevent dysregulation
- Body-based regulation strategies like a cold drink or an invitation to race as you walk from the bus stop to the house, to help them connect to their physical self
- Decreasing the distance between them and a regulated adult, by having them sit closer to the teacher during class
- Structure and boundaries, by getting your clear instructions to stand on the white parking lot line when they get out of the car at the supermarket
- Increased co-regulation, by having you attend a religious class with them
- Remove the stressor, by skipping the religious class and taking them to the park instead

- Body-based regulation strategies, by singing the rhythmic songs your child would be singing at the religious class they are missing.

Really, truly ask yourself: What do I need to change about this situation so my child's success is inevitable? You might not be able to do whatever you come up with. But even if you can't, asking the question and thinking about the answer helps keep the solution focused on the real problem: your child's need for more regulation, connection, and felt safety, which will help them acquire the skills they are missing.

Don't Expect Gratitude

If your child didn't help you come up with the new boundaries and supports, eventually you'll have to communicate to your child what those boundaries and supports are going to be.

You will be so proud of yourself! You are a rockstar parent who isn't punishing but instead gave a lot of thoughtful deliberation to what your child needs to be successful. You are getting really good at using those X-ray vision goggles and seeing your child's behavior as just a clue about what's happening in their inner world.

Your child will not be as impressed.

In fact, they may have a watchdog or possum brain response. This is to be expected, and although exhausting, it's not too big of a deal because you now know how to connect with and calm those parts of your child's brain.

Actually, it is a big deal and I know that. You are tired. Parenting this way is exhausting, isolating, and disheartening. And it requires a huge leap of faith. Is this even going to work? You have to trust in something you can't see: the brain's drive for connection, regulation, and felt safety. Trusting is bold and risky, and sometimes will feel very, very wrong.

It's hard work and it would be great if your child could see how hard you are working to really be on their team. Everyone needs to be seen, including you. Unfortunately, it's not your child's responsibility to be the person who sees you. Seek connections with people who see you. It's my hope that this book will help you feel really seen.

And know this: I see you.

Third: Practice—Playfully!

Play increases resilience, grows our stress response system, and improves learning. It supports connection, feelings of belonging, and problem-solving skills.

I used to be a play therapist, which allowed me to see on a daily basis how play allows children to revisit stressful experiences with new feelings of control and increased regulation. Play decreases shame and increases feelings of competency. Play helps kids develop beliefs like "I'm a really great kid who sometimes does things that I'm not supposed to do."

Play grows the owl brain!

Playfulness is a great way to increase your child's regulation, connection, and felt safety in general, but we can also lean into the power of playfulness in these moments after the watchdog or possum brain is calm and the owl has returned.

When my son was younger, we would play out "the wrong way" and then "the right way" to handle the situation next time.

Playfully do it "wrong" first.

> Me: "Time to start brushing teeth and get ready for bed!"
> Him: "NO!" [And then proceeds to run off down the hall]
> Me: [Sternly] "Get back here right now young man! You will not run off. Get your teeth brushed now and then get your booty in bed."
> Him: [Hides under blankets and doesn't say anything]

Have some fun with this! Be silly. Don't worry that it's teaching your kid not to take these situations seriously. The playfulness is creating enough safety in your child's nervous system and in your relationship to be able to honestly revisit the problem.

Warning! Pause and make sure your expectations of "doing it right" are appropriate. It's okay for children to feel and express their true feelings of disappointment or irritation that they have to do something they don't want to. My point is that when you playfully practice doing something the "right" way, it shouldn't look like this:

> Me: "Time to start brushing teeth and get ready for bed!"
> Him: "Yes mother!!! I will get to that right away! I love you!"

That is never going to happen, and if we ask for it to happen, we are teaching our kids that negative feelings should be avoided at all cost. That does not grow the owl brain.

Doing it the "right" way might look more like this:

Me: "Time to start brushing teeth and get ready for bed!"

Him: "I don't want to go to bed!"

Me: "I know. Ending a fun day and getting ready for bed is a total bummer." [Attunement and validation] "It's 8pm and that's the time we start brushing teeth every day." [Rely on the structure]

Him: [Whines] "I'm playing with cars right now!"

Me: "Playing cars is so fun! You can leave your cars right where they are so you can play again first thing in the morning." [Helps the owl brain see that the fun time will happen again, soon] "I wonder how many HUGE steps it'll take to get to the bathroom from here? Let's count!" [Provides clear structure and boundaries, leans into playfulness, and stays in the owl brain]

See how both me and my child playfully practiced a new way? The responsibility to do something different was never just his. Connection and relationship is always a two-way street.

As he got older, we did fewer playful role-plays. The one role that kept playing was an eye-roll.

Instead, we'd revisit the situation and talk about how to do it differently next time while we were doing something else playful, like arm wrestling. Or I may ask him what he would tell his friend to do differently in the same situation. When my son was a teen, he had a close friend who would happily tell him when he was acting like a doofus. So I might ask him "What would Johnny tell you to do differently?"

Can't Force Play

These conversations and playful practices have to happen while you are both in a playful state of the nervous system. You absolutely cannot force playfulness. Playfulness emerges from a nervous system in connection mode. For obvious reasons, that won't happen if your child is feeling coerced or shamed, or just doesn't want to engage.

Not wanting to playfully practice is fair, and honoring our kid's boundaries is important. If they'll engage in playful practice, it's a huge win because play is so powerful. If they won't, simply move on.

Fourth: Teach Your Child About Their Brain

You're about three-quarters of the way through this book. Does your child know about their owl, watchdog, and possum brain yet?

If not, why not?!

Does it help you to understand that your child's behavior is related to their nervous system? Does it help to picture that wise owl, the growling watchdog, or the dazed and confused looking possum?

It will help your kids, too.

There are so many reasons to teach our kids about their brain! Knowing about the brain:

- Increases mindfulness and self-compassion, both of which grow the owl brain and increase felt safety and regulation
- Teaches kids that they aren't at the mercy of some mysterious system that controls their behaviors. They can learn what the system is, take away the mystery, and increase their own control. This is good
- Promotes self-advocacy skills so your child can eventually get their needs met in situations away from home.

If your kids are younger, you can read picture books to them about the brain. You can download a free PDF of the owl, watchdog, and possum brains (see https://robyngobbel.com/download). Print them and hang them on your fridge. This helps everyone in the family remember that one of your family values is to see behavior as a clue and to get curious about how to calm the watchdog and possum brain.

Use owl, watchdog, and possum language in everyday life! Talk about your watchdog and possum brains. When you talk about other people's behaviors, use owl, watchdog, and possum language. Talk about the characters in books or movies or on TV, and use owl, watchdog, and possum language.

One of my favorite picture books is *Marvin Gets MAD!* by Joseph Theobald. I used to read the book to kids and pause throughout to say something like: "Whoa, Marvin's watchdog brain is getting so active right now! His watchdog brain is telling everyone to back off by growing horns and ferocious teeth!" (You'll have to read it to see Marvin's horns and teeth. They're adorable.) This book also helps create a story for what other people experience when Marvin's watchdog takes over. Marvin's friend Molly gets scared and has some people-pleasing behaviors to try to get Marvin to calm down—her *Trickster* possum takes over! Marvin isn't really able to notice how his watchdog brain behavior is making someone else feel, but if you read about it when the owl brain is in charge, maybe your child will.

When your family is watching *The Avengers* for the 765th time (maybe that's just me—I do love Marvel movies) you can talk about Thor's watchdog brain. Movies like this also help us not make the watchdog brain the bad guy. When aliens are attacking, a watchdog brain response is perfect!

If you haven't already, start talking about the owl, watchdog, and possum brains today. Your family might give you the side-eye and ask what you're talking about, but actually it's been my experience that the language makes so much sense that kids and even spouses just start adopting it without question.

Won't They Use It as an Excuse?
Can't you just hear your child saying "Not my fault, my watchdog brain was in charge!"

Yup. Me too.

Here's what you have to remember. Making excuses and not taking responsibility for something is not a characteristic of the owl brain.

Owl brains are self-reflective and compassionate. The owl brain can tolerate the uncomfortable feeling of taking responsibility for something that didn't go quite right, broke the rules, or hurt someone.

If Your Child Starts Making Excuses, It's Just a Part of the Journey
If you're taking a road trip to Disney World and have to stop at a rest stop for a bathroom break, you know the rest stop isn't the end of the journey. If you were afraid the rest stop was the end, you'd try really hard to skip it and, well, we can all imagine how that would go. Especially if Disney World is more than five hours away from your home.

You are willing to pull into the rest stop because you know it's not the end and you know it's a necessary stop on the journey. You just pull over at the rest stop like it's no big deal.

If your child starts using watchdog and possum brain language as an excuse for their behavior, remind yourself this is just like stopping at a rest stop. It's a necessary part of the journey, and you won't get stuck here.

You're going to keep helping your child's owl brain grow by parenting with regulation, connection, and felt safety. When the owl brain grows big enough, your child will have the regulation to reflect on their behavior. Owl brains want to have connected, cooperative relationships. Promise. For example:

> Child: "I hit my sister because my watchdog brain was in charge. I can't help it! It's not my fault."
>
> Adult: "I know your watchdog brain was in charge, that's for sure! You and I will keep working together to calm your watchdog and grow your owl brain so that your owl brain can have mad feelings without hurting anyone. Whew, it's a lot of hard work but we can do it!"

Growing Your Owl Brain

Maybe by now you're not just seeing your kid's behaviors differently, but you're also seeing your own behaviors differently. I hope so. I know you read parenting books, visit parenting websites, and listen to parenting podcasts. You try hard to respond to your kid's behaviors differently, but goodness, it's hard. Those books and podcasts have really given a lot of information to your owl brain, but it's hard to stay in your owl brain when your kid is flushing squishies or threatening the teacher or hurting themselves on purpose.

Maybe you can understand why knowing isn't even half the battle. It's really not enough to just *know* about the watchdog and possum brains, or even to have a big toolbox full of tools. Just like your kids, you can know a lot of things and still really struggle to do them.

If you want your owl brain to be in charge when you're parenting your child with big, baffling behaviors, we have to tend to and nourish your owl brain. Section 3 will show you just how to do that.

WHY KNOWING ISN'T EVEN HALF THE BATTLE

CHAPTER 10

Why You Can Know How to Respond and Still Not Do It

The temperature outside begins to cool, the fall sunlight streams through the windows, and I put pumpkin spice creamer in the office fridge.

"Sometimes," you say, "it feels like I'm the one with the problem, not Sammie." You do that thing where you take a sip of coffee just as your last word is spoken. It breaks our eye contact and I wonder if it's how you regulate your way through the vulnerability.

"Wow," I say gently and softly. I take a breath and lean back in my chair. As I place my arms on the arm rests, I notice my chest opening toward you, as if expanding to hold your vulnerability. "That's a huge feeling." I pause, intentionally changing my pace to meet you in this slower possum energy.

You take another sip of coffee and I do the same.

"I yelled yesterday. Bad. Said things I should never say. UGH! Why do I do this? I know why she's acting this way! I know that yelling at her is exactly the wrong way to respond. But I still do it! Sometimes I wonder if I'm just not the right mom for Sammie."

I watch a little bit of watchdog energy take hold just before you fall back into a sense of hopelessness. I feel the impulse to say "You're a great mom!" and then hear my owl brain whisper "Why do you want to take away her pain? It's righteous pain. Lean in."

I take another slow inhale and exhale while we lock eyes. I nod slightly—a silent gesture that says "I'm here with you."

After a few moments of silence you say softly, "Like I said, maybe it's me with the problem."

"Raising kids with vulnerable nervous systems is a funny thing," I begin slowly. "Sometimes it's shocking to uncover our own vulnerabilities. Almost every parent I work with at some point will tell me that they don't even recognize themselves."

You nod. The slightest hint of wetness begins to glaze your eyes. Another sip of coffee.

"Here we are. Months into our work together. You know so much more about the brain and behaviors. Your owl brain works so hard during our time together." Our eye contact persists. "But then your owl brain flies away." A nod. "Yeah, and when your owl brain flies away, your watchdog brain comes out. And you yell." Another nod. "So...I think what I'm hearing is that even though you've been coming here for months, you're still human."

I see a little smile and you exhale. Your eyes soften ever so slightly as you wiggle your back and shoulders, looking for a more comfortable position on the couch. You're shaking off that possum energy.

"Okay, yeah, you're right," you agree. "Probably anyone would freak out eventually if they lived in my house."

"Uh, definitely. You know, we've spent a lot of time talking about strengthening Sammie's owl brain. But what about yours?" It's a bit of a rhetorical question because I know the answer. But I'm wondering if you do.

In the months that we've worked together, I've spent a lot of time giving you tools for managing Sammie's behavior by increasing regulation, connection, and felt safety. All along the way, that's exactly what you've been receiving from me: co-regulation, connection, and felt safety.

You've also learned all about the nervous system and why people with sensitized stress response systems flip their lids so easily. We've been talking about Sammie, but actually, we've been talking about you, too. Just less directly. There's always a moment in my work with a family when they realize that all the science of behavior, and the accompanying compassion, applies to them, too.

I go on. "Nervous system energy is contagious, right? If two people can co-regulate, it makes sense that we can co-dysregulate, too. Sammie came to your family with an overactive watchdog brain, and then your watchdog brain grew, too. That's just what happens. I think I remember that on the first day we met, you agreed with me that the energy in your body was just as unpredictable as Sammie's."

"Hmm. True." Your eyes look up and to the side in that way they do when I know you're pondering something. You look back at me, but say nothing.

With a tone of curiosity and not interrogation, I ask, "What happened just now? What came up for you?"

"I was just thinking... I don't think I feel that bad anymore. I felt really bad back when we started. And you're right. You drew that jagged line and yeah, that was exactly me, and exactly Sammie. I think now we're both a little...less jagged?"

"Oh for sure. Sammie definitely is and you must be too, or you wouldn't even be asking these questions."

I thought you'd feel reassured but instead you seem more agitated. "So why do I still freak out at her? I know better!"

I grab my white board and draw two parallel lines really close together. "When you first came here, your window for stress tolerance was teeeeeeny tiny. Like this."

I point at the space in between the two lines and look up. You nod. "Over the months, it's widened a bit. Like this." I draw another set of parallel lines a bit further apart.

"Your nervous system started like this"—jagged lines.

"And now is morphing into something more like this." Still a lot of highs and lows but the second half of the line is smoother.

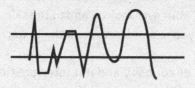

"Both have places where they extend far outside that window of stress tolerance." You nod. "That's all that's happening. We've widened your window and smoothed out the jagged line for sure, but sometimes it still gets a huge surge and pops you right into your watchdog brain."

"So what do we do about that?" You lean closer to me with that laser-focused intensity you sometimes get in your eyes. The watchdog brain always wants an immediate solution.

"We do exactly what we are doing. You keep coming. I keep showing up with my owl brain. You get the connection and co-regulation you need so you can give it to Sammie. You get good coffee, too." I raise my cup to say, "Cheers."

"Wait," you say, as a knowing smile creeps over your face. "I always have coffee when I come here. You're always suggesting that I give Sammie a drink or a snack as a way to help her watchdog brain feel safe." I grin and shrug.

"Do you like that new pumpkin spice creamer?" I ask.

Your Owl Brain

The session I just had with Nat happens with every family I work with. It doesn't always look exactly like this, but parents and caregivers eventually have an "aha" moment, when they realize that everything I've been teaching about their child applies to them, too.

Maybe that happened to you a couple chapters ago. Maybe it's happening right now!

Not only does everything you've learned about the brain and nervous system apply to you, too, but so does all the compassion.

Maybe you've asked yourself the exact same question that Nat asked me. If you know all this stuff about the owl, watchdog, and possum brains, why aren't you doing it perfectly?

Because knowing isn't even half the battle. Just like Sammie, whose owl brain knows she shouldn't punch kids while playing hide and seek, or squeeze all the shampoo down the drain, you can know a whole lot of things and still not do them.

Why? Well, the short answer is exactly what I told Nat. You're human.

I do a lot of things I know I shouldn't do. Sometimes they're small things, like I drive a lot longer than I should on "E" or I don't wash the oatmeal bowl right away. Sometimes they're bigger things, like not putting down my phone when my teenager initiates a conversation, even though I know I should be so grateful for every bit of connection he still makes. Sometimes, they're even bigger things, like when I say something on purpose that I know will hurt my husband's feelings.

If doing the right thing was only based on knowing what the right thing was to do, well, we'd be living in some bizarre made-up fantasy world. It's hard to even imagine what that would look like.

To add a final layer of understanding about why we can know the right thing to do and still not do it, I want to tell you about implicit memory and mental models. But let's start with what's familiar to you: the stress response system.

Your Stress Response System

Just like Sammie, the foundation for your stress response system started to develop even before you were born. As you grew, the co-regulation you experienced, along with your own unique genetics and temperament, nourished (or didn't) your stress response system.

Pause here for just a moment and get curious. How was your stress response system cultivated? Do you imagine that you had a lot of experience feeling safe, seen, soothed, and secure...or not? Or maybe you had some experiences with a caregiver who was mean, weak, or gone.

Now allow your attention to go to your own autonomic nervous system. When you reflect on your stress response system, do you get a sense of openness, maybe even some confidence or contentedness? Or is there constriction? Perhaps some anxiety or sadness comes into your awareness.

Simply paying attention to the sensations in your body is a nourishing act of attunement toward yourself. If uncomfortable sensations and feelings come up, experiment with just noticing those sensations without any judgment. Maybe even send a message of compassion to those uncomfortable sensations.

Believe it or not, those earliest moments of your life impact how you parent. When we parent a child with a hardy nervous system who doesn't seem to be thrown off by that much, our stress response system isn't challenged quite like when we parent a child with a vulnerable nervous system. If you feel like you were a pretty darn good parent until a certain one of your children came along, understanding your own stress response system might help you understand why.

Stressed by Parenting

Parenting is stressful. This is true for all parents, but for special needs parents it's a kind of stress that really can't be described in words. If you're parenting a child whose nervous system is stuck in "danger-danger" mode, then your neuroception is taking in a lot of cues of danger. Your child is in protection mode, and that invites your nervous system into protection mode with them.

And that's just the beginning! The behaviors that emerge from your child's "stuck" nervous system cause a lot of challenges in your life. Maybe you're frequently on the phone with the school—or with the juvenile detention center. Maybe you have to call the police for help, often. Maybe the glass bowl you inherited when your grandma died was smashed into a million pieces, or you had to scrape together thousands of dollars for new duct work because your child was peeing in your vents.

Whatever your particular stress is at any given moment, it adds up. You almost certainly aren't getting the connection and co-regulation that you need in order to keep your stress response system resilient.

Only about 55 percent of the general population gets the kinds of experiences they need as a child to cultivate a resilient stress response system. That means a whole lot of us don't. Add to that the chaos of parenting a child with a vulnerable nervous system, and yeah—it's so easy for your owl brain to fly away.

Luckily, research on chronic stress shows that there are things you can do to care for your body and strengthen your stress response system, even while we wait for the stress in your life to change. In Chapter 11, I'll give you my top four suggestions on how to do just that.

Implicit Memory: Remembered, Not Recalled

The last time I rode a bike, I hopped on and easily rode down the road despite the fact that I've probably only ridden a bike 10 times in my entire adult life. I didn't have to think about how to ride the bike; my body just remembered how to do it.

Implicit memory is all the pieces of memory that we don't consciously notice or think about. Imagine how clunky life would be if we had to think hard about how to do everyday tasks like holding a pencil, getting up from a chair, and driving. Implicit memory is memory, but it doesn't *feel* like remembering. It's this sense that psychologist Paul Sunderland describes as "remembered but not recalled."[1]

Implicit memory supports our survival by helping our bodies and brains work efficiently. If we had to actively remember how to pick up a pencil or get up from a chair every time we did those things, we wouldn't have the resources to attend to anything else. Implicit memory allows us to pick up a pencil while thinking about the address we're about to jot down, to get up from a chair while thinking about where our car keys are, and to navigate to a new location while driving safely enough not to crash our car.

Mental Models

Implicit memory further supports our survival by helping us anticipate what's about to happen next. It does this by relying on a special kind of implicit memory called a mental model. A mental model is a generalization about how the world works based on our unique and oftentimes repeated experiences. Because mental models are implicit memory, these generalizations don't feel like memory, they just feel true.

Let's look at an example. My mental model of dogs is based on previous positive experiences with dogs. Although we didn't have a dog, I had plenty of positive exposure to dogs when I was a kid, both in real life, at my friend's house, and in books, TV shows, and movies. Over time, those experiences combined in my memory to create a mental model that "dogs are safe and fun."

But what if I'd had a previous experience with a dog that was danger-ous? Even just one dangerous experience could completely change my mental model, because the brain is especially cued into things that are dangerous. Including danger in the mental model is protective because it helps me avoid danger in the future. If my mental model was "dogs are dangerous and unpredictable," I would feel and act differently around dogs. That model would even impact how I feel just anticipating being around a dog.

This mental model would also impact my perception of a dog's behav-ior. I'd be much more likely to interpret running, jumping, and barking as aggression rather than playfulness. My mental model that "dogs are dangerous and unpredictable" would flip my brain into protection mode, and I'd respond with fear or maybe even aggression toward a playful dog. Over time, my inaccurate interpretation about this dog's behavior might actually lead the dog to become aggressive. Dogs, like people, often become who we think they are.

Mental models can be built from actual experience but also from observing caregiver reactions. Maybe my mom told me outright: "Dogs are dangerous and unpredictable, don't go near them." But it might have been more subtle than that. Maybe when we went to a friend's house with a dog, I noticed a tightening in her shoulders or a look of anxiety or fear on her face. Maybe she flinched when the dog barked or got too close to me. My mom didn't have to say "Dogs are dangerous and unpredictable" for me to learn it. These behavioral cues could have led to my mental model, though even as an adult, I wouldn't necessarily know *why* I believe dogs are dangerous.

Attachment and Mental Models

Remember in Chapter 3 when you learned about attachment behaviors and the attachment cycle? When babies regularly feel safe, seen, soothed, and secure, they develop mental models like:

- People are good and will take care of me.
- I am good and worth being taken care of.
- I can use my voice and get my needs met.
- I am not bad when I am in distress.
- The world is a safe and predictable place.
- The people who take care of me are safe and don't hurt me.

- Someone cares if I'm in distress and they try to help me feel better.
- I can tolerate my caregiver being out of attunement with me because I know we always fall back into sync.

Some babies don't feel safe, seen, soothed, and secure enough. They might develop mental models like:

- People are unpredictable; sometimes they take care of me and sometimes they don't.
- I cannot use my voice to get my needs met; I'll have to do it a different way.
- I am bad when I am in distress.
- The world is not safe or predictable; I have to be in charge of my own safety. Being controlling helps the world be more predictable.
- People are mean and hurt me, even when I'm already in pain.
- Nobody cares when I'm in distress. I'll be left all alone.
- Being out of attunement with my caregiver feels like agony; I don't know when or if it'll ever get fixed.
- Causing someone else distress is bad and dangerous. To be safe, I must always please other people.

None of us experienced perfect parenting. Even that 55 percent of the population who experienced what attachment researchers label "secure attachment" had plenty of experiences of not feeling safe, seen, soothed, and secure. This is true about our children, of course, but this is true about you and me, too.

How Our Past Impacts Our Now

Sometimes we learn things explicitly, like when our parents *tell* us "dogs are dangerous and unpredictable." When we learn things explicitly like that, it's easy to make sense of why we have the beliefs that we do.

Sometimes, though, we learn things implicitly—like when we pick up subtle cues in our parent's behavior that *show* us that "dogs are dangerous and unpredictable." They may never tell us that. They may even say "dogs are safe and fun!" But we still learn "dogs are dangerous and unpredictable" because of their behavior around dogs.

I grew up in a culture that values "being nice" and "looking good" over being honest and authentic. It's not that anyone ever told me that, but I learned it by watching other people's behaviors. One of the mental models I developed is: "It is dangerous to behave in a way that might cause someone else distress, so I should always try to be perfect and please other people."

Once I ate dinner at a friend's house and forced myself to eat mushrooms because I didn't know that it was okay for me to say "I don't like mushrooms." I knew implicitly, because of a mental model, that it was more important for me to try to take care of my friend's mom's feelings than it was to take care of my own. I learned when I was very, very young that some parts of me hurt other people, and that it was my job to make sure that didn't happen. I didn't want the part of me that doesn't like mushrooms to hurt anyone's feelings, so I ate something I thought was disgusting.

In the grand scheme of life, choking down mushrooms at one dinner isn't that big of a deal.

Or is it? I ate those mushrooms because I believed someone else's feelings were more important than mine. I believed that something about me hurt other people and I was responsible for making sure that didn't happen. I believed it was more important for me to ignore feelings of disgust than it was to set a boundary and say "No thank you."

These beliefs have negatively impacted my life in profound ways, but for the sake of this book, let's stay focused on parenting.

When Being Honest Is Dangerous

When my son was about eight, I chucked a granola bar at his head. Hard. At point-blank range.

I had been packing his lunch when he had sheepishly turned to me and said, "Mom, I decided I don't like those granola bars anymore."

I was furious. My stress response system was vulnerable that morning because I hadn't slept well.

I WANT my son to have that mental model, the one that says, "It is safe to have and express a preference, even if it upsets someone else." But that's in direct contradiction to one of my mental models, so I need my owl brain with me to remember that.

Just a few days earlier, he'd insisted he LOVED those granola bars! So I'd bought a warehouse store-sized box of them. My son knew that changing his mind about the granola bars would frustrate me because now we'd have a year's worth of granola bars no one would eat. But he also knew it was safe for him to express his preference.

Except it wasn't. Not in that moment. With my own brain off-line, my old mental model ("It's dangerous to have and express a preference that upsets someone") got activated.

That's a funny thing about mental models. Mirror neurons help us feel how the other person is feeling, and in that moment, it was intolerable for me to feel my son's cautious comfort with expressing his feelings honestly. Without an owl brain connection, I couldn't access the truth: that it is safe to have and express a preference, even if that preference upsets someone. Ultimately, my watchdog brain believed there was so much danger that I literally attacked.

You know what else my owl brain took when it flew away? The knowledge that it's not okay to throw things at my son. It's not okay to be scary. When my owl brain is in charge, I don't throw things at my son or act scary.

Sometimes my owl brain flies away and I find myself parenting in ways that are out of alignment with my parenting values. In those moments, I can't remember all the things I've learned about how to parent from a place of regulation, connection, and felt safety.

Think back to Chapters 7 and 8. Did you ever notice that sometimes you have a *Back Off!* or even *Attack* watchdog response to your child's behavior that really only warrants a *What's Up?* watchdog response?

Common Parent Mental Models

Here's a list of common parent mental models I've encountered in myself, my husband, and in the parents I work with. Read the list slowly and pay attention to any sensations that may arise:

- I must always be in control.
- It's important we "look good" as a family.
- Achievement and success are the most important things.
- I am bad/a bad parent.
- Having connection rejected is life-threatening.
- Connection is dangerous.
- Being disrespected is dangerous.

- It's important to disregard my feelings in order to make other people happy.
- When bad things happen, it feels like they will never get better.
- Making mistakes is dangerous.
- Good kids have good parents. Bad kids have bad parents.
- Bad behavior makes someone a bad person.

Take a breath. Inhale. Long exhale.

What did you notice? If you noticed tension, constriction, or even shame or embarrassment, it might be because you have that mental model, too. It's common to be unaware of our mental models and it's normal to be surprised when you discover some of them.

Now, reread the list of mental models that are sometimes developed when babies don't feel safe, seen, soothed, and secure enough. Maybe you have some of those beliefs stored deep in your implicit memory:

- People are unpredictable; sometimes they take care of me and sometimes they don't.
- I cannot use my voice to get my needs met; I'll have to do it a different way.
- I am bad when I am in distress.
- The world is not safe or predictable; I have to be in charge of my own safety. Being controlling helps the world be more predictable.
- People are mean and hurt me, even when I'm already in pain.
- Nobody cares when I'm in distress. I'll be left all alone.
- Being out of attunement with my caregiver feels like agony; I don't know when or if it'll ever get fixed.
- It's dangerous to behave in a way that causes someone else distress; I must try to be perfect and always please other people.

These mental models might not seem directly related to parenting, but can you imagine ways they could show up, especially when parenting a child with a vulnerable nervous system who regularly responds with an overactive watchdog brain or a super-scared possum brain?

Big Reaction, Small(er) Problem

Let's look at just a few examples.

Disrespect Is Dangerous

When your child is rude or sassy, it makes sense to have a *What's Up?* watchdog brain response. It's important to help your child learn how to express themselves in a way that respects both themselves and the other person. This skill will help your child have satisfying relationships in the future. Our *What's Up?* watchdog helps us pay attention to our children's rude behavior so that we can help them problem-solve how to express themselves without being rude.

If you have a mental model that "being disrespected is dangerous," then you'll be less able to see that your child's rude behavior may just mean that their *What's Up?* watchdog needs help. Instead, the rude behavior feels personal. When someone's behavior feels personal, the watchdog or possum brain becomes overly active.

Having Connection Rejected Is Life-Threatening

When your child says "I hate you," or "You're the worst mom ever, I wish I had a different family," it makes sense to have a *What's Up?* watchdog brain reaction. Your *What's Up?* watchdog brain wants to work together with your owl brain so you can address this problem with co-regulation, connection, felt safety, and a boundary.

If you have a mental model that "having connection rejected is life-threatening," then you're more likely to have a *Back Off!* or even an *Attack* watchdog brain response when your child says "I hate you." If you have a mental model that "I am bad" or "I am a bad parent," then you're going to have a *Back Off!* or *Attack* watchdog brain response or even a *Shut-Down* possum brain response.

All behavior makes sense. Implicit mental models help us predict the future so we can survive. When you become aware of those mental models, your owl brain can help you decide if those mental models are still true.

We Create What We Expect

Remember just a few pages ago when I said that if I interpret a dog's playful behavior as aggressive, that it's possible that over time that dog might actually become aggressive? This same phenomenon happens in humans. If I see my child's behavior as personally rejecting me, I am going to flip into protection mode and have a big watchdog or possum brain reaction. This teaches my child that I am unsafe and unavailable for connection, which, in turn, leaves them more stuck in protection mode. This will ultimately lead to more behaviors that reject connection, not less.

If I see my child's rejecting behavior as information about the state of their nervous system, and information about their past experiences in relationship, I don't take it personally. The behavior might be unacceptable, but if I don't take it personally, I can usually respond with my *What's Up?* watchdog brain instead of my *Back Off!* or *Attack* watchdog brain. My *What's Up?* watchdog brain works together with my owl brain to respond in a way that solves the real problem by offering co-regulation, connection, and felt safety.

Now What?

It is possible to become aware of your mental models, notice when they are triggered, and ask yourself, "Is it really true?"

"Is it really true?" is a question the *What's Up?* watchdog asks, so the first step in exploring your mental models is widening your window of stress tolerance. That helps your owl brain stick around and work together with your *What's Up?* watchdog to notice your own thoughts, feelings, and body sensations.

It isn't true that you are a bad parent or a bad person. It isn't true that your behaviors define how good, or bad, you are. It isn't true that disrespect is dangerous. It isn't true that it's dangerous when your child rejects your connection.

It is true that those behaviors need to be addressed. But they aren't dangerous. Your child's challenging behaviors come from a nervous system in protection mode. If your watchdog or possum brain believes those behaviors are dangerous, you are going to respond in a way that creates more fear. This doesn't make your child's behavior your fault, but it does mean you miss the opportunity to see the behavior for what it really is—a clue about what's happening in their nervous system.

I know that your child might have behaviors that are truly dangerous. Screaming "I hate you!" while pushing you into a wall is dangerous. When something is dangerous, give your watchdog or possum brain permission to take over and do its job. But screaming "I hate you!" isn't dangerous by itself.

Of course, even if it's not dangerous, it's exhausting. The chronic strain and chaos of overactive watchdog and possum brain behaviors can leave you unbelievably stressed. Your watchdog or possum brain is probably in charge most, if not all, of the time, just like your child's. This is a perfectly normal and adaptive response to a perfectly awful situation.

Let's move on to Chapter 11 and dive into ways to help to grow and strengthen your owl brain, so that you can get some relief.

How to Become More Tolerant of Your Child's Behavior

The first snow falls. November and December are busy months for you, and our weekly appointments stretch to every other week. Over many months of working together, you've internalized my co-regulation, so you need less frequent touchpoints with me. It'll always be hard to be Sammie's mom, but hard things are easier when we do them together. At this point, there's a part of me that will always be with you; we will always be together.

The holiday season is chaotic and unpredictable for both you and Sammie. School parties, class decorations, and lots of sweet treats have Sammie's watchdog brain working overtime. Her window of stress tolerance has decreased, and so has yours.

"Can't we just skip the holidays?" you ask.

I chuckle. "You are probably the fourth person to ask me that—just today! It is so fascinating to me how we all just trudge on with all these holiday expectations. They're supposed to be fun!"

"Are they?" You raise your eyebrows.

"Well, it's finally peppermint mocha season! That's something, right?" I raise my coffee cup toward you, inviting you to clink your mug with mine.

"I'm exhausted and not really being a very good mom. Good grief. What kind of mom is grumpy in December?"

I think you're actually serious. "Um, every mom I've ever known?" Your eyebrows pop up in a look of surprise. "Seriously. Every mom I've ever known! But especially moms of kids with vulnerable nervous systems like Sammie. The sugar, the noise, the special events, the parties, and oh yeah…we end all that with two weeks off school."

Your eyes get wide as you consider that Sammie and Morgan will soon have two weeks at home.

"I'm not cut out for this. What if they got the wrong mom? What if they would be better in someone else's family?"

"Parenting kids with vulnerable nervous systems and sensitive stress response systems is really hard." You nod, quickly and almost reflexively. "No, really," I press. "Do you believe me when I say that? It's really hard."

"Sure, I guess. Yeah, it's really hard."

"And what about when I say you do a really great job at it?" You snort and roll your eyes. "You don't believe me?"

"Well," you say, "I believe that you think I'm a really good mom. But you don't see me at my worst."

"True. Do you think if I did, that would change how I feel?" You look at me squarely for a few moments, really considering this question.

"I guess not."

"If I saw you in your deepest struggles, I'd only feel compassion. I'd feel a deep, deep desire to end your suffering and sadness, even though I know that I can't."

"I doubt you'd feel compassion while you watch me scream my head off." You lock your eyes on mine in an invitation—or maybe a dare—to really, truly see you. I hold your gaze.

"If I saw you at what you believe is your worst parenting moment, behaving in a way you'd never want anyone to see, I'd know I was seeing you in a moment of intense suffering." Our eyes are still locked and it's starting to feel slightly unnatural, but I don't want to be the one who looks away. "I wonder, can you believe that about yourself? That your worst behaviors emerge from your moments of most intense suffering?"

You look away and say nothing.

After a few moments pass, I softly and with curiosity ask, "What happened? Where'd you go?"

"It's weird," you say, still gazing off. "But yeah. I actually do think

I believe you." I take a breath, nod ever so slightly, and say nothing for a few moments.

Then, "What's that like for you?" I ask. "That you believe me?"

"Good? Confusing? I don't know. These past couple years, all I knew was that something was terribly wrong and it was probably all my fault. I had no idea I could feel as bad as I felt. I had no idea I could act as bad as I was acting. I came here because I needed to help Sammie and you were my last resort. But in a way...you've helped me more than you've helped Sammie."

"You know," you go on, my silence an invitation, "I hear your voice in my head." You look at me, almost embarrassed. I take a sip of my peppermint mocha-tinged coffee and notice the trickle of tears behind my eyes. "In my head, I hear you tell me I'm a great mom. You say 'Of course you're freaking out right now!' or 'Sammie's owl brain has flown away!'" I nod. You sip.

"I don't want to spend this December with a family of watch-dogs!" The energy rises and some urgency comes into your voice.

I reach for my binder. "Well! You're in luck! I have an anti-watch-dog family treatment plan right here!" In the back pocket of the binder, I remove a handout that reads "Self-compassion" at the top.

"Here's a list of self-compassion mantras that a group of parents I was working with came up with." I hand it to you and take a few minutes to silently drink my coffee while you read the handout:

The loneliness is real, and it makes sense.

Your messy, whole self is welcome here.

I hear what you are saying, I can see how hard that has to be. It must be very hard. I hope you are taking time to care for yourself.

Keep going, and I hear you.

Hard things are hard. I wish I could take it away for you.

I get it. I hear you. You are weary for a reason. It's okay to be weary. Let's be weary together.

You love so big. It's okay to rest.

That makes sense. I can hold space for you and you are not alone.

You may feel alone, but you are not alone.

This is so hard. There's so much pain. It makes complete sense that you are feeling this way. Thank you for letting me join you in this space.

Even when it feels like you're not enough, you are.

I hear you, and I see you.

You are not alone.

You are doing the best you can with what you have.

This is hard and it gets to be hard. You get to acknowledge how hard it is. I care and understand.

I am, you are, doing the best we can.

I am taking a breath with you.

I am with you. Thank you for sharing your heart with me.

You finally look up at me. I can't quite figure out what the look in your eyes means. It's shock, I think, but really tired shock.

"Hmmmm," I say gently. "What's happening for you?"

"Where did you get this? Who said these things?" You start to say something else, then stop.

"A group of parents who know what it's like to parent Sammie. I wrote down all the things they said to each other, and all the things they said they needed to hear when they felt rage or hopelessness or were so ashamed of how they were acting. Then I asked them: 'Can you say these things to yourself?'"

You look back down at the page. Then back at me.

"Can you?" You don't answer. "If you can't say them to yourself, can you imagine me saying them to you?"

Again, you look back at the page. Then back at me. You look lost. But also found.

"Try. Between now and when I see you again, read these. A lot. Several times a day. Pretend I'm saying them to you, and if you can, say them to yourself." I look at the piece of paper you're holding and I nod. "That? That's going to get you through the holidays. That's going to widen your window of stress tolerance again. Every time you say one of those phrases to yourself, and you really mean it, that's like doing a brain bicep curl for your stress resilience. Promise."

You nod, fold the paper up into quarters, and stick it into your purse.

I smile. "See you next year."

Bicep Curls for the Brain

It is possible to feel better, even if the chaos in your home never changes. Nat's actually one of the lucky ones. Seeing Sammie's behaviors through a new lens and responding with felt safety, connection, and co-regulation has really helped Sammie become a bit more regulated. I don't know if that will happen in your family. I know that even if you don't see your child's behavior change, your child's brain is changing. I can't guarantee when or even if you'll see behavior change.

Even if your child's behavior never changes, you can feel better. There are ways to widen your window of stress tolerance and increase the resilience of your stress response system even if the chaos never calms. It's really hard work and it's not fair that in addition to how hard you have to work to help your child, you also have to work hard to help yourself.

You know that I don't have a magic bullet answer that will help you feel better. If I did, I certainly wouldn't have waited until Chapter 11 to tell you about it! You know I don't have it because if it existed, you would have found it by now.

Small moments of regulation, connection, and felt safety added up and slowly created change for Sammie, and small moments can create change for you, too. Dr Perry's studies of how the nervous system heals from trauma indicate that it's the moments that matter.[1] His research is usually about children, but I've found the same idea applies to us grown-ups. Nat and her relationship with Sammie hasn't changed during that one hour a week with me. It's changed during the weeks, days, hours, minutes, and even seconds of Nat parenting Sammie with a stronger owl brain connection.

I'm going to offer you four different bicep curls for your brain that will help you create a sort of exercise routine for your stress response system. There might be one or two (or even three or four) that feel impossible. That's okay. Start with whatever one feels the least impossible. Over time, small moments will add up to big changes.

- Connection
- Playfulness
- Noticing the good
- Self-compassion.

Connection

When was the last time you spent time with someone who really, truly understood what it's like to parent a child with a vulnerable nervous system? Maybe you're one of the lucky ones and you have a parenting partner who's right there in the trenches with you. Unfortunately, I know many parents are on this journey alone, even if they have a parenting partner. Sometimes our partners have their own challenges with regulation, connection, and felt safety, and they struggle to make this paradigm shift in how they see your child's behaviors. Sometimes our partners agree with the shift but can't really do it. If any of these describe your situation, I have deep compassion for both of you. Yet all the compassion in the world doesn't change that you are still alone.

Research by social scientists Lane Beckes and James Coan suggests that humans don't just need connection.[2] Connection is our baseline; it's our expectation. Since it's our expectation, the absence of connection can initiate a stress response. A chronic lack of connection can lead to the accumulation of toxic stress.

Connection is so powerful that it makes hard things feel less hard. If you're doing something hard with someone else, like climbing a mountain, getting sober from alcohol, or parenting a child with a vulnerable nervous system, your stress response system won't have to work as hard as if you were doing this all alone—even if that someone is a stranger!

Ironically, when we are struggling to raise kids with vulnerable nervous systems, it's easy to let our own needs for connection fall to the bottom of the list. Maybe it's not that you stopped prioritizing connection. Maybe it's that your friends and even your family stopped calling. Very few people know how to support someone who lives in a state of ongoing crisis.

This entire book has been about seeing your child for who they truly are, moment by moment, and offering them connection. Why? Because connection is that powerful. We need it to survive. Where do you receive connection? No, really. Answer the question. Where do you receive connection?

I was working on a presentation for healthcare and child welfare workers on compassion fatigue when I came across research that describes two key experiences that lead to this kind of burn-out. The first is having patients or clients express intense emotions at you while your job is to "be professional." Basically, while a patient is screaming at you, you're expected to suppress all your natural emotions. That's hard, but actually, it's not the hardest part. The hardest part is having no one to turn to when the situation is over. In many stressful work environments, the unspoken rule is to just get over it and move on. Expressing any amount of distress gives the impression you can't handle the job. I experienced this both in my work as a Child Protection Services (CPS) investigator and as a pediatric Emergency Room (ER) social worker in a trauma hospital. I saw horrifying things happen to kids and families and had nowhere to turn to process these horrors. Instead, I locked the office door so I could cry alone without getting caught, after I'd walked with a family down the long empty hallway to meet the folks who would bring their precious boy to the funeral home.

This is exactly what parents of kids with vulnerable nervous systems have to do. Hide their authentic emotions, often out of shame, and try to manage it all with nowhere to turn. The loneliness and isolation can become traumatic.

Moments of Connection Matter

I know it's easier said than done, but you have to find someone who can receive authentic feelings about the hardest parts of your life. Maybe you do have someone, but in the chaos of everyday life, you've let those connections fall by the wayside. Pull out your phone, send a text or two, and start rebuilding those relationships.

Go. Do it now. I'll wait.

You might feel like there is no one. Find a therapist who understands the challenges of parenting a child with a vulnerable nervous system. There are a lot of therapists who see kids with vulnerable nervous systems who would happily see an adult client or two. These child therapists might just really get your family and your struggles.

Google the name of your town and "parent support group." If you're an adoptive family, Google "adoption family support." Reach out to the agency that helped you during your adoption. In this post-pandemic era of Zoom, virtual support groups are easier to find and easier to access. Even well-moderated internet forums can provide a significant amount of support.

Your child needs to feel safe, seen, soothed, and secure, and so do you. If you want to parent your child that way, it's important to find people who can tend to you in the same way, people who don't judge you and who really get you. Connection changes the brain. For your child and for you.

The science of safety is what prompted me to create my virtual community for parents of kids with big, baffling behaviors: The Club.[3] It's based on the same foundational ideas that all of my work is based on: parents working to strengthen connection and co-regulation with their children need to receive connection and co-regulation themselves. I looked at all the ways I've offered those things to parents in my office through the years and figured out how to offer it on a larger scale—to hundreds of parents, all around the world.

I know it's hard to reach out. It feels like one more thing on the unending to-do list. If you've been parenting a child with a vulnerable nervous system for a long time and without a lot of help, then you are undoubtedly exhausted. I get that. Reach out anyway. It's that important.

It might be simpler than you think. You don't have to schedule an adults-only vacation, go to a week-long seminar, or take a girls (or guys!) weekend away. Don't get me wrong—do those things if you can and you want to. But moments of connection can help even if you get them without leaving the house. Sending a text message with a funny meme or even the words "I love you" or "I miss you" will water the seeds of connection. And you'll reap the harvest later, maybe even in the middle of a particularly hard day, when you need it most. My girlfriend and I listen to a podcast "together." When the show airs every week, we text our reactions, favorite quotes, and even just emoji reactions. It's simple and takes about four seconds. We also tell each other "I love you." Remember. Moments matter. Every moment of feeling seen and known and accepted for exactly who you are is a little bicep curl for the brain. They add up.

Playfulness

I have to laugh when I think back to my beginnings as a play therapist. I was a play therapist with a serious aversion to playfulness! I'm not intuitively playful. I can't come up with playful, creative ideas. For the longest time, play felt clunky and awkward.

I also married the most playful man on the planet. Once, a woman walked by while watching my husband and son sword-fighting with 20-pound tubes of ground beef in the grocery store. She laughed, and said, "I want to be in your family!"

But my family definitely isn't fun all the time, and the constant playfulness can even get on my nerves. On the day we met, my husband said to me, "We have a lot to learn from each other before we die," and without question, playfulness has been one of the greatest things I've learned from him. It won't surprise you to know that I was only willing to risk the vulnerability of playfulness after I understood the science of play.

Dr Stuart Brown, a play researcher, says that playfulness:

- Fosters empathy
- Generates optimism
- Makes perseverance fun
- Strengthens immune health.[4]

Most of the parents who came to my office and now to The Club say that, for them, playfulness is long gone. They can't remember the last time they felt playful. In fact, the idea of play and playfulness often leaves parents feeling a mixture of exhaustion, resentment, and even disgust.

What I want you to know is that playfulness isn't something to do—it's a way to be. Just like playfulness strengthens your child's owl brain, playfulness can strengthen yours. I also want you to know that despite the protests I often hear from exhausted parents, I still included it in this book because I think it is that powerful and that important.

Moments of Play Matter

I promise you don't have to do anything new. In fact, I highly recommend you don't. You can infuse playfulness into the mundane tasks you already do every day, like brushing your teeth or washing the dishes. I've gotten to the point where I basically only watch shows if they are funny (or feature Iron Man). I have watched the entire series of *Schitt's Creek* more than once, a lot of it while cleaning the kitchen after dinner. If you don't have 25 minutes to commit to a show, take a page from the teen play-book, and watch funny videos on social media. Go to Google right now and search "toddler laughing." It's impossible not to laugh right along with them. Decorate your home with playful items that spark delight. I have two (uncomfortable) chairs with flamingo upholstery because they make me smile. Look to be delighted by things happening around you. Once on my way out I saw one of our neighbors mowing the hill in their yard with the lawnmower on a rope. I thought this was hysterical. Turns out, it's not even that unusual but I allowed the moment to really delight me.

All of this coming from a recovering play-phobic. I spent too much of my life feeling too highbrow for silly antics. Truthfully, though, I was avoiding the vulnerability of play. I grieve for those lost moments. My family and I are only recently on the other side of a several-year-long serious crisis. Playfulness is one of the main reasons we survived.

Look around. Where could you easily infuse playful energy into your everyday life?

Notice the Good

Neuropsychologist Rick Hanson's book *Hardwiring Happiness*[5] outlines a simple four-step process for shifting out of what he calls "red brain" (watchdog and possum brains) into "green brain" (owl brain). I'm not going to go into his whole process here, but if this section resonates with you, I highly encourage you to check out his book.

His powerful research can be summarized with the suggestion to simply *notice the good*. That's it. Notice things that are good, or at least things that are not bad.

When we spend a lot of time in watchdog or possum brain, we start only noticing things that are bad. You may notice this characteristic in your child who seems to be always complaining and is never happy or satisfied. The watchdog brain and possum brain don't want to risk over-looking something bad, so they focus on everything they think might be bad. It's possible that after all these years of parenting a child with a vulnerable nervous system that your brain has also become hyperfocused on the bad.

I wonder if there are things in your life that are good, or at least not bad, that you've started to overlook? I know that's certainly true in my life! When I first read Dr Hanson's book, I thought the science seemed spot on but I was reluctant to try out his tips. It just felt too vulnerable. Noticing the good felt like it would leave me wide open, unprotected, and the eventual crash of catastrophe would only hurt that much more. Sometimes I was pissed that my life was so bad and this dude was sug-gesting that all I needed to do was think about things that weren't bad. As you can imagine, I was pretty stuck in protection mode, sometimes in my watchdog brain and sometimes in my possum brain.

Dr Hanson's research is not about toxic positivity and pretending things are good when they aren't; it's actually quite the opposite. Dr Hanson is a real proponent for honest self-attunement, which means recognizing things that are just plain crummy. However, he also offers an open invitation to experiment with noticing things that aren't crummy, even when lots of things are.

I'm a sucker for science, and at that point in my life I was feeling pretty darn bad. So I was willing to consider his ideas. I gave myself permission to take gentle baby steps to notice the good. I kept it easy and began with something that I did—and loved—every day: drinking coffee.

Sometimes I go to sleep at night thinking about my morning cup of coffee. Last I counted, there were seven different ways to make coffee in my little kitchen. I bring coffee with me when I travel and I know the coffee pot situation of every hotel and Airbnb I go to before I arrive.

Every morning, I notice how much I love my coffee. (By this point in the book, I'm sure you've noticed it too!) When I have my morning cup of coffee, I notice that it's still dark outside and I'm the only one awake.

I notice the taste of the beans I special order from Mt Comfort in Alabama, and I notice the texture of the fat from the heavy whipping cream I add. I notice how hot it is, and if it isn't hot enough, I put it in the microwave. I like hot drinks really hot.

This is a five, maybe ten, second ordeal. That's it. But it has added up and spilled over to other parts of my life, too.

I've gotten so good at noticing the good that I've kinda become that obnoxious person who walks around in wonderment, pointing out every spring bud on every tree, and every beautiful snowflake frozen on my windshield. I consider myself to be someone who is easily delighted. I cannot believe I just wrote that sentence. Ten years ago I was not someone who was easily delighted. I'm not even sure if I truly understood what "delight" even meant.

Moments of Noticing the Good Matter

Little by little, slowly, one bicep curl for the brain after another, I've grown my owl brain. I went to a doctor once who told me I needed less stress in my life. I laughed at her much the way you would if I told you that you'd feel better if your life was less stressful. That seems obvious! Also, how could I possibly do that?

I didn't. In fact in some ways, my life has only gotten more stressful. My family suffered a serious crisis at the same time as the COVID-19 pandemic swept the globe. I remember once in the middle of this terrible season someone asked me how I was doing. My honest authentic answer was "Actually, pretty good." Despite the darkness we were enduring, my life was also pretty good. I couldn't believe I'd reached a place in my life where both could be true and I *could notice* that both were true. It's possible.

When I'm struggling to notice the good, I marvel at how all I have to do to get a clean glass of water is turn on a faucet in my kitchen. If I turn it one way, it's hot. Really hot! Hot enough to take a luxuriously long shower. This is a miracle. I know this sounds hokey. You maybe just rolled your eyes at me. Sometimes it feels like a terrible injustice that life is so hard that the best thing you can notice is that you have clean, hot water at your beck and call. But they don't have to cancel each other out. There's grief and suffering that exists right next to the good that is clean and hot water. Suffering deserves to be met with compassion.

Self-Compassion

Self-compassion is without question the most powerful tool you could put in your parenting toolbox. It's the most powerful tool you could put in your *humaning* toolbox. If I could give every single parent I worked with just one thing, it would be self-compassion. From the moment Nat walked through my door, I met her with compassion. Similar to playfulness, compassion isn't something to do. Compassion is a way of being. Compassion emerges naturally from the owl brain, but we can also use it as a doorway into the owl brain.

Dr Kristin Neff is a pioneer in the study and teachings of self-compassion. Her book, *Self-Compassion*, defines compassion as "the recognition and clear seeing of suffering. Compassion involves feelings of kindness toward others so that the desire to help, to ameliorate the suffering, emerges."[6]

The definition of self-compassion, then, is simple. *The recognition and clear seeing of suffering in ourselves. Compassion involves feelings of kindness toward ourselves, so that the desire to help, to ameliorate the suffering, emerges.*

The parents I work with are suffering. Deeply.

If you weren't suffering, you wouldn't have picked up this book. You are suffering because there is tremendous grief and hardship in parenting a child with such a vulnerable nervous system. Your home feels unsafe, you can't access the services you need, and you long for a relationship with your child that seemed reasonable to expect yet you now suspect you may never have. You've probably lost friends and you spend your precious free time and hard-earned money on therapy and services. This is suffering. Recognizing your suffering isn't pity and it won't keep you stuck wallowing in sadness. In fact, the research on self-compassion shows exactly the opposite is true. Self-compassion makes it considerably more likely that you'll figure out how to make things better.

Nat is suffering not only because of what she has lost in her parenting journey but also because of how shocked she is by her behavior as a mom. I hear this over and over again from weary parents, many of whom have parented other children and done a pretty darn good job. Suddenly they find themselves saying and acting and feeling in ways that they never dreamed were even possible. Then they shame themselves and are convinced that their behavior just confirms what a horrible person they are.

Your shocking behavior confirms only one thing. Your nervous system is vulnerable and your *Back Off!* or *Attack* watchdog, or perhaps your *Shut-Down* or *Play Dead* possum, are coming out.

I promise you that you could not say something to me about yourself or your child that I have not heard in my office. The intensity of your feelings is in direct proportion with the intensity of your suffering, just like I told you earlier in this book about your child.

I'll say this again because it bears repeating: seeing your own pain does not mean you have to drown in it. You can witness and attune to your own suffering without getting stuck in an endless cycle of self-pity.

Self-pity comes from the watchdog or possum brain. Self-compassion comes from the owl brain. Self-compassion will grow your window of stress tolerance. Self-compassion will strengthen the resilience in your stress response system. Self-compassion will even help you begin to shift your mental models if you discover that some of them are no longer true (more on that in Chapter 12).

If you take nothing from this book but the possibility of being even 5 percent more compassionate to yourself, then I have succeeded. When I'm in my owl brain, my work with Nat is bathed in compassion. There's compassion in my voice, compassion in my eyes, and compassion in my heart. It draws me closer to Nat, and it pulls out of me the desire to end her suffering.

I can't end her suffering, of course. Nat's suffering is righteous and earned, and I have no right to take it away. But I wish I could. What I can do is be with her in her suffering. That doesn't end the suffering. But it ends the loneliness of her suffering.

Moments of Self-Compassion Matter

Parenting this child is hard.

Read that again.

Parenting this child is hard.

I am doing the very best that I can. I am suffering.

Simply because I am human and exist on this earth, I deserve compassion.

How is that? What happens in your stomach and chest as you speak to yourself with compassion? Is it too hard? That's okay. We can scaffold compassion. Here's how we start the scaffolding.

Does Nat deserve compassion? Did you read these pages of me speaking to Nat, and to you, with compassion? Did you believe me?

My therapist used to tell me she felt compassion for me and then asked if I believed her. At first, all I could honestly say was "Well, I don't think you're lying to me." That was true. I didn't think she was someone who would lie to me. I believed her that she felt compassion. I just didn't believe that she would still feel that if she really knew all the worst parts of me. I was always waiting for her to say, "Whoops, never mind. I thought I had compassion for you. Turns out, you actually are just bad. Can't help you anymore."

Well, that never happened. Eventually I believed that I was worthy of compassion even in moments of my worst, most shocking behavior. Especially in those moments. I believe that if she ever saw those parts of me, and let's just say she's come pretty darn close, she would still feel not just compassion but actual adoration for me.

I feel compassion and adoration for Nat. You watched it unfold, slowly over the weeks. Nat deserves compassion because she exists, as we all do. As I got to know her, true adoration for her easily emerged from my heart. If you were in my office, I'd feel the same way toward you, just like I have for every parent who has come to my office. After all, like one of my first mentors Candyce Ossefort-Russell told me, all true selves are loveable. Without question, anytime I'm struggling to adore a client, I know that my own watchdog or possum brain has gotten involved. When this happens, and it does, I soothe my watchdog brain by offering it compassion. If I need, I seek professional consultation. When I lose compassion for a client it isn't an indication that this client isn't worthy of compassion; it's an indication that some of my own implicit memory has been awakened, something that has nothing to do with my client, and it's summoned my watchdog or possum brain into action. It's up to me to do my own inner work.

Scaffolding Self-Compassion

If you can't feel compassion for yourself quite yet, recognize that itself as a moment of suffering but without any agenda to change it. Your watchdog brain is still just slightly on alert and that's okay. What a brave, valiant job your watchdog brain does for you. If you can't feel compassion for yourself, can you bring me into your mind instead? Can you hear the compassion I offer Nat? Can you imagine that I'm offering that to you?

Parents all over the world email me and tell me that they hear my voice in their head. They put their earbuds in and listen to my podcast for their daily (hourly) dose of co-regulation and compassion and, eventually, they hear my words in their head. As if we know each other.

That is an awesome thing for me to contemplate. Awesome in the truest sense of the word, as well as the "way cool!" sense of the word. That's the reason I started a podcast in the first place, and it's working. Awesome!

I've had that experience, too. I'm an avid podcast listener and I know how it starts to feel like the podcast host is a close personal friend. I mean, they are with me while I'm showering, running, driving, doing the dishes, gardening. I spend more time with some of my favorite podcasters than I do with my husband, and we both work from home, so that's really saying something. I used to actually be a little bit ashamed of how connected I could feel to a stranger, but now, understanding the neuroscience of it all, I just marvel at it.

As clients repeatedly told me that, just like Nat, they could hear my voice in their head, I started to wonder if I could offer that voice to thousands of people all over the world.

Turns out, the answer is yes. If you're struggling to hear words of compassion in your mind for yourself, put in your earbuds and listen to my podcast. Hear my voice. I hope that, eventually, you'll hear my voice immediately after you criticize or shame yourself. Eventually, you'll hear it immediately after you find yourself overwhelmed by the grief of parenting a child who has needs that seem bigger than most. And eventually, you'll hear my words—but in your own voice.

Compassion is quite literally the neurobiology of change. In the next chapter, you'll learn how compassion can help you update mental models that are no longer true. Compassion will change your brain, widen your window of stress tolerance, and help you remember something that's been true about you all along: that you are a human who overflows with infinite worth and is worthy of compassion, simply because you exist.

Your Owl Brain Exercise Routine

Wait! Before you turn to the next chapter, I want you to open up the notes app on your phone or find a scrap piece of paper. I suggested four different ways to exercise your owl brain—connection, playfulness, noticing the good, and self-compassion.

Which one seems easiest? Which one seems least hard? Start there. Make a plan. Are you going to text a friend or search for an internet forum with parents of kids with vulnerable nervous systems? Are you going to watch a funny show or set a reminder to Google "toddler laughing" at 8pm every day? Perhaps you noticed that, like me, you have something you do every single day—showering with your favorite shower gel, your morning cup of coffee, or your evening cup of tea. Maybe tomorrow you'll spend just five minutes noticing how much you enjoy that cup of tea. Or maybe you'll download one of the many self-compassion memes you could find on the internet and make it the lock screen on your phone.

Decide now. Which will you try?

CHAPTER 12

How Not to Flip Your Lid—When Your Kid is Flipping Theirs

"Welcome!" I meet you at the coffee station as the final drops trickle into your cup. You look up, your eyes dancing with delight.

"I remembered where you keep the coffee!" you say, taking your first sip and wincing ever so slightly at the temperature.

"Some things will never change." I take a step back in a gesture of "after you," then trail behind you to the office. As you settle into the purple couch, I take in the striking difference between the "you" I see today and the "you" I met at our first session last year. You're sitting just a little straighter, your eyes are clear and relaxed, and you kick your shoes off immediately, drawing your legs under you and settling into a place of familiarity and comfort.

"It's great to see you," I say. "Reconnecting with clients I haven't seen in a while is bittersweet, though. I assume that scheduling an appointment means things are a little tough at home."

"Yeah, kinda. I remembered what you said, though, that if things at home start to go a little sideways, I should call sooner rather than later. It's easier to make small readjustments than wait until we're in crisis mode again. I think we just need a small readjustment."

"I love this! Tell me, what's up?"

"Well, it's probably mostly that the school year is ending so we're facing another huge transition—but Sammie is making some really weird choices. She rides her bike home from school now and..."

"Wait, hold up. Sammie rides her bike to school? And home? Without you?"

"Yes! I know, wild. We weren't sure it would go well but it has! I think getting all that sensory input before and after school really helps her. And she likes the independence. For the most part, it's gone well, no real problems. Until last week. I got a call Tuesday that she rolled her eyes at the crossing guard and told her she was stupid. The next day, she was throwing rocks at cars! I have to admit, when I heard about that, I just about lost it."

"Oh gosh, of course you did. Throwing rocks at cars is serious!" I'm trying to make sense of all of this. I'm in awe that you risked letting Sammie ride her bike to school. That was so brave. I'm in awe that she's been successful! Except now she's throwing rocks at cars.

"Exactly. When I heard about it, I panicked. I had this feeling like I was free falling into a pit, like it was going to get bad again, as bad as when we first came to see you last year. Like it was never going to get better, and I'd be visiting Sammie in jail one day." My eyes wide, I nod. "So, I just noticed it! I noticed I was panicking. And I could hear your voice in my head! You said exactly what you said just now. You said, 'Of course you're panicking.' And I wasn't just panicking, I was pissed. You can't throw rocks at cars! And...I just had a moment of letting myself be pissed. I didn't judge it or shame it or tell myself I was overreacting. I was just pissed."

"Oh Nat, awesome. Awesome." This is exactly what we practiced! Noticing your authentic reaction and then just acknowledging that it's real. Not judging it, not telling yourself to change or be more compassionate or calm or really to do anything different at all.

You're quite pleased with yourself. "Right??" you agree. "And it helped. It really worked. I mean, almost instantly I just felt, oh, I don't know, not judgey. The situation sucked, it was dangerous, and I was pissed. And I mean—I let her know this was serious! She knew I was upset, it's not like I pretended to be calm or anything. But...I didn't freak out. I didn't go bananas." You take a sip of coffee and seem to reflect on everything you just described to me. "Rocks!!! I didn't freak out about throwing rocks at cars!"

You stayed regulated. Not calm.

"Sounds like you did absolutely amazing. So, why are you here?"

"Well," you say. "My kid is throwing rocks at cars and calling the crossing guard stupid. Clearly something is stressing her out. And I'd like to see if we can nip this in the bud before she escalates to property destruction and I have to visit her in juvie."

So we get to work trying to figure out what's going on for Sammie. We could try to solve the mystery of the specific trigger, but we know when it comes right down to it, that's probably impossible. After all, her brain is continuously processing 11 million bits of data. It's the end of the school year and she's facing a huge transition from school to summer. It's not just a transition either; it's a significant loss. She'll never be in that class again with that teacher. She's facing a huge unknown. What will next year's teacher be like? Will the friends she sits with now be in next year's classes?

I ask, "What does Sammie need so she can successfully ride her bike to and from school? Does she need more co-regulation?" We consider the possibility of you riding your bike to school just in time for dismissal so you can ride home with her, or maybe meeting her halfway. Or maybe packing an extra snack she can have at the end of the day, before getting on her bike.

"Can the school give Sammie some information about next year?" I ask. "Help her know who her teacher will be and maybe even arrange a meeting with that teacher?" You like that idea, and you wonder whether Sammie's current teacher might do a whole-class lesson on endings and transitions and missing people.

It's hard to know what will help but you leave the office with a lot of ideas. The door chimes jingle as you walk out, and I wonder if that was the last time I'll see you. Will you call me again next week? Or maybe in a few years, when Sammie's a teenager? Whenever you do, if you do, you'll be welcome.

What a very strange job I have. From the very first session, the goal is to love people so much that I eventually never see them again.

Regulated, Not Calm

It is possible. Like Nat, you could find out your kid is throwing rocks at cars (or worse) and you could not flip your lid.

Which doesn't mean that you won't be mad. Please be mad. Mad is a feeling that says "Hey!!! Something is wrong here! You gotta do something about this!"

It's okay for our kids to see us mad. Did you know you could feel mad and still be regulated? We talked about it way back in Chapter 4, that regulated does not equal calm. Maybe you forgot. That was a while ago.

Regulated does not equal calm.

Who responds to their kids' violent behavior with calm? Someone who isn't being honest with themselves, that's who. You can be mad, and still be regulated enough not to say mean things that hurt your relationship with your child.

Relationships bloom inside authentic and regulated connection. Trust is nurtured when we are honest with ourselves and honest with our kids.

My friend and colleague Lisa Dion says, "Calm isn't the point. Connected to self is the point."[1] Lisa is spot on. We can learn how to stay connected to ourselves, mindful, authentic, and present, while also being happy, mad, sad, calm, or any number of other feelings.

Pause here for a moment and really consider what this means. I'm telling you that you don't have to work to be calm. You can have your authentic feeling and still be regulated.

Does that feel like a relief? Does it feel impossible? Or maybe a little bit of both?

Regulated and Mad

By the time we are adults, one thing our owl brain has learned is to be watchful and pay attention—to ourselves. The owl brain knows you're hungry before you are hangrily snarking at your spouse and mindlessly eating a bag of chips. The owl brain says, "You're getting hungry." And then maybe you have a kiwi instead of the chips. Or maybe you just eat a serving of chips instead of the whole box. Without the help of your owl brain, suddenly you've eaten an entire bag of chips and you have a stomach ache. You know as well as I do: sometimes that happens. Your owl brain will never be in charge 100 percent of the time.

Same with mad! Your owl brain can notice you're mad before you flip your lid. Your owl brain helps your watchdog brain decide: how mad do I need to be? Sometimes, when you're mindful and authentically connected to yourself, you realize that you don't need to be that mad after all. Other times, like when your kid is caught throwing rocks at cars, you realize that mad is a totally appropriate feeling. Mad is a feeling that helps us DO SOMETHING.

Toward the end of our work together, I taught Nat a four-step process for staying regulated—not necessarily calm—when Sammie's watchdog brain takes over. Nat didn't leave my office that day and never flip her lid again. It was more like I'd taught Nat how to shoot a free-throw. She still had to practice. A lot. Miss the shot. A lot. Be willing to keep trying. A lot. And no matter how good she gets, she'll never make it 100 percent of the time.

The process is simple, yet very hard. It takes a lot of practice, and if you practice a lot, it gets easier, not easy:

1. Notice
2. Acknowledge without judgment
3. Self-compassion
4. Release tension.

Step 1: Notice
The very first step is to just notice that you're having a thought, feeling, or sensation. If you don't notice it, you can't do anything else. So noticing is non-negotiable.

Just noticing, even if you don't do any of the other steps, can be extremely powerful. If you can notice that you're having a feeling, your owl brain is still in charge. It's the difference between seeing the feeling and being the feeling.

If you want to be able to notice a feeling in the moment you're having it, you first have to practice noticing the feeling when you are reflecting on the moment. Think about the last time you had what my dear friend and colleague Marshall Lyles calls a $5 reaction to a 50-cent problem. Any problem. It doesn't have to be related to your child.

Think really hard about that situation, and remember what it felt like. When did you start to feel mad? What sensations are present as you remember? What feelings? What thoughts? Do you notice tension in your body, like tight shoulders or balled fists? Think about what comes up for you, and see if you can label it, using neutral words:

> I felt like my head was going to explode! *Sensation*
> I was so mad, I could have spit. *Feeling and behavior*
> I jumped out of my chair. *Behavior*
> My fists were balling up. *Behavior*
> My chest was on fire. *Sensation*
> I am the worst parent ever. *Thought*
> This will never end! *Thought*
> Everything turned red. *Image*

Just notice, and use words that simply describe what was happening.

Step 2: Acknowledge without Judgment

This step is very important and a distinct step from noticing.

Acknowledging your experience means you are attuning to your reality. No judgment, no wishing it was different or trying to "solve" it. Just attunement.

After I've worked with parents for a while, or they've listened to my podcast for a couple months, or they've read 200+ pages of this book, they start to feel like they should "know better" than to still have big reactions. They judge and criticize themselves for having a very human response to a very real problem, like rocks being thrown at cars. They say things like "I know I shouldn't feel this way," or "I know it's not helpful when I...," or "I know I should stay calm," or "I know I should remember their trauma and not react."

"Shoulds" are almost always accompanied by judgment. Judgment comes from a nervous system in protection mode. Can you help your child regulate while you're in protection mode? Nope. And you can't help yourself regulate from there either.

Acknowledging your experience without judgment means that after you notice it, just allow it to be true. "I'm noticing heat rising in my chest." You don't talk yourself out of it, or shame yourself, or blame your child for it. It's simply true.

Step 3: Self-Compassion

I told you I was really committed to the powers of self-compassion! Here it is again. If you flip your lid and parent in a way you regret, you're experiencing a moment of suffering.

Let me say that again. If you respond to your child in a way that is out of alignment with your values and integrity, then you are experiencing a moment of suffering.

A moment of suffering deserves self-compassion.

Shaking from anger is a moment of suffering. When your owl brain flies away and your watchdog screams or puts your hands on your child in a way you regret, that is a moment of suffering. When your possum brain ushers in hopelessness and you give up, feeling like you have no power in your own home and family, that is a moment of suffering.

Once you get really good at practicing self-compassion, described back in Chapter 11, maybe you'll find a familiar mantra or even a gesture that instantly brings in the experience of self-compassion. Maybe you place your hand on your own chest, or you repeat your mantra of "I'm a good parent who is doing the best I can in a very hard situation."

I bring to mind an image of compassion: an owl, confident and gentle, with its wings wrapped around a watchdog and a possum, which are both feeling safe.

Go back to the memory you brought to mind back in Step 1, the memory of the last time you flipped your lid. You noticed the moment you started to feel dysregulated. Then you just allowed it to be true for a second or two. Maybe you said something to yourself like "Huh. Yup. I started to feel mad." Now, right now as you're picturing this moment in your mind, send a message of self-compassion to yourself. The self in your memory. If you're feeling really brave, you can even use words like "Oh sweetheart. That was so hard."

You might even experiment with sending gratitude to your watchdog brain or your possum brain. Remind yourself that you reacted the best way your nervous system knew how. Maybe you, like Sammie, grew up with an overactive watchdog or possum brain, or both. I'm so glad your watchdog brain or your possum brain learned how to keep you safe. Now, you're a strong grown-up with a strong owl brain. Your owl brain can take care of your watchdog or your possum brain so that they can rest and play.

Step 4: Release Tension

How many times when I was with Nat did I tell you I took a breath?

A lot.

Mindfully and intentionally releasing that "accelerator" energy in your body sends a message of "I'm safe!" to your owl brain. Sometimes I release tension by relaxing back in my chair, or, if I'm standing, by sitting down. Sometimes I unclench my thighs. Sometimes I release my fists. It depends on what I notice first. At this point in my journey, thoughts of self-compassion are almost always accompanied by a gesture that releases tension. I seem to have wired together those neurons and now they fire together.

Bring your attention back to your memory of the last time you flipped your lid. We left off with words of compassion, like "Oh sweetheart. That was so hard." Now, right now, as you're having this memory, release tension. Then imagine the "you" in your memory releasing tension. Maybe it's a breath. Maybe you picture yourself sitting down, or softening your spine and lowering your shoulders.

Now You're Regulated, Not Calm

I mean, maybe you're calm, I don't know. Maybe calm is absolutely the appropriate response. But when Nat had to deal with Sammie throwing rocks at cars, calm wasn't really appropriate. In fact, calm could lead Sammie to believe that throwing rocks isn't a big deal.

To reach the point where you can be mad and regulated, you'll have to practice this four-step process a million times.

Just kidding. It won't take a million times. But you do need to practice it a lot. Forever. I still practice this process a lot. It's like any skill. If you stop practicing it or fall back into old habits, you'll lose it. That's normal. Just keep practicing it.

First, you'll practice it the same way we just did it together. You'll reflect back on the moments you flipped your lid and walk yourself through this four-step process.

Eventually, you'll start to hear a tiny whisper of noticing while you're actually still in the moment of freaking out. It'll sound something like this: "You're freaking out."

The intensity of your activation will still be so fast and furious that you probably won't be able to do the other steps. That's okay, though I'll warn you that this might feel like an excruciating step in the journey. Every single client I've ever worked with has gone through the process of developing awareness before having enough regulation to stop the freak-out. It feels confusing and demoralizing, and can bring up feelings of hopelessness.

This step of awareness without the power to change your behavior is an inevitable part of the journey, but it's just one step. Your journey will continue. Remember, you won't get stuck at the rest stop on the way to your dream vacation. Keep practicing this four-step process and doing your window-of-stress-tolerance bicep curls from Chapter 11.

Eventually, you'll hear a voice in your head that says, "You're freaking out." And then you'll notice another beat or two goes by before you actually do freak out. Progress! A lot of progress, actually. Keep practicing.

Then, you'll hear a voice in your head that says, "You're freaking out." And then you'll notice another beat or two goes by where you just let it be true. A wisp of compassion will have time to enter into your awareness—right before you freak out.

You're noticing a theme here. You're going to practice this a lot, make progress that sometimes isn't even noticeable and other times leaves you feeling worse. You're going to work hard and practice this a lot, and still freak out. Pay attention, though. Ask yourself whether you are still getting *as* dysregulated? Is it happening as frequently? Are you recovering more quickly?

Eventually, and yes, this will really happen if you keep practicing, you'll hear a compassionate and non-judgmental voice in your head that says "You're freaking out." And then you'll notice another beat or two goes by where you just let it be true. And then you'll notice a wisp of compassion has time to enter your awareness. And then you'll take a breath.

Now, your owl brain can make a choice about how to respond to your child.

An important warning! Just because your body was regulated enough to do this once doesn't mean it will do it every single time in the future. You'll still have times when you'll flip your lid. The goal isn't for that to never happen. The goal is for you to feel more in control of your own nervous system, for the times of intense dysregulation to happen less often and with less intensity, and for you to recover more quickly.

Remember, when you make a choice about how to respond instead of reacting without mindful awareness, that choice doesn't have to be to respond calmly. You don't have to strike a yoga pose and say "Ohm-mmm..." like the kids in my office do when we first talk about regulation. You can be mad. And regulated.

Maybe when Nat was regulated but not calm, she said something like "Sammie! Rocks! Throwing rocks at cars is very dangerous. I feel mad and scared that someone could have been really hurt and am unsure what to do next. I need my owl brain to make a decision about what to do next, so we will talk about this later when my owl brain is back."

When you express your regulated, authentic feelings to your dysregulated child, you'll have to release any expectations about what is going to happen next. Expressing your feelings in a regulated and authentic way is about being true to yourself, staying connected to your owl brain, and not contributing to more fear and dysregulation in your child. It is not about trying to control what your child does next or how they respond. Chapter 9 offered a lot of ideas about what to do after your and your child's owl brains are back online.

Updating Your Mental Models
When you're with your child in a regulated way that is still authentic to your true feelings, you are taking a step toward widening your window

of stress tolerance. You might also be creating an opportunity to update a mental model you have that is no longer true.

If you can pause long enough to be with yourself with compassion instead of getting pulled into dysregulation, you are creating the perfect set-up to change your implicit mental model. Maybe you have a mental model that tells you it's life-threatening to be rejected by your child.

Eventually, you can strengthen your owl brain enough to see that your reaction is based on an old mental model: "Rejection is life-threatening." Then you can use your owl brain to ask, "Is that still true?"

It's not true, now that you're an adult. But it was true when you were very, very small because, like you learned in Chapter 3, you needed connection to survive. When you notice that it's no longer true, but it feels true, and it used to be true, you can offer yourself compassion—compassion for how painful this feeling is now, and also compassion for how terrifying it was to experience rejection when you were younger.

Compassion is the neurobiology of change! You are healing your nervous system in a way that will lead to long-term, lasting change.

This way of responding to your child's watchdog or possum brain is also exactly what *they* need to have a moment of healing in their own implicit memory and nervous system. Explaining the nitty-gritty of what memory scientists call "the disconfirming experience" goes beyond the scope of this book. A very brief summary is that when your child is dysregulated, they are expecting you to be dysregulated. Not only are they expecting their own dysregulation to be mirrored, but for children who have a history of relationship trauma and disorganized attachment, a dysregulated adult led also to the creation of that dysregulation in the first place. Remember, memory is about how things in the past impact our expectations and experience, both now and in the future. So that dysregulated adult in your child's memory leads them to expect dysregulated adults now, too.

When you are present, mindful, and regulated—not calm—in response to your child's dysregulation, your nervous system surprises their nervous system. This surprise creates the opportunity for the "disconfirming" experience. Their dysregulation receives a brand new experience of being met with regulation, and now a new memory is created.

It might not seem like anything is changing. You will work so hard to stay regulated and there may be no proof that all your hard work is making a difference to your child.

The Brain Is Changing

An ice cube that is 0°F has to warm up 33 degrees before you would ever notice a change—and 33 degrees is a lot! It's the difference between a gorgeous 70°F afternoon and an oppressive 103°F. The ice cube won't change, though, until you cross 33°F. Without the previous warming from 0–32, the observable change when it finally hits 33°F would never be possible.

The same is true for our kids, *and for ourselves.* Change is happening. It simply can't not happen. It's possible you will work hard to stay connected to your owl brain so you can offer your child regulation, connection, and felt safety even in their most difficult moments, and still see very little change in their behavior. The tipping point between inner change and observable behavior could be at some unknown point in the future. It could be next month, next year, or not until your children are grown.

Observable change might not be noticeable until your child has kids, and you see the change in your grandkids. Perhaps in this moment that feels like a lousy consolation prize. Indeed, there is much to grieve about the effort it takes to parent a child with a vulnerable nervous system, especially if you have a vulnerable nervous system, too.

The brain changes inside an attuned, resonant relationship. It is changing. Your brain changed while you read this book because, by some neuroscience miracle, we can create an attuned, resonant relationship through written words, even if we never meet. Your child's brain has changed, too. It simply can't *not* change.

Writing this book for you has changed my brain. After all, teachers teach what they need to practice. Speakers speak what they need to hear. Writers write what they need to read.

Thank you.

Epilogue

I check the office mail and am surprised when I see your last name in the upper left corner of a greeting-card sized envelope. Nestled into my purple couch, I pull the card out and smile. The word "awesome" is stamped above a sketch of a possum.

Awesome possum.

When I open the card, a picture of you falls out. You're beaming. You have one arm wrapped around the shoulder of a less-than-amused pre-teen in a cap and gown. Sammie.

Hey Robyn,

I saw this possum card on Etsy and knew I had to send it to you. 8th grade graduation. Can you believe it? We made it. Don't let that *What's Up?* watchdog face fool you. Sammie seems to be as pleased with herself as I am, though sometimes it's still hard for her to show it. Plus—it was so hot! We were all a little cranky by the end, so we stopped for celebration slushies. A super-cold drink with a straw still helps.

I have to tell you this quick story. A couple weeks ago, Sammie was on a rampage. Honestly, I'm not even sure exactly what was going on—it's hard to keep up with Sammie sometimes. She was full on "ready-for-action!," storming around the house and yelling because she couldn't find the shirt she wanted to wear. She told me it was my fault and said she couldn't find the shirt because I was too lazy to do the laundry. I felt a flash of fury that tried to chase away my owl brain away but then clear as day—almost like I was seeing things—I saw an owl. The owl looked at me like "I got this," and then pulled a grumpy and kinda pathetic looking watchdog into its wide wings.

So yeah, now you have me seeing things that aren't real.

I'm not sure if that owl was taking care of my watchdog or Sammie's watchdog—or both. All I knew was that Sammie needed help. So, I didn't yell at her for being disrespectful or blame her for not looking for her shirt ahead of time. I just knew her tired watchdog brain needed help. I took a breath and helped her find her shirt. When she walked out the front door and climbed on her bike to head to school, she looked over her shoulder and said "Thanks, Mom."

I wanted you to fix Sammie. I wanted you to fix me.

But, neither of us was broken.

Thank you,
Nat

Glossary

Attachment A biological system inherent in everyone; we are born with it. Attachment ensures a child's physical and emotional survival.[1] We all need attachment to survive and thrive. Humans do not outgrow attachment.

Attunement Aligning your internal state with the internal state of someone else; matching someone else with both verbal and non-verbal communication.[2]

Autonomic nervous system The part of our nervous system that is responsible for things that we don't think about and are mostly out of our control, like breathing, digestion, and heart rate. The autonomic nervous system is responsible for the energy and arousal that is fueling all behavior.

Brainstem Located at the bottom of the brain and nestled deep inside, the brainstem is a relay station between the brain and body. The brainstem has multiple functions in the autonomic nervous system. It is largely "wired up and ready for action" in healthy, full-term infants. The brainstem is organized first in connection with rhythms of the pregnant mother. After birth, it continues to organize in relationship to the rhythms of the primary caregiver.

Connection Joining or being joined to something or someone else. True connection includes both linkage (we're the same) and differentiation (we're different).[3]

Cortex The highest and most outside regions of the brain, the cortex is responsible for complex tasks like reasoning, logic, and understanding cause and effect. A calm, regulated, and safe limbic system allows the cortical brain to come online at about 18 to 36 months—when we see a burst in language and improved cognitive skills.

Dissociation A disconnection between parts that are typically connected or associated. This can apply to parts of self, memory networks, mind/

body, and more. Dissociation can be accompanied by a wide variety of sensations, including fuzzy, cloudy, spacey, or a sense of nothingness.

Dysregulation, dysregulated An imbalance in energy and arousal in the autonomic nervous system; difficulty with both monitoring and modifying energy states and emotional reactions.[4]

Felt safety A subjective experience based on an individual's internal experience, relational experience, and their environment.

Implicit memory Feelings, sensations, behavioral impulses, perceptions. Implicit memory is experienced outside of conscious awareness and does not evoke the subjective experience of remembering. Implicit memory is "remembered but not recalled".[5]

Interoception An internal body sense that monitors and transmits signals from inside our body, like hunger and satiation, thirst, or needing to use the bathroom.

Interpersonal Neurobiology (IPNB) Developed by Dr Daniel Siegel, IPNB is an interdisciplinary theory of human development that considers the interplay between the mind, body, and relationships.

Limbic regions Nestled in between the brainstem and the cortex, the limbic regions are involved with relationship, emotion, attachment, and implicit memory. The limbic regions are genetically primed to form connections through relational experiences and co-regulation.[6]

Maladaptive behavior Behavior that hasn't adapted appropriately to new situations, experiences, or environments. No behavior is maladaptive when we understand how the brain creates its own reality in every unfolding moment.

Neuroception The automatic neural process of evaluating risk in the environment and adjusting our physiological response to deal with potential risks subconsciously.[7]

Neurodivergent A brain and nervous system that processes information differently than what would be considered "typical."

Neurodiversity Differences in the human brain are natural and normal. No type of neurocognitive functioning is better or worse than another.

Neuroscience The scientific study of the nervous system (brain, spinal cord, and peripheral nervous system) and its functions.

Scaffolding A form of co-regulation that offers the structure and support children need in order to be successful. Scaffolding may slowly and sequentially be decreased as children gain more skill and regulation.

Toxic stress Unpredictable, extreme, and prolonged experiences of stress[8] that are not met with an adequate amount of safety, support, and co-regulation.

Acknowledgments

I've dreamed of writing the Acknowledgments section in my first book since Mrs Wabeke assigned the "100 Things to Do Before I Die" paper in 11th grade creative writing class. Given that I'll probably never "Compose a symphony that moves people to tears" (#14), it's quite satisfying to at least check off "Write and publish a book." Mrs Wabeke, thank you for helping me find my voice.

Peter Maramaldi, Janie Cravens, and Steve Terrell, you've each had a profound impact on my professional life. Peter—you were the first person who really made me consider that I might have some professional talent to offer the world. And, I'd like to say I've changed my habit of exploding my belongings everywhere and letting them melt like uneaten ice cream, but that would be a complete lie. Janie—you brought me to Adoption Knowledge Affiliates and changed the trajectory of my career. You made me feel special and loved and as though what I contributed was important. And Steve. Steve, you were the first person I knew in real life who loved these challenging, inspiring kids as much as I do. And you showed me it's possible to be bold and brave and tender and compassionate and an absolute smart ass all at the same time.

Obviously there's no me without my mom and dad. Perhaps the one good thing about the pandemic is how much time we were able to spend together in our little quarantine bubble. I never planned on having the opportunity to create an everyday relationship with you in my lifetime. Love you both so much.

Kristen. You are my very best girl. What else is there to say, really?

All my friends from the little blue house. Katie, Suzette, Jason, Christy, and Elisha. The world's best therapists, friends, travel partners, and practice partiers. To be loved and seen and forgiven by people as good as you makes me perhaps the luckiest gal around.

Laura. The universe brought us together—two unlikely but also perfect-for-each-other humans. You've made me a better person, therapist, friend, boss, and collaborator. Never in one billion years could I pull off The Club[1] or Being With[2] without you. So don't quit. Just kidding. Kind of.

Marshall. What did I do to deserve you? I get to be fully me partly because I see in your eyes that "me" is a pretty darn good person to be. Cheers to all the collaborations we've had, and all the collaborations yet to come.

Bonnie. The ideas in this book exist only because of you. I believed them first about my clients and then I risked believing them about myself. Being invited into your life and home has been nothing short of a miracle. I needed the softest place to land so I'd feel safe jumping as high as I could. If I wrote a 100-page letter of thanks, it wouldn't adequately describe how you've impacted my life—my work, my marriage, my parenting, my everything. Thank you.

Juliane. When I pause long enough to reflect on how you've imprinted yourself on my heart and my soul and my mind (many thanks to those mirror neurons, resonance circuitry, and just a whole lotta love), I start to sob and sob and sob. If everyone in the whole wide world had a Juliane, nobody would need a therapist. Luckily, everyone who knows me *does* have a Juliane because you are a part of me.

To a few special folks who have their actual fingerprints on this book:

Anne Heffron!!!! You are simply perfection. I wrote a book! And it started with you. You invited me to play in the clouds and sometimes I even said yes. All y'all reading this book and wondering if you could write one too? You can. Hire a writing coach.

Bethany Saltman. After I read *Strange Situation* I knew I needed to know you. It was gorgeous. Six months of working together writing a book proposal really paid off, in ways far beyond signing a publishing contract. You helped reinvigorate my love for my work, and organized it in a way that makes sense to others. Invaluable.

Stephen Jones. You gave me the freedom to write the book I wanted to write and the opportunity to reach families all over the globe. Thank you for your commitment to publishing books for struggling families, for placing humans over profit, and for staying committed to your values.

Steve Klein. You took the ideas in my head and brought the owl, watchdog, and possum to life. They are exactly right. Having a creative partner while slogging through the final months of completing my manuscript was exactly the inspiration I needed to keep writing.

Holly Timberline. This book brought us together, created a working relationship that far exceeded my hopes, and culminated in a friendship. Working with you as an editor while writing my initial draft turned the project into exactly what it needed to be—a relational experience. Thank you for falling in love with Nat and Sammie. Everyone, including Nat and Sammie, needs as many people as possible to adore them.

Finally, to Ed, Alexander, and the family we've created together—oh, and Ginny, too! Never in my wildest dreams did I imagine I would do life with people like you. I simply wouldn't be Robyn without you. You've given my heart a home. I've erased and rewritten every single sentence in this paragraph because words feel so wrong and so trite. I love you from the North Pole to the South Pole, and all around the world.

Endnotes

Chapter 1

1   Greene, R.W. (2021 [1998]) *The Explosive Child: A New Approach for Understanding and Parenting Easily Frustrated, Chronically Inflexible Children*. Sixth edition. New York: HarperCollins.
2   Josefson, D. (2001) "Rebirthing therapy banned after girl died in 70 minute struggle.'" *BMJ 322*(7293), 1014.
3   Heller, J. and Henkin, W.A. (1986) "Bodywork: Choosing an approach to suit your needs." *Yoga Journal 66*(28), p.56.
4   Siegel, D.J. (2009) *Mindsight: The New Science of Personal Transformation*. New York: Bantam Books.
5   Badenoch, B. (2008) *Being a Brain-Wise Therapist: A Practical Guide to Interpersonal Neurobiology*. New York: W.W. Norton & Company, p.15.
6   Porges, S.W. (2017) "Foreword: Safety is Treatment." In B. Badenoch, *The Heart of Trauma: Healing the Embodied Brain in the Context of Relationships* (pp.ix–xii). New York: W.W. Norton & Company.

Chapter 2

1   Sroufe, A. and Waters, E. (1977) "Attachment as an organizational construct." *Child Development 48*, 1184–1199.
2   Bowlby, J. (1969) *Attachment and Loss, Vol. 1, Attachment*. New York: Basic Books.
3   Porges, S. (2004) "Neuroception: A subconscious system for detecting threats and safety." *Zero to Three 24*(5), 19–24.
4   Riener, A. (2011) "Information injection below conscious awareness: Potential of sensory channels." Available at: https://citeseerx.ist.psu.edu/viewdoc/download?doi=10.1.1.294.5876&rep=rep1&type=pdf
5   Porges, S. (2004) "Neuroception: A subconscious system for detecting threats and safety." *Zero to Three 24*(5), 19–24.
6   Dana, D. (2018) *The Polyvagal Theory in Therapy: Engaging the Rhythm of Regulation* (Norton Series on Interpersonal Neurobiology). New York: W.W. Norton & Company.
7   Damasio, A. (2005) *Descartes' Error: Emotion, Reason, and the Human Brain*. New York: Penguin Books.
8   Siegel, D.J. (2020) *The Developing Mind: How Relationships and the Brain Interact to Shape Who We Are*. Third edition. New York: W.W. Norton & Company.
9   Perry, B.D. and Winfrey, O. (2020) *What Happened to You? Conversations on Trauma, Resilience, and Healing*. New York: Flatiron Books.
10 Perry, B.D. and Winfrey, O. (2020) *What Happened to You? Conversations on Trauma, Resilience, and Healing*. New York: Flatiron Books.

Chapter 3

1   Siegel, D.J. and Payne Bryson, T. (2020) *The Power of Showing Up: How Parental Presence Shapes Who Our Kids Become and How Their Brains Get Wired*. New York: Ballantine Books.
2   Siegel, D.J. and Payne Bryson, T. (2020) *The Power of Showing Up: How Parental Presence Shapes Who Our Kids Become and How Their Brains Get Wired*. New York: Ballantine Books.
3   Powell, B., Cooper, G., Hoffman, K., and Marvin, B. (2016) *The Circle of Security Intervention: Enhancing Attachment in Early Parent–Child Relationships*. New York: The Guilford Press.

Chapter 4

1   Lisa Dion, licensed professional counselor, supervisor, and registered play therapist supervisor, as a guest on my podcast, May 18, 2021, at https://robyngobbel.com/lisadion
2   Siegel, D.J. and Hartzell, M. (2003) *Parenting from the Inside Out: How a Deeper Self-Understanding Can Help You Raise Children Who Thrive*. New York: Tarcher/Putnam, p.202.
3   Siegel, D.J. (2012) *Pocket Guide to Interpersonal Neurobiology: An Integrative Handbook of the Mind* (Norton Series on Interpersonal Neurobiology). New York: W.W. Norton & Company, p.490.
4   Dion, L. (2018) *Aggression in Play Therapy: A Neurobiological Approach for Integrating Intensity*. New York: W.W. Norton & Company.
5   Siegel, D.J. (2012) *Pocket Guide to Interpersonal Neurobiology: An Integrative Handbook of the Mind* (Norton Series on Interpersonal Neurobiology). New York: W.W. Norton & Company.
6   Schore, A. (2000) "Attachment and the regulation of the right brain." *Attachment & Human Development 2*, 1, 23–47.
7   Siegel, D.J. and Hartzell, M. (2003) *Parenting from the Inside Out: How a Deeper Self-Understanding Can Help You Raise Children Who Thrive*. New York: Tarcher/Putnam.
8   Tronick, E. and Gold, C.M. (2020) *The Power of Discord: Why the Ups and Downs of Relationships Are the Secret to Building Intimacy, Resilience, and Trust*. New York: Little, Brown Spark, p.39.
9   Siegel, D.J. (2020) *The Developing Mind: How Relationships and the Brain Interact to Shape Who We Are*. Third edition. New York: W.W. Norton & Company.
10   Cited in Siegel, D.J. (2020) *The Developing Mind: How Relationships and the Brain Interact to Shape Who We Are*. Third edition. New York: W.W. Norton & Company, p.100.
11   Cozolino, L. (2014) *The Neuroscience of Human Relationships: Attachment and the Developing Social Brain* (Norton Series on Interpersonal Neurobiology). Second edition. New York: W.W. Norton & Company.
12   Siegel, D.J. (2012) *Pocket Guide to Interpersonal Neurobiology*. New York: W.W. Norton & Company, p.476.
13   Siegel, D.J. (2020) *The Developing Mind: How Relationships and the Brain Interact to Shape Who We Are*. Third edition. New York: W.W. Norton & Company.
14   Iacoboni, M. (2008) *Mirroring People: The Science of Empathy and How We Connect with Others*. London: Picador.
15   Badenoch, B. (2017) *The Heart of Trauma: Healing the Embodied Brain in the Context of Relationships*. New York: W.W. Norton & Company.
16   Said by Karyn Purvis at an Empowered to Connect conference, based on Cramer, S.C. and Chopp, M. (2000) "Recovery recapitulates oncology." *Trends in Neuroscience 23*, 6, 265–271.

Chapter 5

1   Perry, B.D. and Winfrey, O. (2020) *What Happened to You? Conversations on Trauma, Resilience, and Healing*. New York: Flatiron Books.
2   Perry, B.D. and Winfrey, O. (2020) *What Happened to You? Conversations on Trauma, Resilience, and Healing*. New York: Flatiron Books.
3   Perry, B.D. and Winfrey, O. (2020) *What Happened to You? Conversations on Trauma, Resilience, and Healing*. New York: Flatiron Books.

Chapter 6

1   Rowell, K. (2012) *Love Me, Feed Me: The Adoptive Parent's Guide to Ending the Worry about Weight, Picky Eating Power Struggles and More*. Saint Paul, MN: Family Feeding Dynamics.
2   See https://robyngobbel.com/responsivefeeding
3   See https://robyngobbel.com/responsivefeeding
4   Smith, M.L. (2021) *The Connected Therapist: Relating through the Senses*. Self-published.
5   Siegel, D.J. and Hartzell, M. (2003) *Parenting from the Inside Out: How a Deeper Self-Understanding Can Help You Raise Children Who Thrive*. New York: Tarcher/Putnam, p.103.
6   Powell, B., Cooper, G., Hoffman, K., and Marvin, B. (2016) *The Circle of Security Intervention: Enhancing Attachment in Early Parent–Child Relationships*. New York: The Guilford Press, p.30.
7   Brown, S. with Vaughan, C. (2009) *Play: How It Shapes the Brain, Opens the Imagination, and Invigorates the Soul*. New York: Penguin.

Chapter 7

1   Perry, B.D. and Winfrey, O. (2020) *What Happened to You? Conversations on Trauma, Resilience, and Healing*. New York: Flatiron Books.
2   Porges, S.W. (2017) *The Pocket Guide to the Polyvagal Theory: The Transformative Power of Feeling Safe* (Norton Series on Interpersonal Neurobiology). New York: W.W. Norton & Company.

Chapter 8

1   Perry, B.D. and Winfrey, O. (2020) *What Happened to You? Conversations on Trauma, Resilience, and Healing*. New York: Flatiron Books.
2   Smith, M.L. (2021) *The Connected Therapist: Relating through the Senses*. Self-published.
3   https://app.gonoodle.com
4   Sharma, N. (2016) "Lost Together." In *Wanderings: Poetry from the Dreamer*. Self-published. Poem republished with permission from the author.

Chapter 9

1   https://robyngobbel.com/beingwith

Chapter 10

1   Sunderland, P. (2012) "Lecture on Adoption and Addiction." YouTube. Available at: www.youtube.com/watch?v=Y3pX4C-mtil

Chapter 11

1   Perry, B.D. and Winfrey, O. (2020) *What Happened to You? Conversations on Trauma, Resilience, and Healing*. New York: Flatiron Books.

2   Beckes, L. and Coan, J.A. (2011) "Social baseline theory: The role of social proximity in emotion and economy of action." *Social and Personality Psychology Compass* 5, 976–988.
3   https://robyngobbel.com/theclub
4   Brown, S. with Vaughan, C. (2009) *Play: How It Shapes the Brain, Opens the Imagination, and Invigorates the Soul*. New York: Penguin.
5   Hanson, R. (2013) *Hardwiring Happiness: The New Brain Science of Contentment, Calm, and Confidence*. New York: Harmony Books.
6   Neff, K. (2011) *Self-Compassion: The Proven Power of Being Kind to Yourself*. New York: HarperCollins, p.10.

Chapter 12

1   https://synergeticplaytherapy.com/lessons-from-the-playroom-episode-118-how-trying-to-be-calm-gets-in-the-way-of-regulation

Glossary

1   Bowlby, J. (1988) *A Secure Base*. New York: Basic Books.
2   Siegel, D.J. and Hartzell, M. (2003) *Parenting from the Inside Out: How a Deeper Self-Understanding Can Help You Raise Children Who Thrive*. New York: Tarcher/Putnam.
3   Siegel, D.J. (2012) *Pocket Guide to Interpersonal Neurobiology: An Integrative Handbook of the Mind* (Norton Series on Interpersonal Neurobiology). New York: W.W. Norton & Company.
4   Siegel, D.J. (2012) *Pocket Guide to Interpersonal Neurobiology: An Integrative Handbook of the Mind* (Norton Series on Interpersonal Neurobiology). New York: W.W. Norton & Company.
5   Sunderland, P. (2012) "Lecture on Adoption and Addiction." YouTube. Available at: www.youtube.com/watch?v=Y3pX4C-mtil
6   Badenoch, B. (2008) *Being a Brain-Wise Therapist: A Practical Guide to Interpersonal Neurobiology*. New York: W.W. Norton & Company.
7   Porges, S. (2017) The *Pocket Guide to Polyvagal Theory: The Transformative Power of Feeling Safe*. New York: W.W. Norton & Company.
8   Perry, B.D. and Winfrey, O. (2020) *What Happened to You? Conversations on Trauma, Resilience, and Healing*. New York: Flatiron Books.

Acknowledgments

1   https://robyngobbel.com/theclub
2   https://robyngobbel.com/beingwith

Subject Index

Author Index